£ 1.95

MANIC STREET PREACHERS

mick middles

MANIC STREET PREACHERS

mick middles

OMNIBUS PRESS

Edited by Rob Dimery
Cover designed by P. Gambrill
Picture research by Nikki Lloyd

ISBN: 0.7119.7738.0
Order No: OP 48157

Exclusive Distributors:

Book Sales Limited
8/9 Frith Street,
London W1V 5TZ, UK.

Music Sales Corporation
257 Park Avenue South,
New York, NY 10010, USA.

Five Mile Press
22 Summit Road, Noble Park,
Victoria 3174, Australia.

To the Music Trade only:

Music Sales Limited
8/9 Frith Street,
London W1V 5TZ, UK.

Printed and bound in Great Britain
Typeset by Galleon Typesetting, Ipswich

A catalogue record for this book is available from the British Library.

Visit Omnibus Press at www.omnibuspress.co.uk

CONTENTS

INTRODUCTION

"I do think we are a uniquely fucked up race of people. No two ways about it."

— Nicky Wire

This trendification of Wales. Stop it, please. It's getting embarrassing. They'll be selling harps at the Conran shop next. A Welshman, talented and unpretentious, as Welshmen tend to be, once wrote:

> "I'll dance the dance of Wales Free,
> I'll sing the song of Wales Free,
> And I drink to the dawn of the lovely day,
> The day when every Welshman will be free!"

(Dafydd Iwan)

An infatuated Englishman replies.

Ankle-deep in middle age, head swimming with the kind of career panic that only a long-term freelance journalist, or perhaps a balding punk singer might harbour, I stood on the Porthmadog to Abersoch road, gazing wistfully down upon an eternally comforting sight. The village of Criccieth, a somnolent swathe of grey, bejewelled by yellow lights and curling to meet – forgive my patronising English tone – what always seemed to be the cutest little castle on Earth. A toothy outcrop. Altogether the quintessential Welsh coastal scene. It's a scene that adorns my living room wall, back in Stockport and, no matter how much pressure is applied from design-conscious friends, I will not see it removed. It is my 'Crying Girl'; my 'Monarch Of The Glen'.

I am an Englishman infatuated by Wales and by Welshness. This was once a rare thing to be and I coveted my infatuation proudly. And, unlike all the other weekending Englishers, with their damned jet skis, their phallic yachts, their silver BMWs forever speeding towards the mock Capri that is Abersoch, I actually did appreciate the special quality of the place. For me it was never just an irritating leer in an unwelcoming tap room, or a seemingly deserted village of grey perched en route to seaside frolicking. It was a rich, demanding, endlessly fascinating enigma. Darker, deeper, stronger than anything I could glean from English culture. Maybe Jeremy Paxman, in his newly published study of Englishness, might pull me back on the right track. For I still don't know quite what Englishness is.

As to Welshness; now that was something else. My parents moved to the heart of Gwynedd 18 years ago, as part of the English retirement invasion; loathed by the radicals and yet, to be honest, swallowed whole by the delightful Welsh locals of the village of Llanystumdwy. An ironic and perhaps unusual village, spiced by two hints of celebrity. Lloyd George lies grandly buried there, beside the glorious Afon Dwyfor, a river of diamonds, flowing through damp, wooded beauty. And Jan Morris, writer and Welsh patriot and all round cheery neighbour, works in her library house beside the same river. Both, in their own ways, celebrated beacons of Welshness. Both, paradoxically, born in England.

Welshness didn't immediately envelop my family, rather it descended slowly upon them, like a light mist turning to drizzle. I think the moment of acceptance might have come, again somewhat ironically, at my father's funeral. All our relatives gathered, in that Llanystumdwy house and, in the background, like ghostly shadows, the Welsh neighbours flitted to and from the kitchen, silent and respectful, laying on a monumental spread. After we had eaten and made our funereal chitchat, the shadows returned, gathering up the plates and cutlery, and departing with the discreet swiftness of professional caterers. That is how they do things in that area. To my shame I realised that, aside from a few lovably eccentric local drunks, I had no idea who my Stockport neighbours were. Nor did I have any desire to get to know them. Quite the reverse. This was obviously a very different country.

Until recently I was happy with Wales. I couldn't wait to lose myself in its bewitching drizzle. My favourite moments invariably taking place on Monday mornings. My freelance life allows me that extra day and how lovely it is, when the weekending hoards have departed from 48 hours of relentless rain, to discover the Monday morning sun streaming through the trees. It was my secret. Happy Mondays in a deserted Porthmadog! Drifting into the disproportionate amount of fantastically well-stocked hardware shops. Better than sex, mate.

Part of the allure of Wales was its unshakeable grasp of the unfashionable. As patronising as it may sound, those dour houses, those cheap jeans purchased from the roving markets, those profoundly parochial youths on street corners, a bewildering mix'n'match of fads and fashion, those nicotine-covered pubs, wholly unaware of the pub grubby revolution – it all seemed like freedom to me. A pressure drop. I could relax in Wales.

But times have changed. Once I would, in print and in my living room, champion the inaccessible rock bands of Wales. I would interview, for example, Rhys from intelligent punksters Anrefn, in the Snowdonian village of Llanrwst. That means nothing to you, does it? Well, it didn't back in 1986 either, when seeking out such bands was like venturing into Slovenia and finding some punk enclave which had existed since 1977 peopled by individuals who probably thought that Sid Vicious was still alive. I knew I was reporting from a profoundly foreign culture. It was strangely thrilling.

Alas, no more. It had to happen, didn't it? It is now hyper trendy to declare an affinity to Wales! How awful. A tumble of truly great Welsh rock acts, Manic Street Preachers, Catatonia, Stereophonics, Super Furry Animals, have turned the tables. Back in the old days the only Welsh rock act to penetrate into English record collections, and pretty sad ones at that, was The Alarm. That was fine by me. I was the only person I knew who had read, or had any desire to read Jan Morris's *The Matter Of Wales* – in my opinion, the finest evocation of Welshness to date – and Anrefn didn't manage to secure too many airplays on *Steve Wright In The Afternoon*. As far as the Manics are concerned, did they really have to clothe their latest number one album with a sleeve depicting them windswept on a Harlech beach, with the grand vista of Snowdonia, from Yr Wyddfa to Cader Idris brooding in the background? (That was always the biggest joke in *The Prisoner* TV series. "Where am I?" pleaded Patrick McGoohan, and only an English government minister wouldn't notice Snowdon rising behind him.)

Ah, yes, Snowdon. Or, in Welsh, Yr Wyddfa. That's another thing. How I am tiring of people who wouldn't know Clwyd from Cleethorpes telling me that, "I've done Anthony Hopkins proud: I've sent my twenty pounds to the National Trust. We must save Snowdon!" Do me a favour! They'll be driving to Capel Curig next; and they'll sit in little tents on Snowdon's drizzled upon grass, as if taking part in some massive Mike Leigh play, with a cast of thousands. I joke, but there is a darker fear, a dark irony even, in this recent appropriation of Wales. The heart of Wales is undeniably forged from the experience of a small country – although, as Jan Morris would state, Wales never feels small when you are in it; indeed it feels like a wet India – hinged to the side of a comparatively vast, dominating force. The power of the underdog has fuelled Welshness . . . from Owain Glyndwr to the new Manics album. And yet the incoming flood of Englishness is now partly driven by the success of these fabulous new bands.

But I'm not here to crusade for the Welsh, I'll leave it to far wiser, far more eloquent folk to carry that vast debate. I'm just concerned with me. Yes, it's horribly selfish but, sometimes, that's how it is. When I first went to Wales, as a holidaying schoolboy in the Sixties, I was attracted to corny beach delights, from aromatic paperback bookstands, whitewashed cottages and quaint cafés. Then, slowly, over the years, I glimpsed a lifestyle beyond that surface stuff. The wonderful thing, for me, was that, for a while I seemed to be the only English person seeing it. I was envious, envious of the Welsh. And now we are all envious of the Welsh . . . and it just isn't so much fun any more.

OK, let's not get too carried away.

In any case, it would be immensely patronising of me to even attempt to convey 'Welshness', or Cymreictod as it is proclaimed in its own language, in this book. It would also be a lie, because I don't understand it at all. But I can give an objective view, an observation from across the border, no doubt carrying with it many misconceptions. After all, I am only English. There is also the fact that Welsh bands are now out there, fighting for prominence in the big world and, as such, any kind of parochialism would hardly serve them well. They need to be universal. They need to be understood. This is still a huge problem. The local proliferation of proud Welsh language rock bands of the mid-Eighties carried with it a heavy inevitability. As Rhys Mwn, from the aforementioned Anrefn, told me at the time, "The Welsh language is beautiful to sing. The most poetic language on Earth. But we are not stupid . . . It's fun and it's beautiful but it is never going to change anything." Rhys, himself, was – and is – a paradox. A punk and a schoolteacher. A realist and a nationalist. A benign rebel.

Welsh language rock bands? Mention them now – and there are still some excellent examples; check out Bob Dylan a'r Ebillion from Llwyn – and you will be met with a barrage of vacant stares. "Wales?" a widely travelled American once asked me, adding, "Rock bands from Wales? Do you mean Wales in England?"

To fully appreciate the existence of Welsh rock music, you have to know something about 'the eisteddfod thing'. If you ever wish to seek out the profound gulf between the cultures of Wales and England, then you could do far worse than visit the cultural festival known as eisteddfod. Nothing that England, or anywhere else come to that, has to offer remotely resembles an Eisteddfod. In England we have 'country and county shows' where fruit cakes and grumpy bullocks battle for rosettes. In Wales they have eisteddfods, which are the celebration and affirmation of a rich poetic and musical culture that has existed for centuries. A culture undoubtedly spiced by its eternal battle against its large, bullish neighbour. There are two kinds of eisteddfod. Once a year, The National Eisteddfod is held, alternately in the north and the south. This always occurs during the first week of August. To call it a 'folk festival' certainly does it a huge disservice. It is a vast gathering of every aspect of Welsh culture from the rock band tent, to all manner of literature, song, art and costume. It is attended by all walks of life. (I've attended just one, in Llangollen, and was staggered to find grimacing parochial punks, all studs'n'leather'n'wonky Mohicans, mixing freely with jovial ruddy-faced farmers, precocious choirboys, traditionally garbed harpists and drunken, scowling poets by the score.) From an English perspective, it is utterly bewildering, which, I suppose, is how it should be. It is a Glastonbury that has etched its way into tradition. Then there are the local Eisteddfods. Hundreds of them. Huddled in marquees across the country. Unlike the national event, they do not generally attract stars from across the world, but mainly concentrate on celebrating local talent. (Although it isn't unknown to find a huddle of villagers, in north or south Wales, gathered attentively in their local hall, soaking in the sounds of, say, a visiting Rumanian pianist, or that punk poet from Slovenia.) Here you will find that that corduroy-clad chap who works for the council, and wanders to the pub every evening, is actually a strict metre poet of the highest order. It happens a lot in Wales.

Until the Nineties, the Welsh influence on international rock and pop music was tenuous and disparate to say the least. It is true that, for some of the insular reasons mentioned above, the naturally literate trait of the Welsh people had not translated effectively into its musical exports. If people thought of Welsh music, which was seldom, they thought of Tom Jones; underrated for a long time, largely due to his absurd dance steps and Vegas apparel, but a mighty R'n'B force in his Sixties heyday. And dare I mention Shirley Bassey, that pre-Celine, pre-Whitney Tiger Bay warbler; bejewelled and, until liberated by the Propellerheads in 1998, an archaic reminder of faded showbiz. I personally recall harbouring an unhealthy fondness for meandering prog rock stalwarts Man, certainly one of the more interesting loon-panted ensembles of the mid-Seventies, still plough-ing on, I believe, in pubs and small venues across Britain. Most absurd of all, surely, must be the mighty John Cale whose career, from founder member of the Velvet Underground to his endless string of extraordinarily subversive albums, has seen him established as one of rock's permanently hip figures. Which is, itself, absurd. Cale was never even a 'rock' musician. He came from a classical background, was completely unschooled in rock and yet provided the soul in one of the most influential of all rock bands. If you want a manifestation of the curious, eccentric and understated position of Welshness in the scheme of modern pop culture, then you need look no further than John Cale. I do not, in this skimpy and selective run through, need to think twice about mentioning The Alarm. Unhip and unhinged as they always were, and far too happy to play the role of a second-rate U2 for my liking, they were still the perfect representation of mix'n'match parochial post-punk rebellion. A glorious confusion of styles, as clumsy as the band in a schoolyard hop. Up until the moment Mike Peters was seen playing soccer on a beach with Rod

Stewart, they looked for all the world as if they had been plucked straight from a Welsh bus shelter. And so they had. (Coming from Holywell, or thereabouts, they represented that curious slither of land, where north Wales segued into Scouse.) They weren't without talent, or Welsh pride, as Peters would later prove with his low-key solo career but they would, come 1997, be bettered by the more intellectually gifted Mansun, hailing from just over the border, in and around Chester.

Strangely, until the Manic Street Preachers, the spirit of Wales had been best celebrated by an English band, albeit one of the finest of all English bands and, more to the point, a band uniquely open to soaking up ancient and foreign cultures and fusing them to make one massive, unparalleled universal noise. Led Zeppelin. No other band in rock history has managed to convey the damp, foreboding atmosphere of Wales so effectively. Slate-grey Welshness is shot through the rock of Led Zeppelin, battling with the blues and rock'n'roll. The Welsh spirit was openly celebrated on *Led Zeppelin III*, with 'Bron-Y-Aur Stomp', dedicated to the band's inspirational cottage, which still nestles beneath the shadows of Cader Idris, looking out across Cardigan Bay towards Ireland. It can still be clearly found on any Ordinance Survey map and is visited, regularly, by a straggle of Zeppelin devotees.

As to the Manics. To the legions who were converted in the wake of the staggering *Everything Must Go* album, the Welshness they carried with them, their string of albums, the 'Richey' thing, the latter-day punk image, all these things merely seemed to add to the band's enigma. We hadn't taken that much notice of them, to be honest, and so often we dismissed their punkisms as being little more than sub-Clash affectations. I recall the scorn they received in the local press, and on local television, in Manchester, when the band visited the city in 1991. It was extraordinary. They were treated as little more than naïve no-hopers, a bit of lost rock baggage, tenth-wave punksters not fit to wander such hallowed streets. It must have been so dispiriting for the Manics, given their love of the most literate Manchester bands (Joy Division, New Order), to be treated with such shabby disregard. On the other hand, as Manchester had, somewhat ludicrously, become Madchester, and had garnered praise across the globe, from *Newsweek* in America to *Rocky Magazine* in Australia, and as it clearly believed itself to be the world's most innovative musical city, why should it have opened its ears to a bunch of parochial misfits from the valleys? Perhaps it merely strengthened the band's resolve. One thing I do know: when in 1992, the Radio One DJ Simon Mayo, of all people, started to give repeated plays to the band's exquisite, disarmingly haunting single, 'Motorcycle Emptiness', this writer actually did start to think more seriously about the band. "Have you heard that Manics single?" I would ask friends although, more often than not the question was met with blank stares. The fact is that, to many latter-day Manics fans, the band's initial years were spent in some kind of parallel world and, discovering them, late in the day, was like stumbling across some unexpected treasure chest. Or visiting another planet and finding out who their rock stars were. Welshness has preserved the secret. This might not be the case for the majority of people reading this book but, believe me, for 90 per cent of people whose living rooms suddenly started to reverberate to the sound of 'Design For Life', that's exactly how it was.

There is no doubt that the Manic Street Preachers, as a band, as a phenomenon, are fully immersed in the spirit of their country. There is no doubt, either, that this can sometimes appear trite; quaint even. See Nicky Wire, on stages from Melbourne to Manchester, his amplifier shuddering beneath that Welsh flag. Is this fierce pride or an insular trait? Is it healthy? Does it lock him, as the Manics' chief lyric writer, away from his non-Welsh audience, rather as those Welsh language bands alienated non-Welsh speakers? Doesn't it rather clash with Ian Brown's refreshingly anti-Madchester statement, "It's what you are that matters . . . not where you are from"? To be honest, the Manics, and Catatonia come to that, are guilty of all this, and possibly much more. But that's the price they have to pay for mining inspiration from their home town and their country.

To look at one instance of the band's adherence to their Welsh roots, consider one of the more recent Manics songs, 'Ready For Drowning', from the 1998 album, *This Is My Truth Tell Me Yours*. It is a strange song, set amid a string of strange songs, and it casts a dark glance across the currently rather melancholic psyche of the Welsh people. (Even the rugby lacks the panache of the great days, as if slowly submitting to the encroaching glamour of contemporary football. These days Young Welsh kids growing up to adore Giggs and

Speed, if not Owen and Beckham.) 'Ready For Drowning' is an admittedly ambiguous analogy between this modern Welsh psyche and a ghostly Welsh village, Capel Celyn set in the Treweryn valley that runs down to the Dee from Y Bala. It was the corporation of Liverpool, England, that decided the valley would make a convenient reservoir and the little hamlet was lost beneath the waters. 'Ready For Drowning' uses the story as a metaphor for not only the drowning of the village, but the drowning of Welsh talent, in a flood of alcohol. Indeed, throughout the history of Welsh literature, from Dylan Thomas to Richey Edwards, the alcoholic muse has made regular appearances. The music of the Manic Street Preachers, from the existential 'Motorcycle Emptiness' to 'If You Tolerate This Your Children Will Be Next' contains a sombre heart that is as Welsh as the drizzled upon slate in Blaenau Festiniog. It would be foolish for the band to ignore such heart.

* * *

Blackwood.

Hills of black. Hills of green. Dark, deep, brooding valleys, leaden skies, relentless drizzle tapping off grey slate and fizzing into grass. Wales, north or south, can be demanding, infuriatingly damp and oppressive enough to ensure that a headache continues throughout the day. It can be wildly beautiful too, though that beauty seems to fade at will. How often Snowdonia simply disappears into the murk. And in the south, where the hills are less craggy, softer, perhaps friendlier, they still disappear all too often beneath the dominant drizzle. That's how it is. And that's certainly how it was, in February 1999, when I stood near the top of the Sirhowy Valley near Tredegar, seeing little more than a blanket of grey. Of course there are those (and I'm one of them) who do find a curious comfort in that dense mist. But if you are going to accept Wales as a whole, you have to accept the climate.

If you wanted to see the real Wales, you could do worse than drift through the Sirhowy, or indeed the neighbouring valleys of Rhymney or Ebbw. The ghosts of Welsh resistance seem at home there. Not since the days of Owain Glyndwr, a figure distant to the point of mythology, has Welsh resistance had anything victorious to celebrate. Wales has a culture strong on pride but one which all too often appears reactionary. There has been, as Jan Morris points out in her recently updated *Wales: Epic Views Of A Small Country*, a "national grievance" which has certainly shown in the solemnity of Wales. That and the deeply guarded fact that the Welsh are more literate, more aesthetically aware, more emotive, more sensitive than the Philistine English! At least, that's how it seems to the eyes of proud Welsh patriots and, more often than not, I find myself agreeing with them. The Welsh have contributed much, of course, to this United Kingdom, and so much, in a political and emotive sense, can be attributed to the three valleys which were hiding from me that day, in the February mists.

In nearby Tredegar, Aneurin Bevan, of Charles Street, was elected to the Hospital Committee – closely linked to the Workman's Medical Aid Society in 1923. Twenty-five years later, as Minister of Health, Bevan launched the National Health Service. An outstanding achievement, and one which sits near the top of the heap of noteworthy achievements of the Welsh section of the Labour movement in the 20th century. Proof, if proof were needed, of the passionate conscience and deep intelligence ingrained in such parts.

The Sirhowy Valley snakes down from Tredegar, an archetypal Welsh valley. There are strings of houses, rugby pitches, crumbly bus shelters, and too many eerie graveyards which hint at the mining-related diseases of the past, such as 'the cough'. The valley winds down to the dense grey estates of Oakdale, Penmaen, and Blackwood. By the time you reach the latter, you really feel you are in the heart of something. Blackwood was Neil Kinnock's constituency and that fact alone seems immensely significant. New Labour is a new world. It is somewhere else. For a portion of the later 20th century, the power of the Labour party was here. Now it has gone. To Hampstead, presumably. But some things have changed for the better.

"The Manic Street Preachers are from round here," the bus driver will almost certainly tell you, on noticing your English accent. There would be pride in his voice too, even if you suspect he wouldn't recognise a Manic Street Preacher if he fell over one in the gutter . . . which may well have happened in the not too distant past. The Manic

Street Preachers have been rather glibly labelled 'the most important band in the world', which is debatable at the very least. Unless, of course, you happen to come from one of these valleys, in which case, they may very well be just that. The only band in the world who you could touch, who you could see. And still can, albeit only very occasionally. And they really have changed things. Just a decade ago, Welsh pop culture seemed impenetrable and ferociously conservative. To the outside world it might as well have been poems, pints and leeks in the true Max Boyce style. But this is 1999. Everything has changed. Now people in London invent a Welsh ancestry. The Manics, along with Catatonia, Super Furry Animals and Stereophonics, have changed the image of young Wales. Is that not an immense achievement?

And they came from Blackwood, at the bottom end of the Sirhowy Valley. Everything in that valley, every echo from the past, every political fire and every hopeless struggle, reflects strongly in the band's music which, one now senses, will forever echo around these valleys. It made them the band they are today.

1

IN THE BEGINNING

"When we were winning . . . when our smiles were genuine . . ."
– 'The Everlasting'

James Dean Bradfield, an only child, was born to parents Monty and Sue on February 21, 1969. It was an unexceptional working-class household. Monty and Sue were old-fashioned, in the best possible manner. They were Welsh through and through; nevertheless, they came within a whisker of calling their son after Monty's cinematic hero. James could so easily have been Clint Eastwood Bradfield – which may not have been such a disaster, though his schooldays wouldn't have been stacks of fun. James's grandmother, rather comically, misunderstood a conversation with Sue and duly informed the entire town – and word spreads like a bush fire in such a place – that the new arrival was named Charles.

"I would never name a baby Charles," Sue told the Manics' excellent *11 Commandment* fanzine in 1999, ". . . because people would go and call him Charlie. James doesn't allow Jim or Jimmy or Jimbo. Oh no, his friends would come round and say, ". . . can I talk to Jim?" I would say, "No, because a Jim don't live here." As it was, the newest Bradfield bore the name of an icon of pop culture from day one.

Look around Blackwood, Bargoed and Oakdale. Look at the eerie rising slagheaps dominating the landscape. Kids still hide and play in their shadows. It's not difficult to imagine those oikish faces replaced by the features of a young James Dean Bradfield and his cousin, Sean Moore, slipping around the back alleys, playing soccer in the street. It was always soccer or cricket, incidentally: rugby was a strangely

18

detached world, a sport to be watched, to be worshipped by many locally, but rarely played. Even this image, of grubby kids with scuffed knees and mischief on their minds, now seems of a bygone age, as today's young pretenders are garbed, from baseball cap to trainers, in bewilderingly expensive designer sports gear. (Much of it pirated and purchased from shifty stalls in the local market.) Sue Bradfield: "There were a few little monsters around here . . . but, honestly, never James . . . nor Sean. They were just really nice boys, both of them. I can't remember them ever getting into any trouble."

James and Sean served their time at Pontypridd Junior School, situated at the bottom of the neighbouring Rhondda Valley. Pontypridd is, if anything, even more deeply etched with Welsh history. At Pontypridd you will find the work of Methodist minister William Edwards in the form of a bridge which arches across the River Taff and was erected in 1756. At the time it was the longest single arch bridge in Europe (although there can't have been that many), and it achieved worldwide fame. More than that, it was regarded as a solid, identifiable vision of Welsh achievement. If you travel away from the bridge, along a deadening duel carriageway, you will reach a park where two bronze statues stand. They are not that imposing, to be honest, and local schoolkids treat them rather contemptuously, but they are of considerable significance to our story. They are of Evan James, a Welsh poet who died in 1878, and his son, called, would you believe, James James. They were author and composer of 'Mae Hen Wlad fy Nhadu', which is more familiarly known as 'Land Of My Fathers', the Welsh national anthem. Unlike any other national anthem you might wish to name, it is not a song lost in jingoistic fervour, nor does it tell of dubious and unholy bloody battles in foreign parts. It tells simply of Wales and a desire for Welshness to remain intact, untouched by large and intimidating neighbours. It is a proud anthem, but not aggressive, an essential part of the Welsh psyche and it was written within yards of the primary school attended by Sean and James.

Not, one senses, that they spent too much time debating the anthem's significance while they were at junior school. Undoubtedly it was little more than an irritating task. Thirty squeaky-voiced kids attempting to look solemn, each and every morning, accompanied by a slightly out-of-tune piano. That said, and unlike English schools of the time, hymn singing was treated as an essential part of all grades of education and religious instruction, as fundamental to the curriculum as English or maths, whereas, in England, it was always, and probably still is, regarded as a rather surreal and fairly eccentric diversion from the process of 'real teaching'. James was a good singer, too and, albeit fleetingly, a choir boy. No mean feat in a Welsh junior school in the early Seventies. There is no evidence that he took this activity too seriously. Indeed, the reverse may well be the case, as choirboy prowess is hardly a good way of gaining credibility points in the school playground.

James and Sean, despite the vast gap in their ages – James was born in February 1969, Sean in July 1970, placing James a year ahead in school – were inseparable. When Sean found himself in trouble in the schoolyard, as he occasionally did, James would rush to his aid. Although cousins, their features were strikingly similar and most of the other children thought of them as brothers. In a sense, they did actually become brothers when Sean, at ten years old, suffered from a parental break-up. His father decamped to join the navy, in Plymouth, and Sean moved in with James's family, literally doors away from their MP, Mr Neil Kinnock. As such they shared a bedroom for a full decade, and thus shared their formative years together. There are no reports that the pair ever became distant although they moved with two different circles of school friends. On the contrary, they would tend to share their experiences, compare their experiences of daytime friends, enemies and teachers.

The Bradfields' street was old-fashioned in the sense that a community spirit still prevailed there. Perhaps not quite to the extent that everyone could leave their front doors open, but the local kids would stream from house to house and a general congeniality was indigenous to the area. Burglaries in Blackwood, although not unheard of, were, and indeed still are, rare and are frowned and commented upon, with a fierce and insular gossip network inherent to the local pubs. Difficult to steal and sell a video recorder, unnoticed, in such an area. Of course, there were, and still are, rogues of all descriptions in the locality. But stealing from your own? Generally not tolerated.

The kids played together a great deal in the street. That wasn't necessarily a good thing, as the noise did give rise to pockets of unrest. Cricket was an early passion, sometimes played by teams numbering no more than three a side, with stumps formed from upturned fish crates. James was a good little batsman, powerful, enthusiastic and skilful from the outset. Once they graduated from street to local field, the stakes were duly raised and the ubiquitous tennis ball was replaced by a vicious red bruiser, a vile missile of torn leather and dangling thread. You don't have to be too old to do damage with a cricket ball, as the young James found out to his cost on one painful occasion. A flamboyant attempt to hook a wildly swinging bouncer saw him spinning behind his bat, the momentum turning his face towards the oncoming missile which crashed into his eye, causing him to hurl his bat to the ground and become a sobbing huddle on the grass. Two minutes later he was belting down the road, one eye clasped shut, the other clouded by tears and . . . smack! Straight into the garden gate. He was rushed to hospital and returned with an enormous swelling on his face, though otherwise he was undamaged. Within two weeks another cricket ball had slammed into the same eye, rejuvenating his bulge and kicking off a lifelong psychological trait. Sue: "After that I could always tell when he wasn't feeling well because he would lose control of his eye somehow and it would start to turn in. It never affected his eyesight, though."

James's eye problem instantly became the source of a constant stream of nicknames. Many, as is often the case with childish insults, were genuinely inspired. 'Crossfire Bradfield' was particularly inspired, and rather likeable as it always sounded like the name given to the batty Major in a Sixties' episode of *The Avengers*. Others were rather more cutting. Radar, Terence McCann, He-Man, Joe Ninety and the gloriously inventive 'Squinting Hogg'.

The lads did get into a little trouble, as young boys will. James's local gang were caught, and marched briskly home by the local constabulary, after setting fire to a stack of dustbins behind the local comprehensive school. No action was taken, and James always proclaimed his innocence, stressing that he was 'set up' by the bigger boys in his gang – the ones who constantly ribbed him over his 'wandering eye'. Incidentally, his best-known defence when attention was drawn to his mishap was to state that, "David Bowie had a funny eye, too." Not a statement that would have carried too much weight on the pavements of Pontypridd, but significant in that it suggests James took an early interest in the best pop music of the early Seventies. Then again, perhaps we shouldn't read too much into that. After all, it was football, rather than pop, that fuelled the dreams of these kids. When they weren't annoying their neighbours by playing in the street, they would play, unofficially, on the 'proper' local pitch owned by the Gossard corset factory. Games would stretch into the dark of night, with teams most usually 'picked' at the start of the proceedings. ('30–all' would be a typical score.) Although Gossard were less than happy about such intrusions, most local people did little to discourage the games. After all, it stopped the kids from kicking balls about the streets, it kept them out of serious trouble; and, frankly, there was little else to do around these towns. The more adventurous might try 'bird–nesting', which required dispassionate bravado and a considerable degree of climbing skill. Throwing 'bangers' at rival gangs could transform the annual enormous bonfire parties into sordid territorial squabbles, but at least it provided a bit of excitement. And, come election time, the ripping down of any rogue Conservative signs that might appear in the front gardens of the 'posher' houses provided some diversion.

It might be noted that, in the Seventies if not today, growing up in the Welsh Valleys was a constant battle against mind-numbing boredom. Both James and Sean have spoken fondly about their pre-teen existence, before the horrors of puberty set their hormones ablaze, but there was little in the way of entertainment or adventure readily at hand. School trips to Symonds Yat beauty spot, just over the English border, or the literary haven of Hay-on-Wye were regular and, to young eyes unable to appreciate beauty, mind-blowingly tedious jaunts.

Football was heaven-sent, for children and parents alike, even if Swansea and Cardiff City both consistently failed to cover themselves in glory. Most Welsh kids – apparently still true today, this – maintained an allegiance with Liverpool FC, at this point still very much the dominant force in English and European football. The Merseyside club, even in those pre-Ian Rush times, had strong Welsh connections – the John Toshack legacy very much intact. And the Manic Street Preachers first met on that Gossard football field. James recalled those days in conversation with the author back in 1992: "I can't quite recall the first time we were all together. I'm sure it was for a game of footy, though. That was the highlight of every week . . . every day in summer. Staggering home from an exhausting four-hour game, covered in sweat and mud. It was fantastic. To this day I still miss that. When you were playing, even if it was just against a few kids who just happened to be hanging about, you could fulfil your wildest dreams. It was always Wembley in your head . . ."

Clearly, the memories of being forced to do sports other than football stayed with James – his recollection of the frustration he felt at being denied a chance for glory on the playing field was crystal clear when he was a famous Manic. "You had to do cross-country and cricket in the summer, which everyone hated, and all that athletics stuff," he groaned. "They should have saved the school money and just bought a sack full of footballs. That's all we fucking needed . . . all any kid needs. I remember thinking this when I was about ten."

One day James and Sean were joined by a gangly lad they knew from school. This was Nicky Jones, who swiftly became known as Wire, due to his giraffe-like appearance. He wasn't a bad footballer, though. He adopted the role of centre back, solid in defence and unbeatable coming forward to head in from a corner; Nicky was Jack Charlton without the nasty streak. Immensely likeable and sensitive, Nicky Jones didn't seem to be filled with the daft bonhomie of the street gangs. Moreover, his obvious intelligence made him immediately attractive to James and Sean, both of whom aspired to move up and away from local scummy street-speak. "Right from the very beginning . . . and I mean the very first day we met Nicky properly, as opposed to just seeing him around, something clicked, we thought we were a step above the other kids . . . it was that simple," Sean told the author in 1992. "Nicky was tall so he was the type of kid who you had always seen around but never really got to know until we started playing football. It was like, almost instantly . . . a gang. And when Richey came as well, it just fitted together. Some things are just meant to be. We never doubted it for a second."

Music was always there, lying just behind sport in their affections. The fledgling Manics were 'new Welsh', in aesthetic terms, and were therefore something of a paradox. While they shunned poems'n'pints Welsh culture in favour of the far more contemporary sounds from America and England, a more localised aesthetic awareness still seeped into their psyche. That summary rejection of religion may have seemed total, but there can be something deeply profound about standing in a cool church, experiencing the resonant harmonies of a male voice choir, that can move even the most cynical. True, it may not have been particularly enjoyed by the lads at the time, indeed they will certainly have loathed it on many occasions, but it doubtless made its mark on them.

As to pop, Wales is a very different place now, in 1999. Spearheaded by the Manics it has experienced a genuine resurgence of chart-topping artists, and Welsh pop is probably in a healthier state now than it has ever been before. A far cry from the early Eighties when, The Alarm aside (and notwithstanding the inroads made earlier by Man and John Cale), Welsh pop seemed old and rather cheesy. Tom Jones and Shirley Bassey had grown as rapidly as possible away from their Welsh roots and had yet to return to the public eye as kitsch icons. In the brash early Eighties, the second age of glam, if you like, it was difficult to garner pop credibility if you were Welsh. And from early adolescence the four future Manics knew this and began, right from the outset, to rebel against the unjust stereotype of Welsh pop stars as has-beens or witless no-hopers. Already they were edging towards glam.

Not that it reflected too heavily in the records that kick-started their respective record collections. It has been widely reported that James's first single, proudly purchased after a week of hard saving, was Diana Ross's 'My Old Piano'. He was ribbed about this, and publicly ridiculed later via his metal-loving mates and in Martin Clarke's Manics biography, *Sweet Venom*. As it would turn out, it was his friends who lauded Iron Maiden, Saxon, Samson and Vardis. In fact, 'My Old Piano' was a pretty astute single to buy. Clipped-down, good-time pop, a hint of soul, a hint of gospel and a lovely punchy edge. Well worthy of Ms Ross, and a better 'first' single than most of us could claim. Nicky's first purchase was Black Sabbath's 'Neon Lights', a choice that he once felt obliged to staunchly defend in *NME*: "I don't care what anyone says ... that was a big record for me ... still is. A great monster of emotion. I'm not a metal fan, really, but it is the most misunderstood music form of the past twenty years. So much great stuff has been lost because music press idiots can't listen for themselves."

By comparison, Queen's anthem 'We Are The Champions', Sean's début as a singles buyer, seems an achingly mundane choice. That said, these initial records did, at least, avoid the naff chart fodder that was soundtracking the fledgling Manics' everyday existence at the time. I deliberately avoided mentioning Shakin' Stevens but, in Wales – and elsewhere, I'm afraid – Shaky joined the only slightly more palatable Paul Young, in soundtracking everyone's everyday lives. James: "When we first became musically aware ... well, it wasn't such a great period. I mean there was plenty of good stuff around but you had to filter it from a hell of a lot of crap. And we didn't know how to do that. Nobody did, in Blackwood. So we listened to the crap as well. Lots of it. Gushing into our lives and we just swallowed it up eagerly. Genuinely, a lot of people thought that Shakin' Stevens was as good as Elvis. They couldn't see any difference. Some of them, I'm afraid, still can't. There are people in Blackwood, honestly, who still own Shaky albums ... and still think they are good."

* * *

Richard James Edwards (born December 27, 1969) was a good footballer. Not great – not strong enough to be great – but not at all bad; ask his teen friend, Brian Travers, who used to play 'three-and-in' with him on the local rec. Endless games of soccer tedium, with some vague idea of scoring the winning goal in the World Cup, for Wales, in their heads. At twelve years old, girls began to edge slowly into the picture. Not enough to take over from thoughts of football, of course, but there all the same. Once, or perhaps more than once, Richey and a small gang of fellow footballers sneaked into the bedroom belonging to Brian's older brother. And beneath the bed ... an unholy Grail. A catchment of hard-core porn, ragged faded edges, well-thumbed pages. Brian's brother was obviously an aficionado. The five footballers crouched low, and looked on with intent curiosity, allowing their eyes to wander across the curves, pretending not to be shocked by the central allure of the pictures. The very first time they came upon the mags they were stunned into complete and total silence. For ten full minutes, in a semi-darkened bedroom, their excitement laced by the danger of discovery, they sat and silently stared. Richey suffered the worst. He lasted seven minutes before he got shakily to his knees, crept to the bedroom door and, in a daze, lurched out into the sunshine. His head was spinning. With mounting nausea he staggered out into the street, behind the houses, back onto the football pitch, where he collapsed into an ungainly clump.

He'd been genuinely horrified, as he later confessed: "It was one bloody great shock. It wasn't the nudity, as such, it was the depravation. They were the saddest pictures I ever saw. It wasn't the girls who were sad . . . I felt sad for men. The fact that an appetite existed, out there and, I can't deny, I was part of that appetite . . . it was the violence of those pictures that upset me." The memory of that abrupt entry into a more sexually adult world, and one that he was ill-prepared for, informed his work later as a Manic: ". . . it affected me profoundly and would always haunt me," he recalled to the *Boston Times* in 1993. "You will find references to that experience all over the Manics lyrics. I think we all went through a similar thing. It's that barrier you reach when you realise that, while sexual desire can be incredibly beautiful, it can also be incredibly ugly."

James's first experience of the world of one-handed reading proved to be an altogether less traumatising experience. His friend's dad, obviously loath to keep his porn stash indoors for fear of discovery from his wife, kept a massive and varied stack in his garage. He thought it was his secret but, of course, young boys have a strong nose for such things, and James and his friends were no exception. Breaking into the garage was easy, and there was no rising nausea this time. Just two lads, dazzled by their discovery. No sense of outrage rose in either, and certainly no sense that anyone had been exploited. James found himself hugely turned on by the find and regarded it as a natural 'rite of passage'. Porn would later filter into his own bedroom . . . nothing excessive, nothing hard-core, just top-shelf stuff. As he recalled to *NME*, "I felt guilty in one sense. When you are young and you are hiding it in your bedroom. Then the worst thing that can happen is that your mother finds it. Your mother's got superhuman qualities, hasn't she? I'm not saying pornography's wrong – it brought me through a certain progressive apprenticeship – but in the end you know your mother is not going to want to think of you sitting there wanking away . . ."

Typically, of all the Manics, Richey Edwards was the one who was compelled to articulate his thoughts over this early encounter with pornography; the Manic who suffered the most over something which others, such as James, didn't give a second thought to: "You can understand both sides (of the feminist arguments about pornography)," Richey commented to *Select* in 1994. "Catherine McKinnon said that anybody who looks at page three of the *Sun* is as guilty as anyone who commits a violent crime against a woman. Well, obviously that's not true. But I understand why there needs to be that strain of thought. Why she and Andrea Dworkin are very necessary." Then again, in these early days, Richey's dry humour saved him from over-intellectualising a situation: "We got asked by *For Women* if we would [appear nude]. I have no desire to expose my genitalia. Too small."

The chances of four boys gelling artistically and intellectually, the way James, Sean, Nicky and Richey did, are indeed remote. Nicky and Richey had, literally, been street mates, having lived doors apart. Richey lived in a curious little bungalow which sat at the bottom end of the street. It was a neat building, like so many around it, and the perfect setting for a contented childhood. Living with his parents and grandmother, the young Richey never wanted for anything. He was sharp, quick-witted, humorous, and absolutely devoted to football. In local knockabouts, he was always the first to be picked, and quite often the first to score. Richey seemed to breeze through school too, blessed with the rare ability of being able to attain high marks in every area without seeming to try particularly hard. There was even talk of him taking special exams to attend a 'high achievers' school although it was a possibility that filled him with horror. Indeed, throughout his formative years, Richey seemed to regard his intelligence as something of a burden – something that caused a barrier to spring up between him and the less gifted children with whom he mixed in the playground and the street. His pre-teen credibility swung precipitously in the balance and, to the dismay and bewilderment of his teachers, Richey took great pains to 'dumb down' accordingly, to fit in with the puerile antics of whatever gang he wished to become a part of.

Blessed with kind and supportive parents, Richey never had any serious problems with home life. Working long hours and weekends at their respective hairdressing posts, they left Richey to be tended by his adoring grandmother. No amount of scrutiny could find anything abnormal in this idyllic upbringing; if anything, the reverse may have been true. It has been suggested that Richey might have been too happy, too lost in the lovely maze of childhood and that, as such, perhaps he never really mentally adjusted to the loss of that early comfort zone. Steve Jenkins, one of Richey's childhood friends, remembers him as "... a really happy kid. He just was ... The thing is, when he disappeared and it was all on television ... like everyone else, I started thinking if there was anything, anything at all slightly odd about him and I can honestly say there wasn't. In fact he was a really level-headed kid." Jenkins does recall one incident by which Richey's deceptively hidden strength of character became evident: "(some) kids started ribbing this lad. He was a bit slow, I guess ... The kid was in tears ... Richey seemed to let it go so far and then he just started screaming for them to stop. It was pretty brave because these kids were real big stupid bullies and they would have murdered Richey. But somehow they didn't. They shrugged and backed off and wandered away." There was obviously more going on in young Richey Edwards than met the eye. Even as a young boy, it's clear that there was something of the romantic in him, something idealistic even. Richey Edwards had faith – in himself, in his own ideas of right and wrong. And faith can move meat-heads.

You could probably extend that picture of Richey's childhood contentment to cover all four Manics. Which may seem, to those anticipating signs of embryonic existentialist angst, somewhat disappointing. Curiously, the only place where the gang felt ill at ease (save, presumably, for James the choirboy) was in church. Richey, in particular, loathed the Sunday ritual with a vengeance. In small-town Wales, the pull of religion permeates everyday life, much to Richey's eternal dismay. He was, from an early age, far less affected by this Welsh heritage than his friends, and never fully accepted, even in his latter days, that blanket of national camaraderie. As to religion, it left him cold. Significantly, one of his favourite early songs was 'Religion', the declamatory anti-Christianity monologue from Public Image's début album, in which John Lydon tramples freely over all manner of doctrine. It was not a track that found too much airplay on Welsh radio. But it did in Richey Edwards' bedroom.

* * *

1984. Oakdale Comprehensive. It would be tempting to suggest that the latter-day social estrangement of Richey Edwards could be traced back to an Oakdale classroom in the early Eighties, with a sullen faced teen sulking in the shadowy corners of the playground, avoiding the gazes of bullies and girls and taking solace in a Camus paperback.

It wasn't like that. He had problems, the same problems suffered by any nervy teen crippled by shyness and insecurity. Richey took refuge in the comparatively safe pages of *NME*, where a fascinating, some-what unreal world, built from the egos of rock stars and rock journalists, seemed to offer so much in terms of cultural enlighten-ment. The world conjured up by the weekly inky seemingly so glamorous compared to the world of juvenile Oakdale. To the eyes of a particularly intelligent Oakdale pupil, life in small-town Wales sup-pressed the brightness of dreams, crushing hope and crushing any thoughts of genuine escape. Richey openly loathed it, and loathed everything he believed it to stand for. Like his friends and future bandmates, escape was always on his mind. But how?

Richey wasn't, it must be noted, a rebel. Not openly. He was blush-ingly self-conscious and lived in fear of being asked to read from the Bible at school assembly. He never volunteered to act in school plays and saw little point in seeking any kind of attention from an audience who, for the most part, he must have regarded with the same suspicion as he did Blackwood itself. He was a quiet boy, but not to the degree that he became ostracised. His problems were much the same as any of his contemporaries; his teenage facial skin bubbled a bit, making him more introverted but that's par for the course for most adolescents. Apart from the occasional fling and fumble, girls remained mystical, distant creatures. ("Me and Richey were retards when it came to girls," Nicky told *Vox* in 1996. "Very, very shy. And most people thought we were gay, so they didn't even bother.") He wasn't unpopular, or bullied. His looks weren't good enough to inspire the jealousy of classroom brutes, nor were they bad enough to war-rant mockery. He wasn't a loner on the fringe of school society; on the contrary, he was fairly well liked. His obvious intelligence appealed to his teachers and even earned him their respect, rather than ridicule. He was, however, modest about his abilities and talents. Too modest, perhaps, to make much of an impression on the girls.

Anyway, music dominated his every waking hour at this period of his life, and gave him a whole world to live in that seemed so much more preferable to the one outside his bedroom window. Morrissey was a particular fascination, not so much for the denim-and-greatcoat imagery that seemed to be passed down from the Manc bands of the late Seventies, but for the element of glamour that was so much a part of his image. For Morrissey it was a subtle way of carrying the baton from his beloved New York Dolls, if not the local glam punks, Slaughter And The Dogs, around whom he had famously fluttered. But The Smiths never seemed to quite fit Richey's ideal. His notions were of a more outlandish nature. In the early Eighties he had, much to the angst of his parents, been drawn towards matters Goth, plumbing for long black Oxfam coats – reminiscent of Henry Fonda's outfits in *Once Upon A Time In The West* – eye-liner and, just occasionally, traces of lipstick and rouge. Black was the dominant colour. Black shot with touches of red. Dramatic and mysterious, in a juvenile manner but, at least, it separated him from the casual norm, where market-bought Fred Perrys and Pringles were the order of the day. Richey wasn't keen on the Friday night local discos, either. Not for him the endless soundtrack of Michael Jackson's 'Thriller' and a spate of dreadful dancing. He was a bus stop boy; it was either that, or stay in with a book, *NME* and the latest album purchased the previous Saturday in nearby Newport.

Jonathan Medcroft, a fellow pupil at Oakdale, told me, "He was kind of androgynous even then. And there were early signs of anorexia. I mean, in Wales you don't find that high cheekbones occur naturally... you need to starve yourself." It's difficult to know whether this was merely a comment on the local diet or an observation on the healthily ruddy sheen presented by most Welsh lads. Whatever, the fact is that Richey Edwards looked decidedly un-Welsh. Had he been born a dozen years sooner he would have made a classic Bowie look-alike, circa Ziggy. More glamour than glam, more Bowie or Bolan than Slade or The Sweet, although Richey was probably striving for something between The Sisters of Mercy and The Clash.

According to his school friends, there was always something rather serious about Richey's rock'n'roll affectations. Unlike most of the other kids, it didn't seem like some shallow and transient fad, some half-hearted flutter with *Top Of The Pops*. Pop and its attendant escapist glamour seemed to mean far more to him. He was never playing a role or just messing about with fashion. He was, even then, searching for his own identity. As he reflected to the author in 1991, "It didn't last long but, for a while I was mister daft *NME* reader. There are hundreds, thousands of people like that . . . obviously like everyone else, I learnt the hard way. Doshing out my hard-earned cash on some record that some geek writer in London has raved over . . . probably because he knows the bass player's cousin . . . and when you get home it's the biggest pile of unlistenable shite ever."

Nicky Wire shared Richey's feelings right down the line. "From a really early age, we studied the music press in a really cynical way . . . and I don't think we ever took it too seriously. We could see beyond it. There were kids at College . . . at University even who worshipped the bloody music press. We were picking up on Pinter and they were reading Johnny fucking Cigarettes . . . I mean, no disrespect but let's get things in perspective." Going with gut feeling rather than searching for second-hand credibility became an early Manics maxim, even if that meant flying in the face of received wisdom in matters of taste, as Nicky readily admitted: "There was a lot of heavy metal in our valley . . . it's the music of the valleys and if we liked some of it, as we did, and still do, then why should we give a fuck if some wanker in Camden Town thinks we are naff?"

There were more musical problems in the mid-Eighties than just Shaky. Once the Frankie bubble had exploded, once Live Aid, worthy as it clearly was, had bored us all to tears, there was little else left. The young Manics found new sources of inspiration elsewhere, particularly in literature, and it was that thirst for intellectual stimulation that marked them out as much from their Blackwood peers as from their future pop contemporaries. Richey: "I was doing 'A' Levels. I was learning really fast . . . everything, everywhere. And reading like crazy and we had this intellectual thing going that was beyond the classroom. You know . . . the stuff that was really valuable was stuff that wasn't in the curriculum . . . That's not real education. That's not where wisdom lies.

"Wisdom lies in seeing beyond that and that is where the education system fails. People just are not interested in seeing beyond the narrow scope of their own ambition. I got that from Larkin, from Kerouac . . . Jack Kerouac! Fantastic. The most intelligent bloke who ever lived and he saw genius in people who were basically bohos. Neal

Cassady, for fuck's sake, was the kind of guy who someone who works at Tesco's might regard as a loser. He was a drunken bum who never held a job and shirked all his responsibilities . . . and yet Kerouac saw the real value in that. To Kerouac, one of the sharpest brains America has produced . . . Cassady was a true hero. That, to me, is just beyond everything that Thatcher's fucking Eighties threw up. It was so much wiser, on such a higher plain than those wankers in the British government."

Richey was to become the prime force behind the Manics' lyrics, crafting a style that was equal parts rage, confusion and confession. Literature gave the four adolescents from Blackwood a vocabulary to express their feelings as well as a context for their frustration, the realisation that their predicament was not unique. "We read all the Beats, of course, but also a lot of very English stuff. Books set in the Sixties. Kitchen sink stuff. It could have been through Morrissey that we got into all that. I can't remember but he may have ignited a certain spark there. Stuff like Alan Sillitoe, *Saturday Night, Sunday Morning, The Loneliness Of The Long Distance Runner . . . A Taste Of Honey* . . . It was very much on a par with our lives. Perhaps we really were a bit behind the times in the valleys . . . because a lot of the attitudes we saw in that stuff seemed just like everyday life to us. *A Taste Of Honey* . . . where was that set? Manchester? (Actually Salford and Stockport.) That could have been Blackwood in the mid-Eighties. We still hadn't got rid of that kind of closed mindedness . . . and I hated that about Wales. So those films and books really hit the nail on the head for us. We were brought up in a black-and-white world."

The intellectual learning curve which tied the four lads together grew despite the social and geographical problems of attending different colleges, and given that fact, the bond seems particularly impressive. At any age, and especially as an adolescent, the exciting temptation is to move on, to forge into newer areas, areas that often seem, but rarely are, far more wrapped up in glamour and sophistication. The attraction of becoming a student, and the attendant affectations that all too frequently grow as a result, can rip friendships apart. Indeed, any student returning home from that first spell in halls of residence often has to make a considerable readjustment. Home can seem a narrow, worthless place, peopled by those who have timidly submitted to small-town existence. The experience of a wider culture, of different food, new art, music and books, can suddenly make the place you came from seem small and tame. With the Manics, again almost uniquely I would suggest, this impulse arose before they even left for college, and formed a solid bond between the four. Their intellectual pretensions, such as they were, were not stimulated by their fellow students at all, but by each other and when they reconvened at the end of term, they reaffirmed each others' convictions: number one of which was that Blackwood meant the death of ambition. Years later, Nicky reflected: "I don't think we could have done this if we hadn't grown up in a shithole, where the only way to escape was to create your own reality. We grew up in one of the most deprived areas of Britain. When we go home, nothing's changed. It's such an insular society. We had nothing. We had a cinema but that was closed down when we were twelve. So the only thing left for us to do was retreat into our bedrooms."

* * *

In 1986, *NME* was attempting to reclaim its position on 'indie' ground. The early Eighties had seen the paper's writers move alarmingly into the mainstream, seeing artistic worth in the likes of the Trevor Horn-produced Dollar and Kid Creole, let alone those who have posthumously received more widespread critical blessing, such as Wham! and Frankie Goes To Hollywood. Several genre inventions had occurred since then – Chicago House and the new wave of jangly American rock from the likes of R.E.M. and Green On Red among them – all of which had caused the identifiable readership to diversify beyond belief. As an antidote to this, and, indeed, as a fight back against the older rock market now serviced by the pristine *Q* magazine, *NME* pioneered the bands of boys with guitars (and the occasional girl singer) who would come to define indie music. The dourly clad raggle-taggle legions garbed in Levi's and second-hand Americana, still sheltering under Morrissey's giant shadow and forming scruffily besuited bands who mixed cute pop tunes with buzzing guitars. It was the time of *NME*'s C86 compilation tape, and the bands on that little number, all seemed to fit neatly into one little package. Across the country, meanwhile, small independent labels serviced this small but immediately identifiable market: Ron Johnson, Factory, Creation, In Tape, Play Hard. The bands included The Bodines, McCarthy, The Shop Assistants, Big Flame, The Railway Children, The Wedding Present, Felt, The Train Set, Half Man Half Biscuit and The Woodentops, all floppy of fringe and perfectly placed to provide a student-friendly alternative to Top Forty radio. Though none of the bands built their reputations on musical virtuosity, quite often their curious lack of musical deftness, which reflected in the raw pacing of their set, was nicely countered by an intelligent, lyrical sense of humour. Perhaps the most obvious example of this was The Wedding Present, with their constant battle between thinly stretched guitars and singer David Gedge's dry humour.

It was rock'n'roll, of sorts, and it was the first music encountered live by all four Manics, but at the same time it seemed to lack depth and glamour, sex and funk, excitement and abandonment. As Richey neatly pointed out to *NME* in 1992, "I saw a lot of those bands in Cardiff and Newport and it was very confusing. You never really felt that they meant it. In fact, you always believed that, one day, they would just pack it in and become bank clerks. Maybe some of them were students, I don't know, maybe it was just a bit of fun. But it wasn't what I was into. I knew that, even then. It had to mean everything. I came away from a lot of gigs feeling cheated." Nothing less than heart and soul would do; that was the source of the Manics' burning ambition, and none of them saw the value in anything less.

Punk affected the Manics as soon as they encountered it (though they were all too young to have appreciated its impact first time around). It was in James's front room that all four last sat and watched one of the many compilation films pieced together from Tony Wilson's shambolic but beautiful *So It Goes* programme, filmed in Manchester in 1976 and 1977. Much of what you see on that film is a lie. The Clash at Belle Vue was a furious gig, where many of the audience – including yours truly, Mick Hucknall and sci-fi writer Jeff Noon — crashed the doors and fell into one huge mass pogo. To be honest, the whole thing was driven by the presence of those television cameras; as Siouxsie neatly pointed out, "I think I've just found out who the star of this show is (points to the camera) 'cos that's where all the fucking eyes are looking." *So It Goes* created the illusion of a camaraderie in punk rock that, to this writer, simply didn't exist.

Everyone had their own ideas and, frankly, the punk ideas of a bored kid in Hebden Bridge were just as valid as those of a leather-clad poser in Camden. Punk meant what it did to everyone on a wholly individual basis. Most of the bands loathed each other and no band in the entire beautiful mess, from Throbbing Gristle to The Skids, ever really looked beyond their own ambitions.

Now you wouldn't, and couldn't, appreciate this, if you were a bright valley lad in 1986, sinking his fourth can of Red Stripe of the evening, and watching The Clash, Siouxsie And The Banshees, Penetration, Iggy Pop, X Ray Spex, Elvis Costello, Buzzcocks and Magazine on *So It Goes*. And if you were to mix all those bands together, if you were to slam them in a cocktail shaker and pour it out, the resulting sound wouldn't be too far removed from early Manic Street Preachers. Tony Wilson's televisual trick of the eye was a beguiling vision. And the pre-Manics foursome lapped it all up like eager young puppies. Nothing they saw in the student union halls of 1986 even came close to recreating that visceral thrill.

It was, obviously, The Clash who hit home most immediately. Although this influence, in terms of the music of the early Manics, and certainly in their early image, is often cited, in another sense it remains rather odd. The Manic Street Preachers, from the word go, used intellectual aspirations to move up and away from their roots. Not so The Clash. Nor the Pistols, with the notable exception of Johnny Rotten, come to that. Lads, one and all, they openly aspired downwards in the intellectual sense, The Clash's rather embarrassing latter-day politics being little more than thoughtless sloganeering rants. This is no put-down of The Clash – the times were perfect for a band who would shout before thinking. They were a healthy knee-jerk reaction to years of over-thoughtful fret pondering from prog rock dullards. Yes, quite rightly, The Clash just wanted to rock back to basics. So why would the Manics, four lads attempting to get clean away from the basics, see such worth in a band like The Clash? The truth is that they didn't look too hard. They saw *So It Goes*, saw Joe Strummer's on-stage passion and simply found something that touched them, that stirred their working-class pride. In the context of which, this comment from Mick Jones, plucked from the Manchester fanzine *Ghast Up*, in an interview conducted shortly after that Belle Vue concert, makes for interesting reading:

"Yes, we are for the working classes ... but it's a working-class pride that has been lost. It's all fucking gone and that's it. There's no point in voting any more ... I'd rather have anarchy. I really would. At least it would be honest. You just can't trust anyone, any more. No fucking politician. We were really stunned when a Labour politician objected to us. I thought ... fuck, man, it's like we are the people you are supposed to be supporting. Can't you understand that? ... The Welsh knew it. They gave so much to the Labour movement and they are just shit on these days."

Bored with attending gigs at the flaccid college circuit, James, Sean, Nicky and Richey began to rifle feverishly through rock's history, sparing no thought for modern-day fads or fashions. Richey even managed to secure a copy of Morrissey's scissors-and-paste biography of The New York Dolls and, like Morrissey before them, noticed that a real intelligence lay behind the band's cheap fag glam make-up. Again, the big selling point of the Dolls was the fact that they lived it. The low-rent lifestyle, the drag queen affectation, The New York Dolls were indeed *for real*, and their whole daft rouge and eyeliner appeal was a pure Warholian attempt to embrace celebrity, to force a change, to be somebody. This appealed to Richey perhaps more than the other three, who, at the time, tended to go for the slightly less brash Hanoi Rocks. The Manics' love for all things metal goes back a long way, and they embraced its love of big guitars from an early age. Richey: "A big dichotomy we came across when we were 16, 17, 18 was that the one band we loved for the music they were making was Guns'n'Roses when *Appetite For Destruction* came out ... and then the other band which was saying everything which we couldn't identify with, but at least they sounded pissed off, was Public Enemy. That's what we tried to cross."

University life, although successful for all four, has been latterly and famously seen as a time of trauma. Except, perhaps, for Nicky, whose time at Portsmouth Polytechnic after his mock 'A' Levels had proven less than satisfactory. Poly, and indeed Portsmouth, proved genuinely nightmarish, with Nicky refusing to join his classmates on long nauseous forays into the unusually intense atmosphere of the city's public houses. Newport, Swansea and Cardiff all have their raucous, beery side, but Portsmouth, with the added ingredient of a high percentage of marauding sailors on the lookout for weirdoes to straighten out, was frankly unbearable, if not downright dangerous. With respect, the Poly itself also failed to rise to Nicky's intellectual aspirations and, bored, displaced, he spent long, lonely hours sitting in the austere common room, sinking endless Cokes and writing letters to his three close friends. Long, unusually open letters, mostly slating his Portsmouth existence which seemed, to him, rather pointless. It was his mother who took up his cause. Despite his embarrassed protestations, she harangued Swansea University daily on the telephone until, after two weeks of intense verbal activity, they pushed the rule book aside and allowed Nicky Jones to switch to the politics curriculum. Here Nicky, a profoundly political animal with a seemingly unquenchable thirst for the truth, found the substance to back his explosive, and perhaps rather naïve, personal polemic. A far happier time ensued. Living in the student village set dramatically in the dark, brooding hills above the city, Nicky at last felt some kind of kinship with his fellow students – including Richey – although, throughout the first year at least, he made the short trek back to Blackwood every week.

It was a curious time. Not only did Nicky, and to a lesser extent, Richey, spurn the sounds of late Eighties indie rock with its jangly guitars and cheap production, he also scorned the prevailing ragged student chic. An extraordinary rebellion, this. In a seething mass of dowdy second-hand suits, lengthy coats dripping with threads and ripped pockets, Levi's and Doc Martens shoes, strode Nicky Wire, in middle-aged, and indeed largely middle-class, golfing apparel. He wore Pringle sweaters, not as any kind of ironic mod statement, but as a kickback against student sloppiness. Chequered golf slacks that wouldn't seem amiss at a Palm Springs retirement lunch, or amid Scottish greenery, completed the bizarre ensemble. It wasn't worn entirely for effect. Rather than join any of the myriad social or political activities of his fellow students, Nicky, and occasionally Richey, headed for the local Municipal golf course. In 1995 Nicky told *NME*: "I have always liked golf. I can watch it all day on the television. I find it intensely relaxing. It's a whole parallel world, where nothing really tragic happens and you are guided along by Peter Allis. I don't play golf well . . . it's so incredibly difficult, but it doesn't have to be a place where middle-class businessmen rule. It can be somewhere where everyone can just escape. You can think, you can be in your own world. People made a great deal of my golf playing when I was at university but just because you are a student doesn't mean that you have to act in that clichéd student manner."

This statement, made backstage and under the influence of alcohol some ten years later, certainly hints at an idiosyncratic intelligence that carried Nicky and Richey through their university years without succumbing to the traditional student pastimes. Golf, one senses, and certainly golf gear, helped Nicky retain his sense of identity, his individuality. It also highlighted the natural reactionary streak which would always lie deep within him. But his desire for outward non-conformity was always squarely countered by a profound longing for normality – witness his later love affair with Dyson vacuum cleaners – and might be attributed to an in-built, rock solid personal base. Or, in short, Welshness: a curious desire, as Jan Morris noted, to stay within the comforting confines of the mundane.

It extended beyond Pringles and golf. Not for Nicky a life of binge-drinking bad beer followed by the left-overs of a curry the following morning. Not for him, either, the long spells of uncontrollable giggling over a spliff in some darkened bedroom with the Cocteau Twins on the stereo; nor, indeed, the allure of the rave generation's drug of choice, ecstasy. Nope, in the face of his peers' idea of a good time, Nicky developed a taste for Tizer and Diet Coke, for Britvic Orange and Lemonade. His addiction, such as it was, came from the crystal rooms of fruit machine parlours, the draw of cheap 'n' cheerful gambling. Well, perhaps not all *that* cheap. Although reports vary, Nicky has admitted that his curiously juvenile addiction – for everyone knows that, in any long-term sense, you cannot win on such machines – would contribute heavily to the £3,000 debt he had built up by the time he left university.

During his final year, Nicky survived by purchasing food bought with the money that James, who was not above taking up the occasional bar job in the holidays, regularly mailed him. It was a difficult final year. His one-man rebellion against student life started to affect his outlook on life in general, until he found that he had little faith in the course tutors, or indeed in the course itself. "They never really understood me," he observed years later, "although it can't have been too easy for them. It was different for Richey, who lived to study for a while. For me ... it was only a way, really, of prolonging that awful reality. What was I going to do? Work in a bank? I always knew I could never work in an office. I wasn't practical . . . not in any way. James was. He'd work in bars or whatever to get by but I would have been a fucking embarrassment in a bar . . . or in any kind of work. I'm not proud of that, it was, and still is just the way I am. Bloody lucky that the Manics managed to take off or I would probably still be applying for mature grants or something and blowing it all on fruit machines."

Rather like Nicky, Richey found his own experience of university (at Swansea) disappointing and unfulfilling. His growing thirst for knowledge had helped him soar, seemingly effortlessly, through his 'A' Levels, and the apathy that seemed to surround him in his class he had put down to the lack of ambition one might associate with a small-town mentality. How odd, then, to find that the students of Swansea, in the main, seemed to be equally bored with academia and rather more interested in more traditional student activities, such as prolonged bouts of drinking followed by prolonged bouts of vomiting, or stealing supermarket trollies. It is a delicious paradox that Richey's rock'n'roll ambitions, though still some way from being fulfilled, were initially inspired more by the university library than by the local pubs and clubs. However unlike Nicky he was, Richey did tend to slip into drink, though he did so mainly out of a desire to put himself into a deep sleep and away from the world of his fellow students. Richey's drinking was anti-social. He had nothing in common with the people around him, and it offered him a cheap and effective means of escape. The long-term dangers were not yet apparent.

2

BLACK SHEEP IN BLACKWOOD

"The most beautiful thing in London is McDonalds."
— Richey Edwards

There is a point in everybody's lives when the magic of their surroundings seems to fade away. When familiarity edges into boredom, when parental concern becomes cloying and embarrassing, provoking rebellion. It is the madness of youth and, of course, it is gloriously arrogant, hideously small-minded and great fun even though it perhaps doesn't seem like it at the time.

Nicky Wire, at 19, was an archetypal dissatisfied youth. Black-clad and spidery of frame, he was a well-known local figure in Blackwood and an openly despised one too. Cars would halt, heads would pop out of rear windows and he would hear the familiar greeting "weeeeir-doooooh!" Wire would hunch up and retreat further into the world of books and music that he and his three friends used as a hiding place, a retreat from all that deadening ordinariness out there. Welshness, to the young, punky Nicky Wire, stood for little more than stultifying conservatism. Within a few short years, he would see a genuine appeal in this conservatism, he would even pine to be released back into it, to be freed from the horrors of the pop star world. He would embrace terraced-house domesticity with almost genuine affection and he would bring Welshness into the heart of his music via his natural poetic bent, and a sense of Welsh culture he shared with his older brother, Patrick. All of which would have seemed absurd to the young Wire, as he surveyed dreary, damp Blackwood. The uniform houses lined with wood chip, the bedenimed couples, the Sunday chapel gatherings and the glaring beer-gutted locals in the pubs were anathema to him, symptoms of a world he felt frustrated and held back by. Worst of all was the raging mess of Friday night youth, surging down to the glimmering, chrome discos of Newport. White-shirted boys, reeking of cheap aftershave; red-pocked necks, white socks, black slip-on mock loafers, tight shiny silver trousers, gelled down and wetted hair. By contrast, the girls seemed superior in almost every way, smoking like screen starlets, quick-witted and spiteful, all eyes and make-up, totally in control.

Wire was teetering on the fringe of Goth at the time. Black jeans, black cap sleeve T-shirt, black jacket. His head remained locked in a natural sulk, eyes fixed on his battered plimsolls. Occasionally he would complete the ensemble with a touch of wilful extravagance – a woman's blouse for example, which he would keep hidden beneath his leather jacket or, if he was sitting in the lounge of the Red Lion, Blackwood, a tattered black blazer. There is little doubt that, had he been brought up in Manchester, in London or Sheffield, Wire's mild rebellion would have found a different outlet for its expression. As it was, in Blackwood, he felt like, and *enjoyed* feeling like, Johnny Rotten in Finsbury Park, circa 1976. The stultifying atmosphere of small-town South Wales helped him lead a punk life. Ten years too late.

Girls weren't exactly bowled over by the young Wire and this only served to alienate him further. It's not that he wasn't good looking – he quite obviously was – but his spindly punk form marked him out as just too strange. He was all too often passed over in favour of one of those white-shirted, shaggy-haired lads. It was a classic punk situation. Alienation from raging normality, from those who swarmed the streets of Blackwood or Newport on Friday nights, beery, bleary wastes of space. Wire had seen it all. He had been there, surrounded by mates, on that Friday pub crawl, throwing up in some darkened gutter, soaking in the ale with a tray of greasy chips on the way home. But latterly, he was barely tolerated by the rugby types. There were certain pubs, even in comparatively plush Blackwood, that Wire wouldn't dare enter. It just wasn't worth it. Wire's favourite pub was the Red Lion, a dull, comparatively sedate, profoundly unpretentious boozer soundtracked by a background jukebox and a regular clientele comprised mainly of middle-aged couples and flouncy peroxide blondes. The irony wasn't lost on Wire that his somewhat idiosyncratic dress sense, which caused such friction in younger pubs, was cheerily accepted by the ageing 'straights' of the Red Lion. No one bothered him as he sat in the corner, frayed jeans, scuffed trainers, dour expression and nursed an everlasting half pint of lager. Jenny Watkins-Asnardi, fleetingly Wire's girlfriend at the time, noted to this author, "It was odd for us to drink there, raging rebels in the heart of the valley's petite bourgeoisie . . ."

In so many respects, Wire despised everything he would eventually come to treasure about his Welsh background, including its dogged conservatism. For that, he came to appreciate, was not a weakness, a submission to the system. On the contrary, it is a solid aspect of the Welsh resolve to move at their own pace and not to be pushed forward by their bullish neighbour. In today's world of global communications, the Internet and satellite TV, disaffected local youngsters don't have to leave their hometowns to fundamentally escape. But Nicky Wire needed to.

His songwriting at this stage of his life was highly predictable, at least for a Welsh valley boy with a burgeoning political awareness. Indeed, it's fair to say that the romantic notions of Nicky Wire's art had been forged back in the days of the miners' strike. It's probable that he didn't realise this at the time, but living through such an extreme period undoubtedly fuelled his very Welsh polemic.

Perfectly natural, then, for the embryonic Manic Street Preachers to slip into a parallel world. A wholly insular place, peopled by just the four of them. A film perhaps, containing just four lead characters, with the rest of Blackwood and, indeed, the rest of the world, merely a distant supporting cast. It is a trick that most, if not all, bands achieve to some degree. The nether world, which exists from bedroom to bedroom and is soundtracked by CDs; indeed, the CD rack would become the engine room, fuel to the fire. Outward distractions, girls or football, would only really be tolerated if they actually added to this bonfire of influences. Even the idea of Welshness would be re-assessed in those bedrooms, in terms of what it meant to come from Wales, and to be a Welsh pop star. And this would, perhaps, in time become the Manic Street Preachers' greatest achievement: primarily through them, Wales' rather minimal contribution to the pop canon was kick-started and became something rather sexy, something wholly rock'n'roll.

And in those bedrooms lay a vast cultural world. A scattering of literature and music, all consumed with the ungainly haste of a thirteen year old with a case full of Hula Hoops. There were the Beats – Ginsberg, the mighty Kerouac, Burroughs, Wolfe. Then there were the classic French existentialist authors – Albert Camus (*The Outsider* and *The Fall* were firm favourites), Jean Paul Sartre's *Roads To Freedom*, Joyce's rich and demanding *Ulysses*, Sean O'Casey's autobiographical trilogy *I Knock At The Door*, Beckett's *Waiting For Godot*, Hubert Selby Junior's *Last Exit To Brooklyn*, John Fowles' *The Collector*, Thomas Pynchon's *V*, J D Salinger's *Catcher In The Rye*. A blanket of modern literature, laid down and discussed. Richey's bookshelf was home to J G Ballard's *Atrocity Exhibition*, Wilde's *A Picture Of Dorian Gray*, Jean Jenet's *Miracle Of The Rose*, R D Laing's *Knots*, Kerouac's *Desolation Angels*, Orwell's *1984*, Camus' *Myth Of Sisyphus*, Kafka's *The Trial*, Ken Kesey's *One Flew Over The Cuckoo's Nest*, and Arthur Rimbaud's *A Season In Hell*. One doesn't have to have a PhD. to see themes of alienation and the individual on the fringe of society among those titles. It must have seemed to Richey Edwards that he had much more in common with Joseph K or Winston Smith than with the people he passed every day on the streets of his home town. (Incidentally, more or less the same books adorned the fag-burned coffee table of Mark E. Smith, circa 1977; needless to say, Smith's band were named after the Camus novel.)

To the Manics' credit, their musical preferences were not governed by whatever barriers of credibility had been set in place by the journalists of the day. It was open house with the only parameters being set by their own individual tastes. Nothing wrong then, with playing Guns'n'Roses and Public Enemy, the Velvet Underground and Hanoi Rocks, The Smiths and Kiss, George Clinton and The Clash. A streak of glam, a touch of soul. Sex Pistols and Led Zeppelin. Once warring factions, latterly nothing more than different areas of the same spectrum. Reading matter wouldn't be confined to the modern novel, either, nor to sexual politico tomes or French porn. The four scoured every precious inch of the music press, every sentence of the rock biographies they bought. They soaked in the stories, desperate to sense the mechanics of a particular band – how they worked, what made them great. Were they like other bands? Were they becoming a band? It seemed so, and it was all the more significant, one senses, that the fledgling Manics were effectively slotting their influences into place before they tentatively started to pick up their instruments. Were they like the bands they so admired? The fact is it was impossible to tell as they had absolutely no close reference points; no band anyone had heard of had ever come from Blackwood before.

Undeniably, the fledgling Manics found great enjoyment in creating their own little pocket of elitism. It didn't matter that, beyond local kerbstone gossip, they were completely unknown. In fact, it helped. Between them they concocted a crude manifesto, a ten-point plan to global stardom. It couldn't go wrong! To anyone who might have chanced upon one of their sessions, the extent of their research would have surely seemed obsessive. They even drew up a dossier containing the names and tastes of music journalists. Unheard of, I sense, and quite the antithesis of, say, New Order's cool, where the game was always to ignore, to be downright rude to any passing journos, thereby perversely igniting further journalistic curiosity. Of course, when it came down to it, New Order, and their earlier incarnation, Joy Division, hungered for press coverage just as much as the boys from Blackwood. The groups merely adopted a different approach to achieve the same end. The Manics, rather sweetly, had all the writers lined up before any of them had ever heard of this strange little garishly clad outfit, from, of all places, Wales.

Above all, and like so many of the greatest bands down the years, from The Beatles to The Clash, the four future Manics were a gang. "We always got a kick out of goading people into thinking we were complete tossers," James told the *Toronto Star* in 1992. "Everyone has their own little gang at school and that is what we were like. We realised that, as individuals we were very limited so we had to fabricate ourselves and we took a very academic approach towards being in a band. We were quite clinical. We were like magpies, collecting information. We had intellectual meetings. Discussing books. Sometimes we did read them, sometimes we would rely on Richey, who always read more than the rest of us put together. It was a little bit pretentious, but even that aspect was fun. It was certainly a way to do things differently from the people around us. We were wrong to feel superior. Why were we superior to a local plumber, who worked fucking hard to feed his kids? We weren't. We still aren't. I mean that. But it was something different. We were hungry to learn things at that stage. Things beyond what is expected of four idiots from the valleys. That was the whole point of the group." Like magpies! It was ninety per cent bluff and bluster, of course, but then so is rock'n'roll itself. It didn't matter a jot that such talk made the four sound pretentious. Quoting William Burroughs in your lyrics was a terrific way of stating who and what you were all about, and distinguishing yourself from the pack.

"We had one session," Richey remembered, "when we were actually selecting and rejecting the journalists who would interview us. I know that sounds absolutely pathetic, in fact it sounds downright sad, but that's what we did. The thing is that we actually meant it. We never thought we were being really stupid. We were that arrogant. We knew we were intelligent and we knew we were capable of creating our own world. A world beyond the reach of a lot of the kids on the streets. It wouldn't have really mattered even if we hadn't done well in a commercial sense. Our escape, initially at least, was our sheer collective thirst for literature and music. It was that, more than anything else, that put us on higher ground. That was a fantastic achievement, finding that higher ground."

Oddly, the early Nineties, with the hedonistic dance party of Acid House still dominating, was probably the British music scene's least literary soaked period; a time when the emphasis had swung profoundly away from lyrics towards rhythmic inventiveness. A fabulous time, then, for a punky bunch to start flashing names like Rimbaud and Camus about. It worked for The Smiths – Patti and Mark E – both of whom earned acres of music press space simply because, apart from being damn good, they were considerably better read than The Ramones or The Drones. How cool, then, for an unknown, aggressive young band to be dropping such glorious literary names. Post-punk intellectualism, which produced The Fall, The Pop Group, Throbbing Gristle, PIL, and Doll By Doll to name but a few, was based on exactly the same principles. Stimulate people's aesthetic aspirations – even if they were aspirations they never knew existed – and you have a ready-built audience. That driving force was still there years later, in the opening line of 'A Design For Life': "Libraries give us power." Indeed.

Their musical eclecticism was something else which marked the young Manics apart from their peers. They mixed 'n' matched combinations of genres regardless of prevailing opinions of cool. "People made a lot of our liking of Guns'n'Roses," Richey recalled to *Melody Maker* in 1994. "I think they thought we were being reactionary. Well, we weren't. We didn't love that music just to wind up dumb journalists but, if that's what it did, then that was fantastic. It probably increased our desire to like anything we damn well pleased. I mean, we were all living apart when we started. I was in Swansea, at Uni and the others, apart from Nicky, were at different colleges, but we kept in constant touch. We never really split up. Funny how we all accepted music that a lot of students turned their noses up at. We were beyond them and their petty hipness . . . and we knew it. It made us stronger. And anyway, *Appetite For Destruction* was the best album in the world. You couldn't compare it to those crap student bands.

"I had a period where I just wanted to kick everything in the head and just go over to LA and become a Malibu beach bum. It would have probably had been an impossible thing to do. You would have needed lots of money, but I was envious of the American open attitude towards music and heavy rock music in particular. I thought it was fantastic when Aerosmith did that thing with Run DMC. In England that really blew people's minds. People thought, How could they? But in America nobody gave it a second thought. Of course rock and rap go hand in hand. They always did. It was like owning . . . a Black Sabbath album and a James Brown album in 1970. I mean, why not? Why did people lock themselves into any kind of musical genre? It was so obviously stupid and it was something that bugged me since my early teens. That desire to be part of a particular club. It is pathetic. But it felt fantastic to be intelligent enough to simply rise free from all that. And we were all capable of seeing that broad picture."

If there is a musical heart to the Manics then it must lie with James. The guitar was his vehicle for escape from Blackwood. It was the key. And like every genuine rock star, like Noel Gallagher, Paul Weller and Johnny Marr, James had both ability and determination. Enough determination to be able to lock himself away for hours on end, simply practising and practising like crazy. It was at this point, in late 1988, when the Second Summer of Love was in full swing, that Nicky, taking a cue from his brother, Patrick, a poet and playwright of the old Welsh order, had started to furiously jot down words. Patrick showed Nicky how to channel emotion into words, to capture his natural anger, to funnel it into short, disciplined lyrics. Poetry is at the very heart of Welsh culture, from John Cowper Powys to Dylan Thomas. Patrick Jones, a ferociously political animal, was, and indeed still is, very much a continuum of that culture. And it was Patrick who inspired and guided the artistic direction of young Nick, so that he would be able to plot a course. To do something positive. There was nothing particularly magical in this process. Words formed, more often than not, from the ferocious polemic which burned inside him. His first 'proper' batch of lyrics, almost inevitably, turned out to be a staunch diatribe against the most violent political upheaval that South Wales had experienced in recent times: the 1984 miners' strike, and the subsequent physical and psychological effects it had on the people of Blackwood and beyond.

Sean was drafted into this raggle-taggle band because of his solid musical grounding, forged from many hours spent sitting uncomfortably in an ill-fitting blazer, blowing into a trumpet, as a member of the South Wales Jazz Band. Although not, strictly speaking, a 'brass band', it must be noted that such musical units had long been an important part of local society in many areas of the country, and the subject of genuine working-class pride. Although latterly scorned, it's always wise to note that such outfits often achieve a musicianship of world-class standard, and often for little or no financial reward. Sean had purchased a set of drums in 1988 and was taking to percussion with admirable gusto – indeed, with inspirational dexterity. Initially, the idea was to employ the striking exotic and aforementioned Ms Asnardi as lead singer. It was a role she readily took to and the band entered into months of shambolic rehearsals at James's house, with Nicky feeding Jenny with endless strings of words. Harsh, spiky, political words, unusually laced with literary references and themes picked up from his politics classes.

Lyrically speaking, this embryonic Manic Street Preachers was like The Clash might have been had they bothered to pay attention in class. Of course, the whole point of The Clash was that they did anything *but* pay attention in class and subsequently formed – with the help of manager Bernie Rhodes – an impassioned if ill-informed polemic to back up their songs. With the Manics, the lyrical research was always in place. Musically, much to the distress of anyone within earshot, the Manics were starting to sound like a musically inferior New York Dolls – some achievement – crossed with the most unlistenable fringes of the dismal early Eighties New Wave of British Heavy Metal. In short, they were woeful, artless, parochial, and simmering with boundless enthusiasm. The musical equivalent of a pre-grad art school folder. Perhaps mercifully, this incarnation of the band never dared to emerge from James's front room, although the mere fact that they were in some kind of band at all was enough to grant them some kind of kudos within the local community. It wasn't to last. Jenny and Nicky's relationship fell on stony ground and the band splintered before having a chance to evolve into any kind of remotely palatable unit. However, all was not lost: before the dust had time to settle, another friend, Miles Woodward, more famously referred to as 'Flicker', brought his bass guitar into the equation.

They started again, creating an ungainly thrash which powered through any semblance of melody, James spitting lyrics in the manner of gutter punksters Discharge (from Stoke-on-Trent, a rival to Blackwood in the boredom stakes). Sean's drumming was strong even then, but hampered by a tendency that the others had to speed up, making his role somewhat redundant. On a few occasions, something really did click. Then, once again the disparate elements would come apart, and an inelegant cacophony returned. "Music should be difficulty, a challenge," James proffered at the time, to a resounding thumbs up from the other band members. It's the oldest excuse on the bottom rung of rock. It is the lie at the heart of punk, that passion, commitment and energy are a true substitute for evolving talent. Nonsense, of course. But nobody, least of all the band's friends, could have known that behind the cacophony, lay a genuinely unique talent. It was just so unlikely. There are a thousand bad bands in Britain. One or two, no more, hold the key to excellence. All bands believe they have it.

With Flicker in the picture, a gig of sorts was tentatively arranged at Blackwood's decaying Little Theatre, a dusty amateur-dramatics hall more suited to the ubiquitous mumble of the Mothers Union than dissonant rock'n'roll. In 1988, as Madchester was in mid-explosion, and Londoners circled the M25 in search of raves, the Manic Street Preachers gathered on the austere benches of the Little Theatre's dressing room, and, terrified beyond belief, ran through a set of inelegant retro sub rock. The band's name, Richey told *Boston Globe*, emerged after seeing a particularly bizarre religious ranter in Newport, although they had briefly considered calling themselves 'Betty Blue', after their favourite erotic art flick, 'Blue Generation' or 'The Blues'. Out in the hall, as the meagre but curious crowd gathered, Patrick Jones, commendably eager and encouraging, began setting up his video equipment. The resulting tape shows a band stumbling onto the stage to a dull audience growl. As the chords splattered from the speakers, with the band jumping around in an early version of their famous post-punk pogos, pot-bellied rugby monsters surged to the fore, sprawling onto the stage as if scoring a winning Welsh try, crashing down on top of each other and causing great swathes of brown beer to splatter across the stage and spattering into the amplifiers. James is caught on film, staring in terror – not at the moronic brawl, but at one particular amplifier, fizzing and steaming, on the verge, or so it appeared, of some kind of explosion.

The idiots in the crowd raged on, apparently wholly unaware of the problems band members might face when liquid meets live electricity. The riot, which began in a state of reckless high spirits, soon degenerated into something more serious as a particularly rotund moron flopped onto the stage and began kicking the hapless Flicker. The tension rose further when Nick, spinning around for artistic effect, crashed his guitar into Flicker's side; this caused the bassist to retaliate, grabbing Nick and forcing him to the floor. As a precursor to a mass celebratory scrum, this seemed to work a treat, as the rugby lads crashed on top of the brawling lads. James, heroic to the end, played on, his black jumpers hiding a T-shirt which, somewhat unfathomably or, perhaps optimistically, proclaimed, "I'M SEX!" It was embarrassing, messy stuff, and nobody's idea of a classic début gig. Subsequently, the band decided that the film should under no circumstances be made available to a wider audience.

In retrospect one senses, strongly, that the entire rumpus was inspired by little more than a touch of local jealousy, of prancing, pathetic machismo, aimed at impressing local girls, and putting the band in their place. That glamour of actually being in a band simply had to be crushed. However, despite the debacle they'd just experienced, the Manic Street Preachers returned to their minuscule dressing room in a heady state of elation. They were r'n'r debutantes, and rightly proud of it. Outside, in the hall, the local police constables sifted through the wreckage, wondering what on earth had happened. The few chairs that had been unwisely left in the hall, now lay sadly splintered. A violent crack now decorated the top of a Formica table and two windows had been smashed. Truth be told, it was a small-time, small-town disturbance, nothing more. But to the Manics, it was Altamont, it was The Clash at Belle Vue, it was a flashback to the ill-fated Sex Pistols Anarchy Tour. People knew of them now; they'd started. A second gig, this time at a local pub, proved to be a rather less fractious affair in front of a curiously low-key audience who stared long and hard as the band thrashed about relentlessly, striving to inject some fire into the evening. For reasons that no one quite understood, this second gig proved to be quite the antithesis of the first. Rock'n'roll was proving to be an unpredictable business.

Back in James's bedroom songs were starting to form. Lyrics came first, flowing thick and fast from Nicky and Richey, to be worked up into fuller form on James's unplugged guitar. Richey was not by any means a full band member at this stage, but he was emerging rapidly as a guiding influence, offering snatches of valuable opinion, adding words, muscling naturally into place. Even in this raw company, he couldn't claim any degree of musicianship, but his contributions, his presence even, seemed strangely valuable and, whenever rehearsals took place without him, the band felt slightly lost.

Too early, the band opted to get some of their material recorded in an eight-track studio. Too early, that is, to produce anything remotely original. Not that it mattered. They felt like a real band as they nervously ran through their respective contributions and spent a long night slouched over a small mixing desk, watching and listening as some kind of sound came together. They emerged proudly with four songs: 'Suicide Alley', 'Tennessee (I Feel So Low)', 'Repeat' and 'New Art Riot'. All fairly predictable titles, and neatly complemented by their increasingly low-rent, mock-glam apparel. The band were beginning to look like the kind of lads that Jayne County might take an unhealthy interest in. Cheap tack, plastic and denim, swiped from images of glam period Lou Reed, New York Dolls and Hanoi Rocks and laced with decidedly uncool touches of Guns'n'Roses. (A suede fringe briefly flopped from James's jacket.) Their image put the band violently at odds with the general UK scene which was snowballing into aceeeeeed psychedelia and as far away from trad rock clichés as was humanly possible. The look reflected strongly in the songs, material that could have been recorded by The UK Subs or Angelic Upstarts at the height of the unholy second wave of punk. (Perhaps more significantly, the songs also strongly echoed the first known stirrings of Welsh band, Yr Anrefn.) It was as raw as music is possible to get without having to carry a Salmonella warning and, frankly, unlistenable to anyone not wearing a studded leather jacket and grubby sneakers.

Nevertheless, after playing the tracks to their startled families and friends, the band pooled whatever beer money they had lying around and produced 300 singles. The first 150 were slotted between a photo-montage sleeve by Richey, while the second batch were given a rather more DIY and individual approach. It's rather touching to think of the band, in true punk style, physically sticking the things together and barely containing their mounting excitement as the stack of records in James's bedroom grew larger and larger. The single, 'Suicide Alley', now commands high prices, of course. Not, frankly, that it was particularly deserving or, indeed, intended to be much more than a vinyl demo. Nevertheless, released in August 1989, it can be proudly logged as the début disc by a band with a ferociously prolific capacity for releasing singles. On this occasion they purchased 300 cardboard envelopes and simply mailed the lot, sending them optimistically into the real world. James sat by his phone and waited. Journalists, promoters, record company A&R men – just some of the people who failed to respond. The telephone remained agonisingly silent and the band, frustrated at this early hiccup in their career, began to argue amongst themselves. It's a situation that every band will recognise. How could it be that nobody else could see the talent that they saw all too clearly in themselves? The very first interview with the Manic Street Preachers was up for grabs and there were no takers.

There was even a false dawn – the stunning moment they opened their *NME*s to find that old Mr Irony, Steven Wells, had made the record 'Single Of The Week'. Wells, still carrying the mantle for old, pure punk, had never forgotten the first time he had heard the fabulously raw and loose Undertones single, 'Teenage Kicks', or Stiff Little Fingers' similarly invigorating 'Suspect Device', and held romantic notions of discovering the next low-fi punk classic. Unfortunately, although he had unwittingly discovered the band, Wells' notions of greatness were misplaced with this particular single. For a few brief days the band naïvely believed that such a review was all that was needed to catapult them into the heads of the music industry. Not so. No A&R man listened to more than the first riotous ten seconds before ripping it from their system and sending it spinning towards the bin where, to be perfectly honest, it found its true home. After three days of mounting tension over their spectacular lack of results, bad blood developed between Nicky and Flicker. Band meetings were held in the Red Lion. Intense arguments followed which ended with the disgruntled Flicker being rudely ejected from the band's ranks. Almost instantly, Richey was drafted in on rhythm guitar – although he couldn't play a note – and Nicky switched to bass. By December 11, 1989 the Manic Street Preachers had formed.

Despite the ear-splitting silence and wave of apathy that had greeted 'Suicide Alley', the Manics rediscovered their optimism with Richey in their ranks and even managed to perform in front of a local crowd that was neither openly hostile nor apathetic. A sure sign, they thought, that in Blackwood, people were beginning to regard them as a real band, as musicians, rather than as poncified geeks playing at being pop stars. It was a breakthrough, albeit rather short-lived. During one, long, dreadful week, the band saw themselves refused loans from two nonplussed banks – it might have worked, in London, but Welsh bank and building society managers are a different breed, not so easily swayed by the sight of The Clash meets The New York Dolls striding briskly into their office claiming to be 'the next big thing'. James and Nicky would be naturally attentive during these meetings; Richey spent the meetings flicking his fingers and staring forlornly out of the window like the naughty boy in class. A rock'n'roll affectation, certainly, as Richey was arguably the most eager student of the four. Their public profile, or lack of it, couldn't have helped their cause much. The Manics were, at this point, barely scrambling beyond the 'school band' bottom rung of rock's tortuous hierarchy and with the dance scene still dominant nationwide, what price four ragged archaic, provincial punks?

That fact obviously wasn't lost on Richey, who would later tell *Spin* magazine, "We were always very aware that, in terms of image, in terms of the signals we were sending out, that people would underestimate our intelligence. It was a deliberate ploy. Right from the beginning. Nobody else that we knew about had ever attempted to get the kind of depth of message across in such a format. A crude musical format, if you like. That was what the Manics were all about. Proving to people that we had a brain. And we always knew we were brighter than all the other bands. If we had built that into our image we would have come across like some fucking dull student band and that was never us." Quite the contrary, in fact. It's interesting to note that their collective university experience served to strengthen the Manics' links with their working-class origins. An unfashionable and latterly unique concept in itself. But again, that's another of the fundamental differences between this band and a band such as Happy Mondays, Stone Roses or Oasis – all working-class bands the members of which failed to gain any level of distinction in academic terms, for better or worse. Music became their vocation and, subsequently, none of these bands ever lost that working-class link. By contrast, Jarvis Cocker found himself literally torn from his roots. By the time he was living in London's wealthy Holland Park and making documentary television films about 'outsider art', he openly admitted that he no longer felt comfortable in a Sheffield tap room or, as he courageously put it to the *Sunday Times* in March 1999: "I hope my music, which was working-class music initially, does manage to communicate. But I have trouble personally. I can't go down Meadowhall without having lots of little gits following me around. People attack me in pubs. They think I have moved away from them. Fact is, I never wanted to. But I have. That's life."

Well, sometimes there are things worth moving away to avoid. Witness the night the embryonic Manic Street Preachers stood in the Red Lion, intent on celebrating Richey's birthday without downing twelve pints of bitter and rolling into the Blackwood gutter. Dressed in their usual finery – all leopard-skin and plastic – it's hardly surprising that their appearance that night attracted exactly the wrong kind of attention. It began in the pub, with a few of the younger locals hurling abuse and, as the band exited, throwing the odd mis-timed punch. It exploded nastily later, in a burger joint, when larger, meatier lads started to lash out at Richey. Phrases like "Foookin' fagggottt!" decorated the air; one or two blows connected. James, even then the stockiest of the Manics and the one you would least like to meet in an antagonistic mood in a darkened alley, waded bravely into the fray. There followed a whirling scrum which snowballed around the corner. James became a bloodied mess, with boots smashing into his back and one, unfortunately, crashing into his jaw, splintering the bone. If the yobs' intentions had been to drag the singer away from the microphone, if only for a few months, then their mission was successful.

*   *   *

The gigs flashed by. Nervy, edgy, and improving all the time, the group gradually attracted a small but loyal band of fans. None of their regular contingent made it up to London, however, for the band's début in the capital's Horse and Groom in Great Portland Street – a pub more regularly patronised by publishers and top-ranking medical folk than slogan-bearing punks. It was to be a curious début, with the band tentative and suspicious of everything to do with London. It seems odd in retrospect that a band deemed so unfashionable by those who had actually heard of them, should attract, as they did, a respectable smattering of music journalists. This didn't strike the band as unusual at all: they had no way of knowing just how difficult it is for any new band, let alone a distant outfit from, of all places, Wales, to drag such people into an unlikely pub in Great Portland Street. They had sent leaflets, 'fliers', to all the music papers; they had spent an afternoon screaming down the phone like some kind of absurd Welsh telesales team and had encouraged the few friends they knew who were based in the capital to spread some kind of word. But if they were confident that any of these people would actually turn up, especially in a climate still strongly dominated by baggy and, less so, by scratchy indie rock, they were displaying a great deal of naïvety. Then again, maybe their distance from the general scene was so spikily profound, they actually struck some kind of a chord. That would seem to have been the case. True enough, The Wonderstuff were playing within yards of the Horse and Groom and, apparently by absolute fluke, a gang featuring two full-time music journalists, two major label A&R men and one London-based rock promoter simply 'happened' to float into that very pub within half an hour of the performance. Such things do happen in this area of London, betwixt the

West End and Euston but one must conclude that the Manic Street Preachers had a large dose of luck on their side.

So what did everyone see that night? A brazen mess of Stiff Little Fingers meet Jayne County Clash meet Dolls, Ramones meet Hanoi. A ferocious sound, screaming from the speakers, whirling around the bemused crowd, none of whom could quite comprehend the full-blooded rock'n'roll pastiche that strutted and posed so confidently before them, firing out barbed punkisms, chords and clichés. The bass guitarist leaped towards the room's ceiling (and connected painfully on one occasion), while the lead singer twirled like a pin wheel and the rhythm guitarist affected a Lou Reed glam gorm stare. Faces in the crowd stared in disbelief and applause trickled rather than rippled. Nobody, absolutely nobody in that audience, I'd suggest, could quite believe that such a band could possibly exist, at the start of the Nineties, or that anyone could even have the audacity to perform in such a way. And yet through all that, through all the negativity and prejudice apparent at that gig, something positive did manage to shine through. Nobody could have guessed that this band were capable of evolving into a unit blessed with such a gift for melodic simplicity that its music would one day be used as a highly evocative backing for a Welsh Tourist Board television advertisement.

Record plugger Tony Childs recalls the sheer oddness of the Manics' London début: "It was a really odd night and, thinking back, I don't know why we were there at all. There were a few of us . . . a few record company people. Journalists too, I believe, but I wouldn't have known them. But we had been out for a meal in a little Indian restaurant around the corner . . . I had never been in that pub before and I can't remember anyone saying that there was a gig on. We just didn't feel like going home and went for a drink. Suddenly we were watching this ludicrous band. They were pretty awful. I can't say that it was possible to hear anything interesting in the music at all. Having said that, there was a feel around our little gang of a certain kind of sympathy. For my part I rather admired them, as much for their sheer gall as their music. You would have to be incredibly naïve to try to pull off that glam rock thing at that point in time. Or stupid, or something. We were all a bit stunned, really. It was like being in a time warp and, despite the fact that they were kind of refreshing, I never thought I'd hear their name ever again. You would have bet your mortgage on that."

Bob Stanley, of Saint Etienne, then freelancing for *Melody Maker* in tandem with his lively *Hopelessly Devoted* fanzine, saw much more in the Manics than a mere refreshing gimmick. Penning a short, sharp feature on the band, he hinted that they might well have a future. In a brave attempt to prove this he slapped the Manics song 'UK Channel Boredom' on a flexi-disc and wandered the darkened venues of North London attempting, and more often than not failing, to sell the music of the Manic Street Preachers.

Richey: "We loved London. We always did. I think we understood that London had been so important during the punk years. The Clash, the Pistols, all the reggae thing. It all happened in London. And I think we just fell in love with the place names . . . like any provincial kids. Notting Hill Gate, Camden Town, Tufnell Park. All that stuff. Like Julie Burchill falling for the London Underground map. Having admitted that, we soon worked out how to work the system. We knew we had to do a lot of London gigs and we'd pounce on journalists. We'd befriend them in a really cynical way. We thought we were more intelligent than them but we didn't let them know it . . . That said, some of those venues that sounded really romantic, really rock'n'roll, turned out to be crap little shitholes with three insane drunks and two dogs. But somehow we still thought it was heaven. The thing is that we thought of the people back home. They would know that we were playing gigs in London and that meant something. Well, it didn't. It meant fuck all but they didn't know that. We'd get back and strut around Blackwood like all-conquering heroes."

In truth, the Manics sank swiftly into the system, gigging hard, chatting to journalists from fanzines and music press alike, encouraging tentative followers, and skidding back to Blackwood, taking perverse delight in seeing the hoards drifting out to work as dawn broke, flopping into bed before engaging in the post-gig debrief over tea, toast and *Neighbours* in the afternoon. Although technically still stuck in their Blackwood backwater, they took to playing the rock'n'roll game in London like experts, concentrating their energies and pushed hard at London's curiously parochial music scene.

Nobody, one senses, was too surprised by the way the major labels reacted, or rather, failed to. They did come to watch, but if the Manics expected their dressing rooms to be besieged by enthusiastic A&R men, waving wads and contracts, they were heartbreakingly disappointed. In truth, they were not seen by anyone in command of a budget large enough to finance a new rock act. It just didn't work that way. The indie route, therefore, appeared to be the only option. This obviously dismayed Richey, who never shared that particular dream. "I wanted a big label," he remembered, "big money right from the outset because I thought we were worth it and I didn't want us to be seen as another band just farting about, getting nowhere because nobody around them had any money. That was never the case with the Pistols or The Clash, was it? The whole point was to get the money and move on. OK, so Buzzcocks and Joy Division did it the indie way but I always thought that was simply because no big labels were interested at first." (Absolutely correct, as it happens. Ian Curtis always dreamed of signing to RCA. Pete Shelley used Buzzcocks' own New Hormones label to lever a decent wedge out of United Artists. You would have to be pretty short-sighted to fall for the indie ethic *per se*. Many did though.)

That said, although the Manic Street Preachers would have signed a twenty-album deal with Sony if it was on offer, they simply weren't ready to face the hidden traumas of life with a major label. They would have been swamped by the deadening professionalism of it all, by an overzealous A&R man, or by a professional producer welded to a contract and intent on imposing his musical authority. As such, and despite their understandable misgivings, the Manics' anti-indie stance capitulated immediately the moment they were approached, in the most casual of circumstances: a pub. The Bull and Gate in Kentish Town, to be precise. The first person to make the Manics a genuine offer was Ian Ballard whose label, Damaged Goods, had been named after the scorching Gang Of Four song of the same name. It was an indie legacy, of sorts. But Ballard must be heartily commended. Not only had he picked up on a band that had been seen by representatives from most major labels, he had sensed something about them that had eluded those so-called experts.

A handshake in Walthamstow resulted in the release of the 'New Art Riot' EP, which surfaced noisily in June 1990. It was, of course, pacy, ragged and lost in a murk of swift, cheap recording techniques. Alas, as with most latter-day punk discs, it failed to grasp the adrenaline rush of, say, Buzzcocks' classic, 'Spiral Scratch' or those early outings from Stiff Little Fingers or The Undertones. It was rather more reminiscent of punk's tedious, uninspired second wave: the flood of bandwagon-jumpers topped by 999, The Drones, The Lurkers ... (Cue one thousand dreary names which paved the well-trodden path between the Sex Pistols and Discharge.) Four songs, again with titles that proclaimed the Manics' manifesto: 'New Art Riot' (an out-take from sessions for the first single), 'Strip It Down', 'Last Exit On Yesterday' and 'Teenage 20/20'. Each title, let alone each song, simply screams the most achingly obvious influences – The Fall, SLF, Hubert Selby Junior and The Ramones respectively. Frankly, the music itself was a bit of a letdown compared to the kind of rush associated with the bands who were clearly such an influence on it. That said, there was a market ready and all too willing to swing against the dance pulse of Madchester and, to such ears, any kind of spirited rock thrash would be welcomed. There was also the small fact that the Manic Street Preachers looked unlike virtually every other rock act in Britain at the time. An A&R man with vision – a rarity, I know – might well take a long look and wonder if these pretty, glammed-up Welsh boys might just be the ones to lead the backlash against dance music.

And curiously, the Manics' first meeting with their management team – Hall Or Nothing – would come via a link with the very Madchester scene they so naturally opposed. Indeed, a link with the kings of baggy themselves, The Stone Roses. Stone Roses' Manager Gareth Evans: "Throughout the heyday of the Roses I worked extensively with Philip Hall. He became my best friend. In fact, more than that, he became the only person who I genuinely trusted within the music business. He worked on PR for the Roses and worked it all quite beautifully. He got to know the band. He understood their music in a way that, to be really honest, was always a bit beyond me. I was more of an ex-Mod. Philip more or less created an image out of nothing because the Roses, despite John Squire's artwork, were pretty hopeless in terms of image. They just came across as four dull boys in interviews but Philip even helped to turn that around so they started to appear distant and enigmatic. It was very subtle. I'm not sure even the band realised it, but it worked.

"As soon as I heard that he was getting involved with the Maniac (sic) Street Preachers I knew they would be massive. I didn't know much about them apart from the fact that they were like The Clash which, from a Manchester perspective, sounded incredibly dumb, to be honest. But I knew he would work on that and entice something of value out of them. He would turn their image around into something positive. That's what he could do. That's what he did. He called me once. One night. Very late, which was unusual and he was absolutely exploding with enthusiasm. The thing is, Philip wasn't normally like that, not with me. He was a pretty cool kind of bloke but he obviously saw something within this band that he had never come across before. I remember him telling me that 'they write me letters all the time. Long, rambling letters.' He thought this was amazing and so did I. I tried to imagine Ian Brown writing me a letter. Or John. It would never happen in a million years, so in a way I was a bit jealous even though they were nothing at the time. They were obviously intelligent and willing to listen and learn. That sounded like a dream to me."

Philip Hall was an ex-*Record Mirror* writer who drifted into the PR side of the music industry. That sentence alone explains a great deal. Rarely celebrated at the time or since, *Record Mirror* was the most visually (and dance) conscious of all the music magazines of the Seventies and Eighties. Caring not for the streetwise credibility cultivated by *NME*, *Melody Maker* and *Sounds*, *Record Mirror* – situated above the *Sounds* office over Covent Garden tube station – worked in tandem with the pop fringe of the music business. As such, Hall came to understand how hype worked and it was perhaps no surprise when, following a spell at EMI, he joined the Stiff Records hype machine as Head of Press. At Stiff he cleverly helped develop an essential sense of humour and built it into many press campaigns. It was a fantastic tactic as it helped bring on board the dour, pretentious music writers from the inkies: if it was fun, the hype could be justified. (Though it was not enough to prevent Stiff from sliding from prominence as the major labels moved bullishly in to take charge of the Eighties pop boom.) Hall's own company, Hall Or Nothing, swiftly established itself on the back of his expertise, and record companies and journalists alike found it an intelligent and approachable company, refreshingly lacking in the cold aloofness that generally hovers around London-based music-related PR companies. (Hall Or Nothing didn't even force its female employees to adopt ludicrous names on taking up their positions; an extraordinary breakthrough, that one.) Hall remained a refreshing oddity. Swayed neither by trend nor A&R bullshit, he forced himself to actually listen to demo tapes that might pass his way. He would actually read the accompanying letters. He believed in his own ability to seek something out. That said, he had absolutely no idea quite what he was looking for.

The Manic Street Preachers, having finally understood the workings of bottom rung rock'n'roll, correctly decided that it was a numbers game. Talent, commitment and originality are pointless attributes if the music doesn't manage to reach any important ears. From a Blackwood base, there was only one way around this. They would gather in James's bedroom, from which they would send out copies of their EP accompanied by long-winded, ludicrous letters claiming genius and, eventually, world domination. They were learning fast. The letters were poked behind a striking photograph of the band, in full regalia, made up to trash Dolls standard. Richey: "If you take the daftest, most naïve, most juvenile fanzines, then maybe you will have some idea about the kind of crap we used to put in those letters. And I'd put in endless literary quotes. It was incredibly pretentious really, really dumb. But, as time passed, the letters became more and more surreal. It's strange but, in a way, maybe there was a certain honesty about those letters that appealed to people. We were just dumb hicks trying to be clever. But we knew that most people would just hurl the whole package in the bin. So we actually sat down and had a discussion and decided that there was only one way around it. Everybody ... and I mean everybody in the London music business, would be approached. We simply reasoned that somewhere, somehow, it would land on the right desk at the right time."

Philip Hall was the man at the right desk at the right time. He had received a flood of similar packages that week and, as usual, wasn't sure quite what to do with any of them. The Manic Street Preachers were, at least, unexpected and strangely fresh. Although he wasn't immediately knocked out by the EP, he did listen hard enough to hear something intriguing within the music. As he was hugely involved with the comparatively sophisticated Stone Roses, one can only conclude that he had remarkable ears or, indeed, remarkable vision. Perhaps it was Hall who had decided to plan for the rave kickback. Perhaps this was it – this strikingly retro bunch from, of all places, a Welsh valley. It was so unlikely, it was positively perverse.

Philip and his younger brother, Martin, ventured forth to Blackwood. To Newbridge School, to be precise, used by the band for rehearsal purposes. It was, to say the least, an unusually austere venue, especially as the band had wandered into the school 'glammed' to the nines, with rouge, eye-liner and the obligatory spray-painted shirts bearing slogans such as 'Lonesome Aesthete', 'Culture of Destruction' and 'London Death Sentence Heritage'. The Halls looked on in utter disbelief while the band slammed through their set, as Philip Hall later recalled to Manchester's *City Life* magazine: "There was something about them, even then. I didn't know whether to laugh or applaud at first. But after about two or three numbers I knew they had a life beyond their image. It was strange because we had been conditioned to thinking that music had evolved in a certain way and everyone was into the Manchester baggy thing and, in a sense, it was incredibly courageous of the Manics to be the way they were. They were far from stupid . . . in fact, they were incredibly intelligent and that intelligence really did shine through . . . that is probably what convinced me. I thought they were going to be enormous, which is a pretty naïve thing to think."

Hall's days at the terminally unhip *Record Mirror* were still etched into him. Back then, he established a resolve that saw far beyond the soundbite mentality of the hipper music press and, with the Manics, he was confronted by a talent so distanced from the mindset of the average music press reader that that in itself started to make them seem like an attractive proposition. He also surmised that the band's intelligence was a real ace in the hole, and that their music would gain melodic stature as they developed. It could go wrong. Horribly wrong. Indeed, the odds would be stacked against them. But he knew before he left that school, that he would sign the Manics to a management contract.

The band couldn't really tell anything from the visit. The Halls stood before them and seemed genuine enough. They seemed interested, too. The only problem was – and it was a major source of tension on the night – that none of the Manics had a clue just what it was that the Halls did, or what, if anything, they wanted to do with the band. The apparent sweetness of the band was, I sense, somewhat overstated. They bombarded Hall with letters following the visit. Either he would tire of their precocity or he would admire their unbounded enthusiasm. Luckily for the Manics, who, by now, urgently wanted to join the vast army of the London Welsh – Blackwood couldn't contain them; let's be fair – Hall fell for their unusual charms. In a well-documented and somewhat comedic interlude, the entire band went on to occupy the flat he shared with his wife in Queens Park. As related in Martin Clarke's *Sweet Venom*, far from adopting the lifestyle of disaffected Nineties punks, the Manic Street Preachers, spurred on by Nicky Wire, proved to be quite the perfect house guests, endlessly cleaning and preparing the evening meal for the returning work-weary Halls. This little scenario can be seen as a microcosm of the Manics role in the run of things. A critic might perhaps label them 'pseudo punks', an intelligent, strangely polite band engaged in dumbing down to catch a growing street audience. But that would be to miss the point. Although intellectually they had little if anything in common with The Clash, and could hardly be said to be relating to the cider-quaffing tartan and leather-clad strays who terrorise tourists in Leicester Square, they were honest enough to follow their own line of influence. The music press, of course, remained reticent to say the least, but Philip Hall had started to discover the true hidden depths of the band.

Gareth Evans: "I still couldn't see it, to be honest, but (Philip Hall) was obviously one hundred per cent convinced. I had never known such conviction. Most band managers are conspirational (sic) between each other. They are quite cynical about their artists but I could tell that Philip had fallen hook, line and sinker for them. And his enthusiasm started rubbing off on me. I started believing him. So it is easy to see how he started to turn heads. Because he completely and utterly believed in the band himself. When I mentioned this to people in Manchester at the time . . . to Tony Wilson, I seem to remember, it was met with something approaching anger. 'How can he like that crap?' That kind of thing. It was really snobbish but the Manchester people thought they were beyond all that . . . but they hadn't listened. I always listened to Philip. Incredibly intelligent man."

If nothing else, the Manic Street Preachers of 1990 were young and beautiful, the first sighting of an unprecedented Welsh presence in pop. The new, upbeat, cosmopolitan Wales. Not a Wales of ruddy cheeks and beery torsos, of the insular locale, the brooding undercurrent of anti-British resentment, but a bright, vivacious, sexy, sharp Wales. They were a band of the world, ready for anything, gorgeous and highly intelligent. While their Welsh forebears, The Alarm, skidded back to start singing songs about saving their local town hall steps, and making folksy ditties in Welsh, the Manics were stretching to catch hold of the distant coat-tails of Guns'n'Roses. They hailed from a completely different planet to, say, Shaun Ryder or Clint Boon, or any one of a hundred droopy baggies. The Manics wanted glamour. Seen in this context, rather than as another bunch of 999-style sub-punks, it was difficult to think of another band in Britain who shared their dreams.

If there were any early cracks in the band dynamic, they kept them hidden from Philip Hall. The spotless house and cooked and ready pasta masked the fact that, during band meetings, Richey would occasionally slink into the background to be caught, five minutes later, hacking into his skin with a small sharp blade. It wasn't taken too seriously at first; the wounds were of a schoolboyish nature. Richey was the cleverest member of a clever band. It was just a fleeting affectation, surely, part and parcel, the band felt, of the cult of 'dressing up', being different, marking yourself out. In the band's experience, the easiest way to rise from Blackwood's deadening ambience was to slap on some of your mother's eye-liner.

"Things changed a bit when we arrived in London," James confessed to the *Toronto Star*'s Lenny Stoute in 1992. "For the first time we found out that most of the people on the streets were considerably weirder than we ever could be. It was a bit soul-destroying, to be honest. We had a few meetings about that. We knew we had to do something else to stand out." So it was that, masterminded quite beautifully by Hall, the Manic Street Preachers emerged into the Nineties and into the music press, firing loose broadsides here and there, attacking every band, every journalist, in fact, everything on the scene, in a manner not seen since Ian McCulloch reached his noisy puberty. It was, they would later admit, a purely cynical ploy. And, overnight it seemed, they became a band big in print, though small in vinyl output. A courageous and precarious ploy, to say the least. Hall must have understood this. He must have known that, with so little of substance to back up the band's lippy image, they had to make a big noise somehow.

Despite Hall's inherent PR professionalism, or perhaps encouraged by it, the band continued to scribble their letters of wild self-promotion. Nobody seems able to recall whether it was Philip Hall who passed a typical letter across to his friend, Jeff Barrett, head of the small but intensely hip label, Heavenly. At that point, Heavenly was enjoying a surge of media attention, much of which revolved around the striking spectacle of Flowered Up, a horrendous Madchester parody who gar-nered a flood of unwarranted music press superlatives. Flowered Up's subsequent failure to progress beyond first base wasn't, of course, apparent at the moment the Manic Street Preachers met, liked and signed a brisk no-nonsense two-single deal with Heavenly at the close of 1990. Perhaps it didn't matter. Although they respected Barrett and were gushingly grateful for the chance to release some of their more recent, vastly superior songs at last, nobody involved in the band believed the move to be anything other than a convenient stepping stone to a major label. Which is exactly what it proved to be. Few people, however, expected the band to immediately deliver a single as powerful as 'Motown Junk'. A layered rock growl masking a curiously delicate love tale and, just simmering in the undertone, a previously absent hint of soaring melody. For the first time there was undeniably something worth listening to here; the record bore the distinct trace of future glories. The title itself was confrontational, evocative, intrigu-ing. One doubts whether the sharp little guitars and spiked lyrics would have lingered in the memory of the fans for so long, had the track not possessed such a memorable monicker. *NME* had no doubts, giving the Manics their second 'Single Of The Week'. From here on in they would be taken rather more seriously.

Around the same time, a photograph of Richey, his shirt emblazoned with the awful portent 'Kill Yourself', adorned the cover of *Sounds*, once the leading champion of punk. Years later, fans would stare, misty eyed, at the image, not daring to guess whether Richey's masterplan, if there was one, had already started to glimmer in his mind at this early stage in the band's career.

*   *   *

Think back to that quote at the start of this chapter. He meant it. Yellow and red plastic artlessness. Prole food for spotty brats in track suits, guzzling thick milk shakes, chomping through the cotton wool, a brazen affront to London's 'foodie' Mafioso; the middle classes who seem to control the media, the rock business come to that, openly sneer at this ultimate corporate nightmare. And far worse than McDonalds, was the brief Eighties spread of 'upmarket' burger joints, places that, in charging £9.99 for a home-made burger and a clump of coleslaw, totally missed the whole point of fast food. "I loathe the places really," Richey confessed, "but at least they provide a sense of continuity. You can sit in a McDonalds in Manhattan, Malibu, London or Cardiff and you know exactly where you are. Course, the food is shit and, in England, the staff are usually stupid but even that seems perfect. Strangely beautiful . . . McDonalds."

He would repeat the phrase, in May 1991, to *NME*'s James Brown who, at the start of his quest for 'lad' culture, greedily gobbled up the concept, and decided that, alongside Happy Mondays, whose laddish credentials could never be in question, the Manic Street Preachers, with their sprightly new single, 'You Love Us', their Clash references and their trashy clobber, were quite the perfect scream for some kind of new rock'n'roll dream. Four lads being noisy and messy and pretty damn obnoxious. The fact is though, in Manchester, we just laughed. Manchester saw the Manics as being quite the epitome of uncool. It was a two-way street, in Manchester, in 1991. Either people embraced dance culture with a vengeance, or they still clung to the dowdy old indie dream, dressing darkly and still finding some kind of hidden worth in Fall albums. Either way, a band who were apparently intent on dragging the whole thing back to the days when The Clash made their trail-blazing first album, adopted urban terrorist chic and – this was possibly the lowest point of punk – posed moodily in Belfast, turned the whole punk idea into little more than a shallow and rather flippant sham. Mancunians with long memories had been there before – they remembered The Drones – which is why, when the Manic Street Preachers cropped up on *Granada Tonight*, the news and magazine programme covering the North West of England, they were treated as some kind of freak band who had no relevance to the youth of the region. Things weren't much better at a gig of the time either (at The Gallery, now defunct), where retro punks garnered from the sticks mixed testily with a few curious students. The Fall's Mark E. Smith had little time for what he saw as four punk opportunists: "They are probably the most pathetic band in Britain," he sneered to the author in a 1991 TV interview. "Very bad Clash copyists with no innovative ability of their own. They are a pantomime act and, to be honest, it is beneath me to even spend time thinking about them. I mean, one of the reasons we started The Fall back in 1977 was to provide an alternative to all that dumb politico punk shit. We injected intelligence. Even The Worst had intelligence. (They did?) So why would anyone want to listen to a bad version of The Clash in 1991?"

It was becoming clear that the Manic Street Preachers were, in many ways, sending the wrong signals. Their love of Guns'n'Roses and their tendency to play around with cartoon visuals of rock'n'roll, which was so refreshing in so many respects, would be met with derision by many of their peers, as well as many punters. Perhaps they shouldn't have worried about it all too much. But, the thing was, they genuinely *cared*. As Richey said, "I know that people look at us in a really shallow way. But the thing is, that is their fucking problem, not ours. If their prejudices are so strong that they can't see beyond what is put in front of them, then I couldn't give a shit, really. We are not fucking Clash Two! Which is their neat little pigeon-hole and has nothing to do with us at all. The fact is that we are intelligent enough to see something like Guns'n'Roses and understand it for what it is. We see the worth in it. It's not our fault if British music journalists are just too stupid to see beyond their particular fave genre of the moment. Fuck 'em."

That bravado was mixed with a good deal of hurt. In *NME*, Nicky Wire expanded on the theme: "When Steve Clarke out of Def Leppard died, a man who had written songs that sold 60 million, or whatever, why did he get about that much (holds up thumb and forefinger, millimetres apart) in the press? Yet when Shaun Ryder, talentless and brain dead, has a baby, he gets a page. Why does he deserve it?" It seemed that for a while there back in the early Nineties, the only people the Manic Street Preachers saw eye-to-eye with were themselves.

The Manics themselves were not without their prejudices, and often launched into similar attacks on The Stone Roses – curiously vitriolic put-downs, considering the friendship between Manics manager Philip Hall and Roses idiosyncratic man in charge, Gareth Evans. It's possible that the venom of their criticism could be pinned down to the fact that, while the world was grasping everything the

Roses did with uncritical fervour, the Manics seemingly still couldn't put a foot right. Not where it really mattered. "When we started the UK was in the grip of dance, rap and acid house," Richey told the *Toronto Star* in 1992. "All that Manchester stuff sounded so contrived. The Roses were flaccid. The only real rock'n'roll was coming out of America. We had to do something to bring it back." Maybe the Manics were tiring of their classic rock'n'roll lifestyle, surviving on £5 per day when they were touring, crammed like sardines into a tour bus filled with discarded curry cartons, crisp packets, crushed beer cans, fag packets and music magazines. It was more than a mite wearing, back in 1991, for a band so desperate to set the world alight.

At the start of the Nineties, the Manics stood accused, not of plagiarism, not of rock dullness either, but of parading their influences too obviously, whether in their music, or their clothes. It was a strange period this. A time when, if you wandered through Oxford or Cambridge, you would see the brightest young students in the country, all too often from middle-class backgrounds, sporting T-shirts boasting their allegiance to the aforementioned Happy Mondays. It was a pre-*Loaded* social dumb-down, a time when every 'chap' aspired backwards, to laddishness. A laddishness where kudos could be gained from having a streetwise knowledge of the international dance scene rather than a selective knowledge of rock, literature and film. Indeed, in Manchester at the time, street culture seemed destined to become synonymous with street gangs, many of whom succeeded in squeezing themselves into the prevailing clubland. No place here for a traditional-looking rock combo.

As to those avenues of influence, the Manics were scattering them around their interviews like smarties, to be greedily snapped up by anyone who cared to listen. Some of them obvious, some curiously obscure. Films? Try *Watership Down*, *The Apartment*, *Thelma And Louise*, *Stardust*, *Carrie*, *Apocalypse Now*, *Being There*, *Days Of Wine And Roses*, *Taxi Driver*, *Betty Blue*, *Quadrophrenia* and *One Flew Over The Cuckoo's Nest*. You get the picture. It would be difficult to claim to be a serious rock band without being headily swayed by *Taxi Driver* at some point in your late adolescence. Same, too, might be said of *One Flew Over The Cuckoo's Nest* and, certainly, *Apocalypse Now*. The choice of *Betty Blue* might have been driven by pure lust, which is fair enough. But citing *Watership Down* is just plain wilfulness.

Perhaps more telling is the Manics' 'Desert Island Disc' list which appeared in an August 1991 *NME*:

> *Never Mind The Bollocks* – Sex Pistols
> *London Calling* – The Clash (Of course.)
> 'True Blue' – The Faces
> *Exile On Main Street* – Rolling Stones
> *My Generation* – The Who
> *It Takes A Nation of Millions* . . . and *Fear Of A Black Planet*
>   – Public Enemy
> *Shake Yer Money Maker* – The Black Crowes
> 'Sweet Emotion' – Aerosmith
> *Appetite For Destruction* – Guns'n'Roses
> 'Misty Mountain Hop' – Led Zeppelin
> 'Boulevard Of Broken Dreams' – Hanoi Rocks
> *What's Going On* – Marvin Gaye

Not exactly Hacienda playlist stuff. The heavy accent on American contemporary rock and classic English rock is no surprise, and one can hear all that in the music of the Manics. Only Marvin Gaye seems oddly placed, although pure strength of talent could have prompted that choice. Most tellingly, there is undeniable quality in every one of these selections although, with the exception of Marvin and the two punk albums, there is hardly anything that the average *NME* reader would place at the front of his or her CD collection.

In April 1991, the Manics toured Ireland, North and South. Perhaps not the wisest move for a band wishing to shed their infernal Clash comparisons. It wasn't simple bland posturing this time around, though. Clearly the place had a real effect on the young Welshmen. "I was really happy experiencing Belfast because you read so much about it. Then you go and experience it and you come down here and no one gives a fuck," Richey told *NME*'s James Brown in May 1991. "That report last week said that 80% of the Republic couldn't give a fuck. I wish we could have done a residency there. Johnny Hero, he's a DJ and promoter, took us round, showed us the place where those soldiers drove into that funeral. We went up the Falls Road and then down through areas where they go joy riding. The IRA and the soldiers tried to stop them joy riding but they still do it. There's burnt out cars along the side of the road. The people who came to our gig told us they couldn't take seriously any of the reporting of the Gulf War because they have seen the way television reports incidents they have actually experienced in Belfast city centre and it's so inaccurate."

Their short, spiky tour hinted that Ireland might be slightly more willing to swallow the whole Manics package than mainland Britain had been. For their part, the band's interviews over there seemed unusually reverential. The journalists certainly seemed more interested in finding out more about the band's ideas than merely sniping at them from a distance. Even the audiences seemed more attentive. Perhaps the link between Blackwood – which does have a look of northern Ireland at times, with its sullen housing and leaden skies – and life on the Emerald Isle is stronger than one might suspect. Whether this could be seen as a link between the Welsh and the Irish psyche is a dubious claim. It's probably more of a provincial thing, that slight mistrust of the power of London, that sense of aloofness. "In Coleraine these kids who had come from some small place told us that the only thing they did for excitement was walk into the railway tunnel and then squeeze into the manhole in the wall when the train came through," Richey told *NME* in 1991. "All the oxygen gets sucked out when the train goes through. That's all they have got for kicks." Of equal significance were the comments from the two 16-year-old boys who hitched 50 miles to Waterford to catch the band live. In between throwing up over the club's tables, they managed to splutter these encouraging words. "Manic Street Preachers are the first rock band we have liked, before it was only Public Enemy and NWA that meant anything . . . there is only one copy of 'Motown Junk' in our village and we all share it."

Fantastic. And such instances would begin to filter through to the band on a regular level. That kind of belief seemed generally more prevalent in Ireland but now it also seemed to be increasingly true of the mainland. Somehow the band's message, their influence, was managing to reach the people who really mattered. Not to rock hacks sitting in Camden eateries thinking of little beyond their own careers, but the young kids, out in the sticks perhaps, who couldn't empathise with the endless party spirit of Happy Mondays. Kids who would sense, in the Manics, something their older, cooler brothers and sisters had dismissed as plain old hat. Compare the rock scene of the early Seventies, when prog rock aficionados would hide in their bedrooms, slapping Wishbone Ash onto their stereos, and dismissing the vibrant, sexy pop of, say, Marc Bolan, as commercial pap. The Manics, while they still had their musical shortcomings, possessed an intelligence and a sense of melody that was all too often missed by the music press and many of its readers. James (to *NME* in 1991): "We get compared to the greatest bands ever and are accused of being crap. If you start comparing music journalists to the greatest writers ever you'd still see how shit they are, too."

The singer expanded on this point to *Selling England* fanzine: "The problem is that you don't really get too much time to grow, to develop naturally. Yes, we shoot our mouths off and all of that . . . and perhaps we shouldn't. Perhaps it smacks of desperation and a lack of patience. I understand that, but we are young lads and we want it all now. The problem with that is that you get yourselves into the public eye and they scrutinise all your little mistakes. It's good in a way because it sharpens you as a band. Journalists may often be idiots but, in a sense, they are right. It's their job to criticise. We are learning and learning fast . . . but we are still learning. If that makes any sense. But you have to be out there or you would be playing fucking pubs for the next twenty years. You'd end up playing old R'n'B numbers to three beer-bellied mechanics in Newport. No thanks. We'd rather get right out there and fuck up completely."

The Manics were clearly emboldened by the experience of their support in Northern Ireland and encouraged by a music press who, suddenly, seemed to have awoken to their rapidly unfolding potential. A potential hinted at by the feisty single 'You Love Us', which contained strong echoes of the best anthemic punk songs, from The Clash's 'White Riot' to Sham 69's irritatingly infectious 'If The Kids Are United', which was destined to become the hinge of their set for many years. Philip Hall could sense the rise in interest, in the constantly ringing phone, in the increasingly raucous crowd reactions at gigs in Northern Ireland and the modest string of dates back in England which followed them. As for the band, a spate of quick-fire song writing had added depth to their set, energising their performances to a degree that, years later, long-term fans would cite these early Manics outings as the finest gigs they had ever seen. At the same time,

the band hovered on the brink of poverty. In fact, they were dig-
ging deeply into Philip Hall's pockets at this point. They were, quite
literally, crushed into a Ford Transit, heading into unknown towns,
where they joyfully discovered pockets of devotees whose support
would sustain them for several years. But it was all so finely, so
precariously, balanced on the flip side of almost everything else that
was happening in music. And there, hovering in the shadows, but
still frustratingly out of reach, the promise of a major record contract. One way or another, the Manic Street Preachers knew that
they were precariously poised on the brink of greatness. Bands were
flowering and fading all around them, on a week-to-week basis it
seemed, but the Manics, beginning at last to realise their potential,
were now living the rock'n'roll dream. Who cared if they were career-
ing into cliché? Not them. Not as midnight approached and, awash
with alcohol, they would crash instruments into amplifiers, overin-
dulge in on-stage theatrics and slam into each other, more often than
not falling into an ungainly heap with the audience spilling onto the
stage around them.

Then again, what's a punk band without a riot? The Manics' biggest
and best came at the Downing College May Ball in Cambridge. It was a
marquee event and the band were blind drunk. Famously, if mystify-
ingly, Nicky attempted to give James a blow-job, mid set. This was a
scenario that James didn't find altogether welcome, and after issu-
ing a warning to his bassist, he stepped back, hitting his speaker
stack. Richey fell backwards into the opposite speaker at the precise
moment that Nicky's reckless foot connected with the monitor. The
crowd, who were equally beered-up and looking for excitement,
took this as a sign to heighten their celebrations a little further.
Whereupon the security team slammed off the electricity, and the
entire tent plunged into a scene of ugly disorder. The band reacted
first, trashing their gear in classic fashion before turning to see a
small army of surprisingly beefy students clambering onto the stage.
Fists began to fly and the whole sorry affair, by now strongly resembling the spidery walk of a moveable rugby scrum, careered into the
dressing room area. Richey reacted to the event with predictable
scorn: "It was entirely the fault of the fucking students. I loathed
students when I was at university and I wasn't surprised to find that
Cambridge had the most stupid students in the country . . . and that is

saying something. Privileged twats with no idea about anything. I despise them ... they are beneath me. I love the fact that they are drawn towards rock'n'roll. I hope it changes them but I have more respect, a lot more respect for a chip shop owner in Blackwood than idiots like that. They have golden futures. But none of it is real.

"I may not be much of anything. But I mean what I do. My entire heart is in this band, and I'm the worst musician in the band. In fact I'm no musician at all, never will be. But it's about communication. I know I am intelligent. I know, also, that financial circumstances, jobs, everyday life, survival, causes people to lose track of what's really important. Well, if the Manics can just help pull a few people back to some kind of real belief, that's all I want. We are not particularly clever ... not really. It's just rock'n'roll and it's fundamentally dumb. But it's real. And few things are real. That's the point."

Richey's fascinating comments surfaced in Shrewsbury fanzine *Castle Walls*. (Shrewsbury, an English border town, no less.) When I met Chris Jenkins, the author of the fanzine's Manics article, in a Chester wine bar, he told me that Richey was the most intense person that he had ever met. He added that Richey talked to this tiny, insignificant fanzine as if it was *Rolling Stone*, and that he was the only pop star who didn't seem remotely patronising. He didn't seem like he was making a point. (The week before, Jenkins had met Johnny Marr and that was a completely different story.) I read the interview over and over again. Much of it was typical rocky guff, semi-inebriated bluster. But the above passage screamed out. The overriding message is that Richey Edwards was 'FOR REAL'. And if he really was that unique, if he really was in rock'n'roll because he believed in its potential to make a difference, it didn't matter a jot if he had absolutely no talent at all. He had belief in himself and in his band, and that says more about music's potential for revolutionary change than any amount of musicianship. I am not going to analyse the overly hyped occasion, at Norwich, when the same Richey literally carved the words FOR REAL into his forearm in the shocked presence of Steve Lamacq, then of *NME* in 1991.

Lamacq came into the scene carrying with him a well known distrust of the Manics and their leanings towards rock of the 1977 variety. He approached the interview with an unusual degree of trepidation, fully expecting to be confronted by a Rottenesque broadside, perhaps from all four corners, delivered in vitriolic Welsh. What he found, in fact, were four boys of considerable intelligence. Each question was slowly digested, passed around freely, debated, argued upon perhaps. Not just in the interview, either, but in their curiously conciliatory general attitude. The interview has been published, in full, several times and it seems pointless to languish too fully on it here. What can be ascertained is that Lamacq simply didn't trust the Manics hype. It was a fully understandable distrust. Too often, he had seen bands adopt a stance, any stance, simply to grasp attention. And the saddest sight in the rock world, frankly, is a band who, having made that initial splash, force themselves to live within it. I am referring particularly to the swell of post punk copyists, of which there were simply hundreds, who lapsed into blank, thoughtless sloganeering. The fact is that the Manics were not like that at all, as they would later prove. But no one could blame Lamacq for his distrust.

It didn't seem very likely . . . did it?

Richey knew this, completely. He knew that a cloud of distrust had gathered around the band. He understood it fully. All the Manics understood it. Completely . . . and it was their quest, if you like, to power through it, to prove their uniqueness, to prove that they were not just living out some sad punk dream.

The difference between Richey and the others was very simple. He felt crowded by frustration and unable, perhaps, to utilise his musicality in such a liberating way. He wasn't a sham and he simply had to prove it.

"I know you don't like us but we are for real," he explained. "When I was a teenager I never had a band who said anything about my life . . ."

Lamacq sighed, wanting to believe, and stood back, amazed as Richey carved FOR REAL in straight gashes, deep into his left forearm.

It was Lamacq who called for the ambulance.

Entire fanzines have been written about this incident. It has been debated endlessly in the music press and its shadow lingers on. For what it's worth, I still find it a dull, wearisome tale. Richey was a man of sincerity . . . of profundity perhaps, but this story weakens his continuing enigma, rather than strengthens it. He was more worthy, really, than such a crass rock'n'roll act . . .

* * *

Although it was reported in the music trade papers that the Manics were the subject of a 'Dutch Auction', involving as many as half a dozen big labels, the reality was rather different. Converting that interest into a suitable deal is rarely as simple as it might appear. Hall knew the golden rule: that the individual A&R person who signs the band, who will work closely with them during the difficult time that follows and who will, naturally, be the one solid link between artist and company, is the most important person in any record deal. Furthermore, a 'key man' clause inserted into the contract would effectively tie the band to that A&R person and reduce, though not completely wipe out, the risk of the band becoming imprisoned on a label whose enthusiasm has waned, but which might not be prepared to let the band go. And that's every manager's worst nightmare. Rob Shreeve, of Sony/Columbia, certainly seemed the most promising party. And his MD, Tim Bowen – a long-standing Clash fan whose punk enthusiasm had been rekindled after seeing a Manics gig at Guildford – seemed to share Shreeve's determination to make something of this band. This made Hall's decision relatively simple. The contract was realistic. Although, naturally, weighted with yearly options in favour of the company, it offered a £400,000 commitment for the first album, the first year, and an attitude-softening initial advance of £250,000. Hall, who had seen The Stone Roses sign for a fraction of this, knew the dangers, but also knew that it was unlikely to be bettered. They signed to Sony.

3

BACK IN IRELAND: APRIL 1992

"They look like someone doing The Clash in a school play."
                    – Steve Hanley, The Fall

In retrospect, the Manics' fond return to Ireland might be seen as something of a training exercise for their latter-day domination of awards ceremonies – Brits, Brats and the rest. In 1992 they attended the Irish equivalent of The Brits, and Sony pulled out all the stops, badgering the organisers into supplying the band with their own corner and their own stab at post-event socialising. Not, perhaps, the wisest thing the mega-label have ever done as the Manics, despite their lyrical sophistication, despite their thoughtful eloquence, were still more than capable of disgracing themselves with the demon drink. They were still arrogant enough to stake a claim as being punks at heart and an industry bash was an open invitation for them to become just that. Among the tables laden with sumptuous food and wine, amid the chatter of music biz camaraderie, the Manics let fly. They were unsophisticated Blackwood boys, spitting at the bus stop; they swore too loudly, drank too much, and caused great disruption among people who didn't know quite whether to applaud or turn away in disgust. It was all pretty harmless stuff – indeed, it generated decent copy for Dublin papers, for the Irish music mag *Hot Press*, for the odd predatory English journo and even for a huddle of American and Japanese freelancers who were present and who adopted a collective look of disgust at the Manics' behaviour reminiscent of a group of Surrey housewives caught in a tube carriage with a gang of Millwall fans.

"You're scum. You are all scum. You should be thrown out of here!" The outburst came from a tweed-suited female not, one assumes, normally accustomed to the hedonistic antics of an up-and-coming rock act. There was Richey, grasping the ice bucket that had been employed as the table's elegant centrepiece, emptying the contents of six bottles of Chablis and a bottle of Châteauneuf De Pape into the bucket (the philistine) and completing his juvenile trick by adding liberal sprinklings of salt, pepper and English mustard. He then sat back and admired his handiwork.

Richey remained quite unapologetic about his antics: "It's nice to feel that you still have something of that obnoxious little imp in you," he argued. "I think all rock'n'roll bands have to have that. It's the Sid Vicious thing, isn't it? Everyone knew that Sid wasn't tough at all. He was just someone who refused to grow up. He must have been incredibly obnoxious to be around but, then again, there was some kind of glory in that, in not maturing into a fucking clerk at the DHSS. That's the poetic escape of rock'n'roll. It's not the whole point but it's a fucking good starting point and it sometimes keeps us together. We are all intelligent people but we still like to mess about and if these people (swings arm in wide arch around the room) can't accept it from us . . . then they are the ones in the wrong business. Not us."

That went for Nicky Wire too, it seems, who spent a mischievous ten minutes leaping about, popping the balloons that had originally formed part of a display of the republican tricolour before, no doubt reeling from the intake of wine, falling slap-bang onto the table and sliding to the floor, muttering sundry insults. Perhaps the target of Wire's venom had been the presenter of the live televised event who had unfortunately made a number of remarks along the lines of "the Manics are dull Clash copyists" on an earlier programme – alas, the band had seen it in their hotel bedrooms. James, unable to forgive this slight, confronted the startled presenter and, as his verbal onslaught began to border on the physical, had to be pulled away by a couple of bouncers. Throughout the affray, and throughout the entire broadcast, Sean hurled insults towards the stage, at one point standing on the table screaming something along the lines of, "Boooring bastards . . ." while the same bouncers, by now baying for blood, hovered menacingly in the shadows. The band caused some concern among the depleted Sony ranks by 'vanishing' suddenly (to a nearby pub, as it happens) and the final memento of their part in the event was the sight of the food-splattered Sony table being carried out of the hall. On witnessing the event, one local reporter penned a hilarious "Punk Band From Hell Wreck Awards Shock" story. Had the story surfaced in 1976, it would probably have gained national coverage and made the Manics something of a talking point. As it was, nobody seemed particularly interested.

It would, of course, all be forgotten by the next morning. Especially by the Manics, who spent the afternoon watching in horror as England trounced Wales in the Five Nations rugby international. This made for a trauma-ridden afternoon in that hotel room, where every try and drop goal was met with cries of anguish. It might be noted that, despite the lads' collective preference for cricket and soccer, rugby is, and always has been, *the* game of South Wales. The physical game always seemed to be the embodiment of the South Wales character, especially that of the valley boy (James and Sean are both the valley boy archetype). It is a game that suits stockiness and swift changes of speed. It is a tough, fiery, sprinters' game. The gathering of a Welsh crowd, especially at the now-defunct Cardiff Arms Park, was always quite unlike the gathering of any other sporting crowd on Earth. Welsh rugby fans never merely turned up to watch a sporting event. They turned up to take part, exhibiting a tremendous sense of 'oneness' that went beyond camaraderie, beyond national pride even. It seemed to be the very soul of the country out there, often against an England team superior in performance, but not blessed with such a solid heart of support. The international rugby match exhibits, even today, the true heart of Wales.

And it still prevails. You can feel it in the music of the Manics, especially in the later period with *This Is My Truth Tell Me Yours*, an album haunted by Welsh passions – obviously within the framework of the lyrics, but also in the melodic undertones which, in places, echo Welsh male voice choirs. Latterly, after Welsh pop attained an unlikely hipness, Welsh bands would exhibit a similar affection for their country that would seem unlikely to be replicated by English bands. Thus, Cerys from Catatonia's celebratory "Every day when I wake up, I thank the Lord I'm Welsh." Of course, the Welsh love of rugby has softened, in recent years, partially because of the distractions of the satellite TV age, of soccer and basketball, and partially because most Welsh games – with the odd glorious exception, such as the Welsh victory over France in 1999 – have ended in a long dull groan of defeat. A long, long way from the sheer exhilaration of the days of JPR Williams, when it would take a tank battalion, or a New Zealander, to stop the surging red flow of probably the most inspiring rugby team of all time.

But one Manic felt quite differently about the national sport. Richey Edwards had long since pulled free from the allure of 'Welshness'; indeed, more than that, had positively rebelled against it, seeing it as restrictive, an oppressive force. And while the other three remained glued to the TV set that day, he found greater entertainment in the pop-orientated children's television on a different channel. Richey saw great significance in even the most puerile of programmes. "Children's television is fantastic," he enthused. "It's really sharp and not cluttered up by any kind of pretension and that's what I really like. Kids aren't stupid. They know what they like and they also are bright enough not to read too much into it. They like their pop music to be disposable. What's wrong with that? It *is* fucking disposable. Give me a kid to some old serious git who reads every review in *Q*, or takes *Record Collector* . . . give me that kid, any day." For Richey, the individual always took precedence over the mass, and national pride was regarded with extreme suspicion: "I see the dangers in being too nationalistic or whatever. I'm fully aware of what the English have done to Wales but I don't go about blaming every Englishman that I meet . . . Welshness doesn't do it for me. I'm not sure I have much in common with some fat drunken thug in Swansea, to be honest."

Even at this relatively early stage of the Manic Street Preachers' career, Richey was beginning to be seen as a mouthpiece for the band, the one (along with Nicky Wire) who could come up with the perfect quotation that seemed to crystallise what the Manics were all about. To Sylvia Patterson, respected veteran rock hackette, moonlighting in April 1992 for *Smash Hits* – much to the delight of all the band who had temporarily fallen out with *NME* – Richey confessed his utter contempt for the average member of his own sex. "Men are full of hate and obsessed by power and sex and everything. I hate men," he spat. "We get lots of girls at our gigs and we get criticised for that because these people are saying that girls aren't proper fans. Like they can't possibly like or understand the music and they are not going to have thirteen pints of lager, have a big mosh down the front and have a curry on the way home. And they should be at home reading *Jackie* and thinking about blokes. It's crap! In terms of sensitivity and intelligence, girls understand so much more than men." And, of course, sensitivity and intelligence were qualities that Richey himself displayed in spades. Indeed, it was the fact that perhaps he possessed both qualities in too great a dose that was to make life increasingly more difficult to bear for the young Manic as time went on. The intellectual voraciousness that he displayed seemed to backfire; the more he learned, the less he seemed able to cope with what he knew. Witness his comments to Patterson on sexuality: "The Manics are all sad, lonely people. I have never had a girlfriend and that makes me sad. I don't really believe in relationships because men and women just aren't compatible. Men are just too selfish. It doesn't really matter because we will all be wiped off the face of the world, anyway. It's true. In three generations 75% of the animal species of the world will be wiped out and it's all our fault. We have only got five generations of man left if you ask me and maybe it's just as well. Mankind is the worst thing that has ever happened to this planet." From his original theme, Richey expands until he's discussing the destruction of human life; every sentence offers a new and alarmingly pessimistic view of life. And this to a *Smash Hits* writer.

* * *

To the rock historian surveying the past 15 years of British music, the problem with the Manic Street Preachers would surely be one of placement. We have already focused on the bands existential distance from virtually anything else that was happening in the country at the time, but there are still times when the dates and instances seem all at sea. How could this band be playing this kind of music in the middle of this particular era? The Manic Street Preachers' début album, *Generation Terrorists* is a classic example, emerging, as it did, three full years after The Stone Roses' eponymous début. Three years after the peak of 'baggy'. Five years after the break-up of The Smiths. Five years after the celebrated Second Summer of Love. *Ten* years after hip-hop first broke!

Perhaps it's because, as the Manics would prove, Britain was all too entangled in fad and trend, in hipness, fashion, youth and image. The successful glossy music magazines were now being designed specifically to catch the idle and all too fleeting attention span of readers whose allegiance to music was competing with many other leisure interests. Even *Q* magazine, once revered and seemingly reactionary, was reduced to tabloidesque fervour, to the short, sharp, stupid and the sexy and, like America's *Rolling Stone*, simply a mouthpiece for the record companies whose expensive full-page adverts infringed more and more on their sycophantic editorials. Lagging behind, at least in terms of circulation, an inky music press similarly was dumbed down, unrecognisable to anyone who spent long days attempting to understand its pretentious blabberings of the late Seventies. But back then, amid all that wordy, deep and meaningless guff, *NME*, *Melody Maker* and *Sounds* could still manage to peer beyond the obvious, beyond the charts and the hype. By late 1991, this had become difficult, nay impossible. You were what you wore. You lived and died by the cut of your garb, the flash on your trainers. Given such a context, the Manics were sending strong and confusing signals from day one. One reason, I'd suggest, why the Manic Street Preachers' first album, a spiked and savage beauty floating a disarming array of ear-catching melodies and one of the truly great rock débuts of the past twenty years, received its fair share of unceremonious slapping at the hands of spotty oiks clad in combat trousers tapping pseudo street venom into their London computers. It was February 1992. People were confused by young punks with loud guitars. Fair enough.

And perhaps the hacks weren't wholly to blame. After all, this lanky, pale-skinned leopard-skin-topped crew were still bouncing around like a latter-day 999 to audiences full of confused and displaced youth. In a sense though, this displacement suited both band and audience, for it fuelled their spirit, added that barbed edge to their determination. It was the Manics against the world. That's how things stood as 1991 began to fade and Sony started to prod the Halls, pleading with them to send the band into the studio to record their début album.

As far as the band were concerned, confidence was sky high. Songs were stacking up, with Richey and Nicky riding a wave of inspired prolificacy. This lyrical focus mirrored the band's general stance, that Richey was the spirit and fire of the band, despite, or possibly because of, his lack of musical ability. Richey could write lyrics with effortless ease; he had an enigmatic presence on stage, however limited his actual musical contribution. And anyway, his questionable musicianship wasn't an issue, as James and Sean's practice sessions had seen them break into new musical ground. Richey was a sensitive Sid Vicious, blessed with a literate brain and a fierce desire to create rather than dumbly destroy. Add on Nicky Wire, his erudite partner, and you had a heady cocktail. The entire band were convinced that their idiosyncratic blend of talent and self-belief would produce an album capable of stunning the rock world. Famously, they told the world that sixteen million people would scurry instantly to their local Our Price or Tower Records to snap it up. And that having released this record-breaking album they would then split up, in perfect punk style, before they got old and boring. Of course, they couldn't quite grasp the fact that their sparse smattering of reviews, mini-features and news items hadn't been feverishly gobbled up by every music-hungry teenager in the land, that they weren't – not then, anyway – the band everyone was waiting for. But the Manics believed they had truly arrived. Nicky Wire: "I had started to tire of the cynicism of the small venue circuit. The all-knowing look on the faces of the venue owners, the stupid local sound crews, the negative audiences. It wears you down. When we signed to Sony, it seemed like we were leaving all that. And, in a sense, we did. Not like we imagined . . . but suddenly, for the first time in our lives, we weren't scraping around for change, trying to rustle money together to get a pint, that kind of thing. It felt like luxury. All false, of course, but it was a game completely new to us. I think it did go to our heads a bit. We weren't stupid. But it does kind of grab you and take you somewhere else. Richey was definitely the most vulnerable in that aspect. But we were all too excited to be worried."

Sony must have looked on in horror as the Manics booked themselves into Black Barn Studios in Ripley, Surrey. At £1,125 per day, plus rock'n'roll excesses. Black Barn was undoubtedly at the very top of the Manics' price range. There was some objection to this at first as Sony, quite understandably, queried the band's reasons for their choice. Why would such an expensive polish be needed for a band who, as far as the company were concerned, had built their reputation on producing raucous punk? As no one could ever deny, the finest punk singles were all recorded in downbeat circumstances. As it would turn out, Black Barn was to be an inspired choice, as producers Steve Brown and Matt Ollivier would, with the help of the musical strengths of Bradfield and Moore in particular, turn in an album of genuine clarity and freshness that the Manics, for all their future glories, would never recapture. Not that the album – a double album as it would turn out to be, perhaps unfortunately, as double albums traditionally lack the clarity and impact of the single version – would be without its problems. It should have been sliced in half, for a start, but its sheer energy was still a valuable enough commodity, at the start of the Nineties.

Although lyrically indebted to Richey, the album's musical side survived perfectly well without him. He was at the recordings, although his fleeting ghost-like presence didn't transfer all that successfully onto the tape. Like most nervous young musicians, his insecurity ballooned in the studio environment, within a subterranean hierarchy patrolled by studio engineers who, more often than not, plugged away in bands considerably less successful and yet, in their eyes, considerably more talented, than the one they were recording. It wasn't quite like that at Black Barn, where the camaraderie would have made Richey feel comfortable with as little hassle as possible. But it was like that in Richey's head. He flickered into the melodies like a spiritual shadow. A few people did question the value of his presence, as tends to happen when record companies are geared to keeping the expenses of their acts to a bare minimum. Sony's accountants would have been hard pressed to explain such a . . . *conceptual* presence.

Not that it mattered. His work had been done and his splintered lyricism more than made up for his musical inadequacies. It was better for Richey Edwards to opt out, to drift into London, into Soho apparently, where he'd take great delight in succumbing to the promises of titillation from bored 'door girls' and their heavy, heavy shadows. Richey Edwards must have seemed like a present from heaven, to the sundry spivs and club owners. Here was a beautiful young man, dripping in rock star cliché and flashing plastic like a character in a Brett Easton Ellis novel. There were a number of reports of him hanging around Wardour Street's infamous rock'n'roll pub The Ship, where he would catch hold of the shirt-tails of anyone who looked like a pop star.

Damned drummer Rat Scabies: "Yeah ... I do recall this guy. A geeky rock'n'roll guy. I knew about the Manics, though I thought he was a kick-back to The Clash, really. But he was sweet. One of those people who you would always sort of see around and yet never quite know what he did. That was it, really. Lots of kids like that. You had no way of knowing whether they were any good or were just posers, they all looked the fucking same. Wandering into The Ship, looking lost and famous ... just like The Damned twenty years ago. Fucking sad, ain't it?"

Richey Edwards, lost and aloof, wandering drunkenly through a maze of black and neon, in search of some downbeat form of glamour, possibly for a Soho that had ceased to exist, a pre-café bar Soho. A hopelessly romantic mess of mirrors and glass, scuffed floorboards and matriarchal landladies. Who knows, he may even have sought out The Coach And Horses, hoping to 'eyeball' an inebriated Jeffrey Bernard. The Sony deal had, so perfectly, provided him with the means to live out a dream – the boy from Blackwood at the seamy heart of London itself. In retrospect, the image of Richey's nomadic wandering rather eclipses the comparatively dull evenings spent by the band in that darkened studio, recording and re-recording, mixing and listening and mixing again. It was as if he was living out their fantasies and they felt strangely proud of this. It was glorious, really. Richey was Sid with a brain. Too much of a brain. Richey was the only member of the Manic Street Preachers who one could never, ever ... envisage working in the Building Society, having friends over for dinner on a Friday night; enjoying 'normal' life. That was the key. He may well have been one of the last people on planet Earth to believe in the rock'n'roll dream. There is something undeniably heroic in that Richey, carrying the weight of old rock'n'roll, such a tattered old dream in the Nineties. So incredibly un-English, so gloriously unhip.

Personal note. Back in 1989, I spent three months in Los Angeles. During that spell, I caught a concert by ... well, by Guns'n'Roses. I went into that gig loathing the band. Hey! I was a Mancunian! I'd followed every inch of New Order's career. I understood dance culture; The Hacienda was my home town club. And that one concert completely wiped me away. I just couldn't deny its brilliance. How could we, sometime during the Eighties, have lost that passion for simple rock'n'roll? I knew that, to a huge number of super-hip students in Manchester, if not London, Guns'n'Roses would have been laughed at before a single chord had been played. But how incredibly exciting was that gig?

Well, there are echoes of that same spirit in *Generation Terrorists*. It was an album that just didn't give a damn, from the first, gloriously derivative chord on 'Slash'n'Burn', which will always remind this writer of a demonic blast-through of Cream's 'Sunshine Of Your Love' crossed with The Rolling Stones' 'Under Cover Of The Night'. British groups, you see, just shouldn't display their naff influences in such a fashion. That was the point for so many – so many music journalists in particular. *Generation Terrorists* – a title straight out of that damned Nineties' New Wave of New Wave – was exactly that refreshing. But surely that was all there was to the band. Few expected anything else, not from the tight-white-jeaned Manic Street Preachers. I certainly didn't expect mind-blowing beauty. But there it was. Three songs in. Amid a wild mass of slash and riff, hearing it for the first time was like being knocked down by a neurotic courier on Oxford Street. A song that would soar way beyond any expectations one might have had of the Manic Street Preachers, a gripping portent of future greatnesss. The song, 'Motorcycle Emptiness', didn't belong on this album. It was awesome, massive, wide-screen cinematic, existentially grandiose and worthy of the album price alone. To believe it to be little more than a corny tale of 'Harley Davidson' freedom, of burning down the Pacific Coast Highway, a companion rider to Neil Young's 'Unknown Legend' perhaps, would be to take the song purely on its most immediate level. There is no doubt, in my mind, that 'Motorcycle Emptiness' spills the beans on Richey's inebriated forays across Soho. It speaks of a rock'n'roll dream that had been lost in England, probably since 'God Save The Queen'. On the album sleeve, the track was accompanied by a Sylvia Plath quote, "I talk to God, but the sky is empty". Visions here of wandering alone, estranged from society, no job, no future, just the beauty of an endless dream.

'Natwest-Barclays-Midlands-Lloyds', another standout track, takes a heavy-handed glimpse at the strangulatory grip of the credit scam:

"Blackhorse apocalypse/Death sanitised through credit". It seems, at first glance, nothing more than a punkism, a full-blooded attack on the man in the suit. But although the imagery may, at first, appear clumsy, it does echo a genuine belief held by many that credit, be it the massive debt of a nation or the glaring redness of your monthly bank statement, is all part of one giant global conspiracy, where all wealth rises to the top of the pyramid, wherever that may be. And who sits aloft this fiscal hierarchy? Again, theories abound. Rather ironically, one of them is that Sony, the Manics record label, are the ultimate controllers. (A somewhat fanciful notion, as Sony were, at the time, teetering on mega-debt.) Rather more rash theorising places Freemasons at the top of the tree and, beyond them, through them . . . who knows? The point is that, as the Manics noisily state, banking has a dark heart and its eventual aim is, naturally, to drain away any money we might fleetingly be able to call our own. Amen to that.

The subject of alienation, the eternal Manics theme, be it individual, national or global alienation, surfaces on 'Love's Sweet Exile'. One senses, in this case, the lyric is dealing with an individual's estrangement from his own nation, with the song's protagonist deserting rain-swept Wales for, presumably, a life in London. He strongly resents his forced exile, however, and longs to be able to live the kind of life he would wish without having to abandon the culture of his home country. It's a topic, of course, that has been an important part of Irish culture for two hundred years. Ireland, perhaps more than any other country in the world, has become truly a 'country of the heart', scattering its influence across the globe and, in particular, to the USA. The influence of Welsh culture has always been rather more subtle, its music finding new places to settle with less spectacular effect. One wondered, upon first hearing this song, whether the Manics might, once having achieved greater success, feel the need to move to London.

'Little Baby Nothing' took up the feminist cause, balancing a somewhat pathetic view of men with a response from a stronger, though exploited, woman. The woman pulled in to perform the vocal was Traci Lords, the American porn star who, it transpired, had appeared in nearly forty porn films before her 16th birthday. Lords flew in from the States, met the band backstage at a London gig and added her vocals the very next day. The track worked out nicely, too, Lords' voice fitting in neatly with the Manics' sound. Originally the band had attempted to hire the vocal talents of petite pop star Kylie Minogue, who had thrown herself into the lifestyle of a London-based socialite and was at the time seeking some kind of hipness to drag her away from the dreaded Stock, Aitken and Waterman. Minogue would eventually achieve her goal, signing to hip dance label Deconstruction, and indeed would work superbly with Bradfield (the single 'Some Kind Of Blue' was co-written by James and Sean; James would also produce her 1997 album, originally titled *Impossible Princess*, famously delayed, and released under a different title, after the death of Princess Diana). However, at the time, she presumably didn't see the band as providers of the kind of credibility she was seeking. Plus, she demanded an outrageous wedge. There was, and still is, a hard-faced professional cynicism to Kylie which may be applauded by the Julie Burchill school of battling career girls, but is ultimately as shallow as 'I Should Be So Lucky'. As it turned out, Kylie's image, of a girl slowly, deliberately taking control over her own career, would have suited the theme of 'Little Baby Nothing', but the childhood exploitation of Lords carried far greater resonance. Although her involvement seems more than appropriate given the context of the song, and any attempt, on an album as long as this, to vary the sound should have been welcomed, most critics slammed the band for spreading a female vocal too thinly over a heavy rock background. (Kylie's voice would have sounded even more bizarre, one senses.)

The connection with Lords was only one of a number of potential collaborations talked up by the band, literally while in the studio. The idea of bringing in Public Enemy to produce the entire affair, which resulted in nothing more than an excessive remixing of the single, 'Repeat', was never really a serious option. In the months to come, Nicky Wire would repeatedly thank Public Enemy for turning the Manics down, with self-effacing statements such as, "They would have been too good for us . . . it would have been utterly embarrassing." As it happens, the collaboration might have proved very interesting indeed although one sensed that the Manics had a need to lay down a base sound of pure white rock before any subsequent experimentation could be allowed to take place.

Fittingly, *Generation Terrorists* was a rock album, adrift in post-rave, pre-Brit Pop Britain. As we noted at the start of this chapter, it was a courageous and lonely stance and encouraged detractors to moan about its derivative nature. They had a point. The album fairly reeked of the spirit of 1977. After all, the original title – 'Culture, Alienation, Boredom and Despair' – was, in effect, just another way of saying 'No Future'. The sleeve depicts Richey's tattooed arm, a rose peeking from above a 'Generation Terrorists' slogan, and the no-nonsense simplistic aural assault could all have combined to have made the album that 999 always dreamed of making.

The title was brittle, abrasive and young. So young, in fact, it was about the fall in expectations that occurs between the ages of 12 and 17, when individuals leave school and are expected to slot into place in society. A 'Generation Terrorist' is someone who breaks from that system, if only for a while, one who challenges the accepted notion of maturity; someone headstrong and, perhaps, naïve. Such an individual is driven to seek out the kind of freedom that comes with the limitless possibilities of life before grim reality begins to kick in. The extension of that freedom, and the final cries of that kind of self-belief, is at the heart of punk rock.

The fact that it was an 18-track double album offered for the price of a single, recalled The Clash's ambitious *London Calling* set; and that, too, would have benefited from a little tidy editing. There were also obvious echoes of The Sex Pistols' *Never Mind The Bollocks*. I'm not suggesting, for one second, that *Generation Terrorists* managed to capture the essential ferocity of that album – it couldn't; we were living in different times and the Pistols were very much the focal point for an absurdly outraged media. Such a statement could no longer be made; life was rather more complex in 1992. However, it was encouraging to note that the Manics were prepared to step beyond the rebel-as-hedonist stance, previously set in our minds by Happy Mondays. The notion of a rebel with a brain, a thinking punk band, seemed most peculiar in the early Nineties. It was easy to knock, but without the fire of *Generation Terrorists*, the subtleties of *This Is My Truth Tell Me Yours* wouldn't have seemed so striking.

It was an album that simply begged for, and duly received, a critical pasting. The targets were certainly plain enough for all to see. The scissors'n'paste element of the lyrics; the band's parochial glam visuals; their tendency to emulate American-style power rock – Guns'n'Roses guitarist Slash haunts the entire album. Surely, nobody at Sony could have been surprised by the mauling *Generation Ter-rorists* received. However, there was undeniably a rather liberating aspect to all this. The Manics, unwittingly I'm sure, were carrying the mantle for all the artists who wished to follow their natural instincts – to begin with the punk basics if needs be, however unfashionable it may be at the time. And the fact that, within a handful of years, it would be quite acceptable, even critically applauded, to use punk's year zero as a starting point – step up Ash, Republica, Three Colours Red – is testament to the Manics' strength of character. Ironically, the band were severely brutalised, in print, and especially in the broad-sheets, for attempting to cash in on a punk revival (The New Wave Of New Wave) that didn't really exist at the time. And what a pity, one might conclude, that the more positive aspects of *Generation Ter-rorists* were not heartily applauded.

The Fall's Mark E. Smith, interviewed by this writer at the time of the album's release, offered a surprisingly forgiving view of the Manics. Especially as he was already most famously on record for unceremoniously slamming them. (See previous chapter.) Still, enter-taining contradictions have always been his forté. Smith admitted, "No ... I don't fucking mind them at all. A lot of these Manchester bands think they are above all that, but they are just deluding them-selves. Same with that Seattle lot. (The Seattle grunge scene was just in the process of breaking world-wide.) The Fall are massive in Seattle and all those people, Nirvana and that lot, we throw off the bus. They go on and on about spirit of punk. It's crap, man. But the Manics have a much more honest attitude. At least they are just doing what they do and couldn't give a damn what anyone else thinks. That's a punk kind of spirit. That's what we have always done. Good luck to them."

Strange bedfellows, one might think, The Fall and the Manic Street Preachers, although there are certain similarities. The Fall, in their embryonic 1977 form, were, unlike the Manics, musically spindly and inept. However, the highly literate if under-educated Smith did use references to Sartre, Camus, Nietzsche, Rimbaud, Burroughs, Miller, Joyce, Wilson and Larkin in his lyrics, and on The Fall's self-parodying DIY album sleeves. The concept was simple: to marry the low art of an emergent rock band with aspirational references of literary merit. This worked superbly, immediately elevating The Fall above many of their peers. In 1992, the Manic Street Preachers were reclaiming this intellectual high ground for the spirit of punk and hard rock, the former having been dragged through all the tired clichés of Garry Bushell's 'Oi' movement and the latter lost in a sea of dumb sexual braggadocio and devil worship. Here, at last perhaps, were a brash young band filled with ambition and holding on tight to the rock'n'roll dream.

And whether their approach insulted the post grads of the music press or not was of little consequence. For the average music fan in Llanryst, to purchase *Generation Terrorists*, and to be confronted with quotes from Burroughs, Plath, Nietzsche and Orwell, must have been a particularly positive form of subversion. It was a young album. 'Slash'n'Burn'. 'Stay Beautiful'. 'Methadone Pretty'. 'Condemned To Rock'n'Roll'. (Yeah, OK, that last title slides straight off an old Iron Maiden album. Maybe that was one cliché too far.) But if the Manics were guilty of anything, it was simply a case of bad PR. Their pre-release announcements that it would be "... the best album for ten years..." (*Melody Maker*) did little to offset the critical backlash and even infused a sense of anticlimax into the first listen. It obviously didn't have the scope and depth of a classic, and it should have been cut in half, but it contained more fire, verve and spirit than any-thing else that existed in the pre-Brit pop vacuum. As to the accusa-tions that the band were merely a recycling engine, it seems almost too obvious to point out that *Never Mind The Bollocks,* for all its undoubted class, contained precious few moments of genuine innova-tion. Much of the worst music of the past 20 years has been what was regarded at the time as front line stuff, constantly, and often rather pointlessly, striving for innovation for the sake of it. Sometimes it's better to simply pull in the reins, understand one's own limitations, and work within them.

However, a strange and rather worrying paradox was beginning to develop around the Manics. Already chastised in England for produc-ing an album which wore its punk and heavy metal influences all too clearly tattooed on its arm, more than one critic was now beginning to suggest that the allure of greed had already started to pull the band towards the American marketplace, where trad rock is actively encouraged. To suggest this was to completely misread the band's early avenues of influence. To British eyes it may have appeared naïve, parochial even, but the Manics could never differentiate between the excitement they drew from Sex Pistols songs and the inspiration they received from Guns'n'Roses. And quite rightly so. One might reasonably expect Sony, never a company to shirk from the lure of the Yankee dollar, to be rubbing their hands with glee at this situation. After all, Britain had been exporting fey young rock acts to America, with little success, for some considerable time. (Indeed, Suede would soon be hurtled States-wards, only to return, tail between legs, falling out with each other and smarting over being upstaged by support act, The Cranberries.)

At least Sony had a band with considerable attack. No one ever accused the Manics of not being able to rock. However, the label felt the need to massage the album a little for the US market. Despite the Aerosmithian nature of the title, they cut 'Condemned To Rock'n'Roll' from the album, presumably in the belief that its out-break of hard line rock'n'drunk lyrics, including a violent burst of vulgar Americanisms towards the end, would be too much for the delicate ears of, say, Seattle youth. Although the band meekly protested, via fax, Sony argued for, and got, a slimmed-down single album version of *Generation Terrorists*; the band's backdown was seen as something of a compromise. In retrospect it's a great pity that Sony didn't impose the same degree of editing on the English release. Perhaps rather less in keeping with the band's ethics, such as they were, was the re-production on four songs, smoothing the edges, tailoring the band in the hope that they wouldn't seem too 'spiky' for American radio.

The album sold 'steadily'. A babbling trickle, rather than a rush, that would eventually climb to respectable sales figures of 350,000 before the LP eventually slipped into the 'reduced' bins; later Manics albums would commend far greater attention. As the band had preco-ciously forecasted multi-platinum sales, *Generation Terrorists* might be deemed a failure. But it was all part of their learning curve. All four band members would later admit that, to allow all their recordings to sprawl across a double album, rather than tighten it onto a sharp, single album remaining musically in line with, say, 'Motown Junk', was both artistically and commercially naïve. None of them, however, would admit to regretting the double album. As to the band's desire to produce a ground-breaking statement which would shake the British music scene to its foundations, Richey would later tell this writer (in a phone interview to the *Manchester Evening News* in 1993), "I think that perhaps we were a bit naïve in that respect. It's not that we didn't have the capabilities. In fact it was all there, in that album, but the world had changed, perhaps more than we realised. People didn't care about such things any more. It wasn't like 1977, when you could really make a statement and get taken seriously. I don't blame people for becoming that apathetic . . . that selfish. They get on with their own lives. Because music had been so important to us we just thought it would still be just as important for people on a massive level . . . and it wasn't. I do think we cared more than most people, though."

Richey was quite right in suggesting that in the Nineties it was impossible to galvanise public feeling against apathy in the same way that the Pistols did in 1977. But he was being somewhat precious to suggest that the Manics were, in any way, more openly caring than the average man in the street.

* * *

It would evolve into arguably the most puzzling failure in modern pop times. By the end of 1998, with the market outside the States slobbering at their feet, the Manic Street Preachers had evolved into a formidable rock beast. But not to American ears. Indeed, the Yanks' apparent disregard for the Welsh band had started to verge on arrogance. Even a full-blooded endorsement from Michael Stipe, in *Rolling Stone* for God's sake, couldn't seem to shift the blockage.

At the time it seemed a certainty that the Manics would take America by storm. This writer spent nights sitting in a wooden shack on Malibu Beach listening to the diminutive DJ and ferocious socialite, Rodney Bingenhiemer repeatedly playing 'Slash'n'Burn' and agreeing with sundry in-studio sycophants that this would be ". . . the most important English (sic) band to hit American shores since The Clash." The vast American college radio circuit seemed equally willing to follow the Bingenhiemer line. Whether this translates across to the FM stations is always another matter: witness the difference between the US fortunes of Suede (failed) and The Cranberries (succeeded massively, but their Irishness – and work ethic – would always be a trump card in the States).

91

Welshness has seeped into the States, but it exists in tiny scattered pockets. It is undoubtedly a fact that while Americans have taken warmly to a number of Welsh artists – Tom Jones, Shirley Bassey and the unique John Cale to name but three – they would rarely have any idea that these artists were from a culture so at odds with its dominant English neighbour. This seems particularly odd, especially as the causes of the historically suppressed Scots and, of course, the Irish (by 1924, 26% of all New Yorkers were of Irish origin), have soaked so fully into the fabric of American society and culture. But Welshness has very little American resonance. That, of course, would be wholly immaterial, if the Manic Street Preachers were actually a rock band entrenched in America cliché (like, for instance, The Alarm, who were fleetingly successful in the States). But if their music still seems so obviously transatlantic in its powerful attack, their lyrics and, indeed, their attitude seem, to the casual American listener, difficult and, fittingly, obscure. Which is possibly why 'Slash'n'Burn', actually a full-blooded attack on the shrinkage of Brazilian rainforests, was so wholly misunderstood by Rodney Bingenhiemer and, indeed, everybody else, who seemed to regard it as some kind of pseudo-romantic soundtrack to footage of the riots of South Central Los Angeles which raged during the band's visit. It was suggested that this misconception genuinely upset the band, and this is an indication of the culture gap. It is, after all, a pretty understandable mistake. The song comes across with all the ferocity of an ancient Dead Kennedys' single and the lyrics "Slash'n'burn, Kill to live, Kill for kicks . . ." do nothing to dispel the illusion of a hedonistic, live-for-today lifestyle. The very next line in the song is, "Third world to the first, Kill to live," but, by this time the damage had been done. This was a band who looked like The Clash after ransacking the cosmetics counter in Bloomingdales. Of course the Americans would grasp the wrong end of the stick. It would be naïve to expect anything else.

And there's more. Anyone who believes the English music business to be more than just a sycophantic swirl of shady corporate oiks, proffering handshakes while, at all times, promoting their own careers, should spend five minutes at, say, The New Music Seminar in New York, where the American music industry gathers for three days of unashamed backslapping and brown-nosing. Nothing, in England, and certainly not in Wales, compares to this. American record companies are heavy at the top – very heavy – and crumble away towards the fat bottom of the hierarchical pyramid, a place where absolutely nobody is to be trusted and young bands, fresh from across the Atlantic, are often overwhelmed in sickly gush. There is little point in fighting this. New Order used to hurtle sarcasm straight back at the smiley smile face of American A&R, only to be met with an even larger grin and a retort along the lines of, "Oh you English. Always joking. Now, about lunch." That said, it is all too easy to react against such smarminess, and therefore fail to see the commercial intelligence that lies behind it. And so you have to play the game. But how did it feel, for four intelligent post-punk Welsh lads, glammed-up ready to attack, to be faced with such overt superficiality? One can safely assume that the Manic Street Preachers had mixed feelings that bright day in April 1992, when their limo swept into Manhattan for the first time, the band cowering beneath an ambuscade of record company people. The latter professed long-term friendship and devotion, while a couple of dubious New York-based journos sought to find an angle on this raggle-taggle Welsh crew. The raggle-taggle Welsh crew, quite understandably, sought solace in booze before, finally, punching through a lacklustre early morning set in front of a jaded and apathetic crowd at the Limelight Club, a venue more reminiscent of a wine bar in Yeovil than anything that the band might have envisaged for their first New York show. It was all terrifyingly low key. The gig was actually reviewed in *Village Voice* where the reviewer, deserving of an endurance medal for being the only reporter who didn't keel over and get carried out before the band took the stage, saw the Manics as, "an excitable bunch. They ran around the stage like nervous chickens, thrashing out a punk screech that was familiar but not entirely unwelcome." It was a good, if rather lukewarm, review.

Things were better in LA, where radio play had managed to stir a little local interest. Indeed, the free music tabloid *Santa Monica Freeway*, a hard rock 'What's On' guide staffed entirely by stunning Goths, even devoted a full-page welcome for the band. In the more bizarre clubs, such as The Cathouse and The Den, the Manics were already regarded as emergent heroes. This was LA, after all, and Gangsta Rap was still balanced by a fair slab of leather and studs rock'n'roll. Somehow the locals managed to slot the Manics into this image. There was even an anticipatory party held for the band in The Kings Head English Pub in Santa Monica, arguably the one bar in the entire mass of LA that knew exactly where Wales was. Flagged Dragons drooped over the bar, obscuring the photographs of Ian Botham; but the Manics, alas, didn't show. At the gig, however, the Rodney Bingenhiemer entourage, plus the usual rock glitterati did, at least, attend and seemed generally pleased with the spirited set. The band, however, felt uneasy amid the flood of compliments ("Hey man, you were so hot tonight") and seemed unusually subdued. While Bradfield grasped his obligatory and omnipresent bottle of Corona, and chatted with the humous-munching liggers backstage, the rest of the band seemed less inclined to swap niceties, and kept to a tight huddle, retreating to their hotel as soon as possible. Although they later turned tourist, tripping down to Anaheim for a day at Disneyland – *NME* in tow – one couldn't say the Manics accepted America with open-mouthed awe. In LA, in particular, they just didn't know how to square their small-town socialism with such a garish and vulgar explosion of rampant capitalism. To many, LA is both a cruel and sexy city, buzzing with the absurd and the crazed, an irresistible frisson between wealth and poverty. But the city's terrible beauty was lost on the band, who remained as insular and sullen as a group of schoolboys forced to go on a day trip to the Peak District.

Nicky Wire, at least, had the grace to admit that, as a bunch of valley boys with little experience of the big world, they weren't exactly qualified to pass comment on the social atmosphere of large American cities. It was odd though to note that, as they were in LA during a time of explosive social friction, they didn't seem to find it a bit more stimulating. Though to their credit, they displayed a commendable maintenance of their standards. While they were in the city, three magazines attempted to get them to pose colourfully on the street corners of Watts. Quite rightly, they refused, but it is difficult to imagine The Clash in their heyday, pushed and hurried by ferociously opportunistic manager Bernie Rhodes, passing up such an opportunity. Perhaps, as time has passed, we have all matured a little. While The Clash believed themselves to be an integral part of, say, Notting Hill discontent in 1976, and used the riot, literally, as the backdrop to their sellable angst, the Manic Street Preachers were fully aware that, for all their genuine integrity, they were still just a rock band and, in such a socially volatile context as Watts, could only be seen as flippant, superficial and highly patronising.

Back in New York, following a string of gigs at small venues, the band finally arrived on the street that was home to the US punk scene in the late Seventies: The Bowery. Halfway down this downbeat strip, an unassuming darkened entrance beckoned them in and a long, slim, blackened room unfolded to present them with a grim little stage. Nevertheless, it was sufficient, at last, to stop the Manics in their tracks. For this was CBGBs, the spiritual home of punk, where once The Ramones, Talking Heads, New York Dolls, Jayne County, Television, Patti Smith and Blondie would jostle for attention, a mess of ego and talent, unwittingly changing the course of music. Unless you were to reconstruct London's long-dead Roxy Venue, it would be difficult to imagine a more fitting venue for the Manics to play at this stage of their career. Richey, in particular, seemed massively affected by the ghosts of this tiny room and even tinier dressing room. The place had a definite power, still, reflected in the unusually excitable nature of the crowd who drifted in that evening, seeking inebriation and some kind of hard rock. It was, by far, the finest gig of the whole tour, a universe away, or so it seemed, from the swirling sycophancy of LA. "No matter how big we get we will never play a better club than that," Richey told a *Village Voice* journalist. It was obvious that the Manics regarded the gig as some kind of important stepping stone in their career path, even though for a number of years the club had been host to many of the more hopelessly adrift artists of New York's largely derivative rock scene.

One encouraging development that resulted from the US tour was a noticeable swell of support for the band in America's underground press. The Manic Street Preachers? In tune with underground America? Well, not quite but many of this particular batch of interviews seem strangely significant in retrospect. It was lovely, for instance, to see Richey Edwards attacking the notion of the Manics as a rock'n'roll cliché outfit in the excellent, though appallingly named, *Check This Out* magazine. Commenting on the idea of a young American kid, heavily into Guns'n'Roses, purchasing 'Slash'n'Burn' and attempting to come to terms with the fractured lyrical vision of that song, Richey observed, "I think that is the best thing about us. Because, for us, corny, cliché-ridden bands singing songs about girls or livin' in New Jersey or Harley Davidsons or, like, 'I got my tattoo done on Sunset Strip . . .' it's all so pathetic and shit. I mean, rock music is the music we like. But that brain-dead metal mentality pisses us off so much. And that's why a band like Nirvana getting so big and on the covers of . . . basically, metal magazines, can only be a good thing because these kids have grown up with all the crap that goes with it. You know, cocaine party. I sniffed coke off 23 models last night . . . that's got nothing to do with real life."

Richey's comments to *Rock Blues* – from Detroit – reveal a double-edged attitude to the New World. He clearly found it both exhilarating and somewhat alarming at the same time: "Just like in England we find there are pockets of fans, of people who have been waiting for a band like us and haven't found anything in the music press, or wherever, to suit them. But you lot. You do seem to take us so seriously, it's frightening. You know all the lyrics, you analyse them. You make assumptions but you are not usually far wrong. And, anyway, even if you don't grasp our meaning, which can be pretty ambiguous sometimes, it doesn't matter at all. In England they don't tend to bother. They say we are like The Clash but, I mean, have you ever compared The Clash's lyrics to ours?"

The American tour was neatly sandwiched by two singles from *Generation Terrorists*. The first, 'Slash'n'Burn' had, of course, alerted the more perceptive American radio stations to the punkier edges of this new band, and the cheer which had greeted the song at CBGBs was an indication that an American fan base, albeit comprising Seventies throwbacks in studs and leather, was in the process of building. The next release, however, was the first true indication that this band would eventually transcend their embryonic punk state and create music of fine and rare majesty. It was, of course, 'Motorcycle Emptiness', a song written – incredibly – three years before its release. It was the song which finally seemed to suggest that the Manics could transcend their cult status and appeal to the casual music fan in search of a song. There are famous posters and photographs of the band, in all their long-legged, white-jeaned elegance amid a thronging Japanese street from this period (Japan being the exotic venue for the 'Motorcycle Emptiness' video). Extremely inappropriate actually, as the song begged for a vision of a Californian highway and an expansive desert vista flanked by craggy mountains.

A riot of my own, 1990, left to right: Nicky, Richey, Sean & James. *(Joe Dilworth/S.I.N.)*

Peroxide pudding bowls and acne, 1990. *(Joe Dilworth/S.I.N.)*

Anarchy in Blackwood, 1990. *(Steve Double/S.I.N.)*

A bomb in Wardour Street, 1991. *(Martin Goodacre/S.I.N.)*

The Manics in Cambridge, 1991. *(Tim Paton/S.I.N.)*

Backstage boredom: Richey in Cardiff, 1992. *(Tim Paton/S.I.N.)*

Richey and Nicky in lager frenzy. *(Justin Thomas/All Action)*

James

Sean

Nicky

Richey

(Kim Tonelli/S/I/N)

Nicky: The 'Dot Cotton' era. *(Fred Duval/Famous)*

Richey *(Martin Goodacre/S.I.N.)*

This is my truth…, the Manics in 1998. *(Steve Double/Retna:Paul Bergen/Redferns)*

Performing 'You Stole The Sun From My Heart' at the Brits, 1999. *(Mick Hutson/Redferns)*

Still, as the band were fond of paradox, perhaps a seething, crowded Japan was a neatly absurd choice. The track reached a respectable number 17 in the British charts, one place behind the peak position of 'You Love Us', although few people would argue that 'Motorcycle Emptiness' broke considerable new ground.

Although it is tempting to ignore the next, rather sordid little episode in the band's career, one feels that it remains a significant part of their story. Therefore, direct your attention towards Nicky Wire's anti-New-Age-Travellers remarks which first appeared in the pages of *NME*. Wire attacked the crusties' universal loathing of besuited politicians, calling this attitude naïve and dumb. He added, "I think they should be treated more harshly. I wouldn't care if they were rounded up and put on an island. I don't think they do any good." It was fascinating to see such an argument from the lips of someone previously seen to be flying the dumbed-down banner of punk. In effect, Wire's outburst merely echoed the sentiments of countless intolerant ivory towered columnists of Fleet Street, all hoping to gain right wing cred points in the wake of Julie Burchill's public swing at liberalism. Indeed, at the time it was hip to be hard line. A 'lock 'em up, flog 'em, chuck away the key' stance seemed to be heartily accepted by broadsheet-reading media types, worried by the increasing likelihood that they would return from work to find that their trusty Apple Mac had been unceremoniously spirited away.

The 'crusties' debate was raging, with all manner of woolly-jumpered, green-booted ex-liberals suddenly crying 'Get a job' at mud-splattered New Agers protesting against the construction of new bypasses. Crusties, 'New Age Travellers', 'hippies', call them what you will, are a gang drawn from across the class spectrum who generally gather under the cause of eco warriors. Their PR isn't generally too good, especially as, all too often, they are seen tramping, en masse, through pristine little villages and spots of noted rural beauty. All this was particularly evident in Wales, and on Welsh television, where they were seen adding significantly to the worries of struggling wholesome farmers. Nicky Wire's little broadside, therefore, was absolutely no different from statements made in Welsh homes from Newport to Llandudno, from Aberystwyth to Offa's Dike. Both Richey Edwards and James would subsequently attempt to diffuse the situation by noting that, "The Manics do tend to shoot their mouths off..." Needless to say, to the rather easily offended *NME* readership, then going firmly through one of its most precious pre-lad stages, Wire's objection to crusties was inexcusable, the infamous letters page bristling with indignance. Some of it, to be fair, was understandable. Wire had, after all, been attacking a group of people prepared to stand by, and live by their principles. Whether agreeing with them or not, surely one had to admire their tenacity and strength of mind in delivering on what they preached?

Wire showed little remorse. His infamous "I think they deserve total hatred and contempt," remark would never be retracted. Years later, when interviewed on Radio One by Steve Lamacq, Wire expanded upon this theme: "It wasn't just an ill-informed pop star trying to make a splash. Neither were these people living outside society. You just have to be intelligent enough to see through that kind of bullshit. They were walking all over land that people had worked very hard to own. It wasn't free land. They had no right to be there. That was my point... and I don't think it was particularly controversial. Most people certainly agreed with me."

They did, too, although they weren't the kind of people who tended to write to music papers. What comes across as so fascinating about the whole episode is the notion of a rock band, and a fairly outspoken, politically aware rock band at that, voicing the views of the silent majority and antagonising those who would see themselves as rebels. Yet again we find an instance where the Manics differed from The Clash, who, for all their musical brilliance, would undoubtedly have seen the New Age Travellers as romantic rebels and offered to do a benefit gig for them.

All of which added colour and spice to the public image of the Manics. James Dean Bradfield's conciliatory remark that, "... if we stir things up a bit, it doesn't matter if you agree with us, does it," seemed to placate those who bayed for Wire's blood and by the time the band were blasting through a show-stealing set at the Reading Festival, any trace of friction, even amongst the mud-splattered revellers – most of whom strongly resembled New Age Travellers at this point – was noticeably absent. As far as *NME* was concerned, it was generally perceived that 'mouthy' acts sold copies, whether the act in question was Mark E. Smith or Madonna. Wire's opinionated musings had more or less guaranteed acres of space in terms of future coverage.

At Reading the band were outstanding, revelling in the swaying mass before them, the crazed dancing during 'Slash'n'Burn' and the awestruck attention that 'Motorcycle Emptiness' received. Most reviewers saw the Manics' performance that day as sheer magic, an exuberant display exemplified by Nicky Wire's standard festival act of holding his bass aloft and crashing it into the speakers. Even this seemed curiously apt, as British gig-goers appeared to have retreated, bedenimed and long haired, back into the field, back into the mud, back into the dubiously romantic notion of the 'Summer of Festivals'. Indeed, festival mentality-drifting from Reading to Glastonbury to Phoenix etc, had seemingly been reborn. Suddenly the notion of travelling cheaply, camping in fields of mud and purchasing New Age trinkets from fifty year olds dressed in velvet didn't seem quite so old hat. It was a pity, however, that Wire's battered bass, dripping with snapped strings, had been hurtled towards the crowd. Initially there was a ripple of amusement as the said instrument crashed into two security guards until, however, it became apparent that both sustained injuries. (It was an accident, of course, and both men received, and apparently accepted, sincere apologies from the band.)

NME, in keeping with their tradition of producing utterly contemporary compilation albums, and tapes, requested that the Manics offer a track for their celebratory 40th anniversary release, *Ruby Trax*, offering the proceeds to the Spastics Society. It was a good opportunity for the band to slip out of their natural recording routine, and indulge in something less demanding: a cover version. They had enjoyed recording Alice Cooper's 'Under My Wheels' for the flip side of 'Motorcycle Emptiness' and the track seemed to suit them. The notion of continuing with the Cooper connection, by covering either 'School's Out' – which would have been rather obvious – or, more bizarrely 'I Love The Dead' from the *School's Out* album, was seriously considered, as was Iggy Pop's 'Search And Destroy' which, to be honest, I would have loved to have heard. Instead, following Nicky Wire's suggestion, they opted for 'Suicide Is Painless', the once-banned theme from the 1970 film and subsequent TV series, *M.A.S.H.* Wire had always been attracted by the audacious bad taste of the song, and recalled watching the film through an early drunken haze, back in his late school days. The film's influence is, perhaps, of relevance here. Through a horrific splattering of mobile hospital tents in the Korean War, two hugely overworked surgeons, Trapper John McCintyre and Hawkeye Pierce, manage to rise above their grim task by creating their own world of flippancy and sarcasm. The duo play golf, drink Vodka Martinis and chase nurses while death and destruction rages, apparently needlessly, all around. The film's inspirational central theme was that of the power of mind over matter, the notion that, with thought and application, anything can be achieved and overcome. As the kind of film that made you walk from the cinema feeling strangely emboldened, it always appealed to Wire. That said, the band entered into the recording, in a Cardiff eight-track, in a loose and carefree spirit. None of the brow-beating traumas of the *Generation Terrorists* sessions here. And, if it didn't work, the only thing wasted was the minuscule £80 studio fee. This loose atmosphere undoubtedly translated into a recording which, much to the band's astonishment, climbed to the dizzying heights of number seven, in September 1992. Detractors may argue that the single's charity status certainly encouraged sales, but the fact remained that the Manic Street Preachers had now had their first genuine top ten hit.

Despite the thrill of a hit single, there were no signs of any possible relaxation as 1992 melted into 1993. Nicky Wire took it upon himself to deliver what was to become his most infamous comment, onstage at the band's celebratory Christmas show at London's Kilburn National. Following on from the rumours at the time – false rumours, thankfully – that R.E.M.'s enigmatic singer Michael Stipe had registered HIV positive, Wire opined, "In this season of goodwill, let's hope Michael Stipe goes the same way as Freddie Mercury pretty soon."

It was shock for the sake of shock and one might have been forgiven for surmising that Nicky Wire, if not the rest of the Manics, had started to lose their grip a little. Was the remark made out of envy of R.E.M.'s worldwide success? Certainly, having just released the globally successful *Automatic For The People*, R.E.M. were at a commercial peak. (At the time of Wire's original remark, much had been made of the fact that Stipe had remained silent, neither confirming nor denying the story. Of course, given his naturally somewhat emaciated appearance, this only served to increase the rumours about his welfare at the time.) The Manics wouldn't have been the first band to be frustrated by their own failure to break through to the mainstream. When pressed to defend himself, Wire argued that he was merely making a point about the deification of celebrities over the average person in the street; that the suffering of ordinary people was no less genuine than that of pop stars. Fair enough, but even so, Wire was still guilty of attempting to make his point in an exceptionally clumsy and genuinely offensive manner. And, through the barrage of loathing that instantly flew straight back at him, it became clear that he was, not for the first or last time, radically out of step with prevailing opinion. Years later, in *Q* magazine, Wire admitted, "The one thing I might be pushed into showing a morsel of regret about is the Michael Stipe statement."

It was a pity this tentative apology didn't arrive earlier although it's interesting to note that Michael Stipe would later refer warmly to the Manic Street Preachers, perceptively telling a startled journalist from *Spin* magazine that, ". . . I love them, there is something very warm, very human about their spirit. Maybe it's in their background, but you do tend to believe in what they are doing."

Stipe's generous comment raises once more the subject of the band's Welsh roots. Certainly as the most intelligently fey American rock star since Jobriath, Stipe sensed the small-town heart of the band. Even more strangely, and much later, Michael Stipe would feature alongside James Dean Bradfield and Cerys Matthews on the cover of the *Q* magazine's Awards Special edition in January 1999. Inside, both Stipe and Wire dispelled any suspicions of lingering frostiness between them.

Stipe: "Oh, I didn't know who they were so it didn't matter. (Laughs). It just seemed so dumb-headed. I mean, c'mon, I don't hold a grudge. Against something like that, no, that's just stupidness."

Nicky Wire: "I just feel really embarrassed. We met Peter Buck in San Francisco on the last American tour and he was very nice. And the biggest irony of all is that I still consider R.E.M. one of my favourite bands. When R.E.M. were on *The Tube* doing 'Driver 8' and Michael Stipe had purple eyeliner on, that was the first time I'd seen them on telly and I thought fucking hell, that's fantastic. So, anyway, I don't expect any of them to ever talk to me again."

Case closed.

4

GOLD AGAINST THE SOUL

"Our manifesto is, 'Don't do it, kids, never get past the age of 13.'"
– Richey Edwards

Condemned by their own pronouncements, castigated even by some of their own fans, the Manic Street Preachers had backed themselves into a corner by the start of 1993. "We are going to make one great album and then split," they said, a number of times in a number of magazines and in a number of different ways. They must have meant it. Should this band be even thinking about recording a second album? To exceed the limits they deliberately set themselves would be to devalue any statements they made in future . . . wouldn't it? Of course, by this time they should have smashed through to global dominance . . . and that hadn't happened. They were still wedged in cultish obscurity, worshipped by little pockets of devotees from the most unlikely corners of Europe (massive in Slovenia, I'm told) and yet they could still freely wander the streets of Blackwood.

The band transcended the 'you said you would split up' criticism with graceful ease. "Yeah, well we fucking lied, didn't we," was James's curt response when approached by Dave Owens, editor of *Welsh Rock* fanzine, late one Swansea night. Richey's much-publicised statement was rather more eloquent. "Well, we were proved right. When we made those statements we knew all these stupid people would come gunning for us. Of course we were never going to sell 16 million records. We were just creating a fuss, partly just for the hell of it. Why not? It grabbed people's attention." Nicky Wire was resolutely defiant when questioned about the success of the Manics' first album:

"We actually sold an awful lot of records," he insisted. "Nothing like our prediction but that tended to spur us on. We knew we would never split up. Especially if we actually had sold 16 million. But it was a more artistic thing. We were getting better and we knew it. It would have been ludicrous to call it a day. Richey was handing me lots of lyrics, James and Sean were taking us into whole new areas musically speaking and I was kind of lodged between those two extremes. Rehearsals were getting very exciting. The music was writing itself. It was just rolling along effortlessly. How could we stop it?"

In some respects, a superficial big time had already arrived. 'Generation Terrorists' had sold 100,000 copies in the UK alone. Hardly Garth Brooks levels, but enough to convince the record company to pull the band onto the next level. The general consensus was that a more mature sound could now be achieved. The rougher punk edges could be polished a little, allowing something a little more grandiose (and, perhaps, more commercial?) to develop. Curiously, although they would ultimately fail with this next album, the same approach would eventually lead the band to their first major breakthrough. Whatever, those 100,000 sales had generated record company confidence, a confidence that increased after a batch of fairly rough demos had been handed over. For the Manics would now be allowed to enter, and indeed, to indulge in, the softly lit atmosphere of the luxury studio, a strange subterranean world resembling a Star Trek set, where the rigours of everyday life are assuaged by recording and re-recording, by daytime coffee and night-time alcohol, by games of pool, by mysterious outside caterers bringing in endless trays of food. For those wishing to break from the rigours of recording, a swimming pool beckoned. It was an unreal blast of wall-to-wall comfort, a place where hard work and relaxation existed side by side. And it would be home for the Manic Street Preachers for a full five months.

The studio in question was Hook End Manor, a Berkshire retreat that cost Sony £2,000 per day. The luxuries, naturally, would extend into the actual studio, a particularly grand affair and a dream for any producer wishing to extend a band's sound to its very limits. Such a situation was fraught with danger, of course, and a battle to keep control over an individualistic sound would undoubtedly ensue. How would the Manics, with a sound as stripped down as any band in the country, be able to come to terms with such a vast array of musical possibilities?

Then again, the band's finest moment to date had been the sprawling, anthemic 'Motorcycle Emptiness'; perhaps time spent in a studio with facilities to spare could result in more of the same. The man responsible for producing the Manics' sophomore set was Dave Eringa, who had particularly impressed the band by his work on 'Motown Junk'. Eringa had also worked as engineer on the latest demos which had so impressed the record company. Nevertheless, it was a courageous decision to insert Eringa as producer; indeed, it was equally courageous of Eringa to accept, to be written into the band's contract, to take on the immense responsibility of creating with them a more expansive sound, without sacrificing the power of that début album.

From the outset, the sessions for the album that would eventually become *Gold Against The Soul* were edgy. If anything, the band took too many songs into the recordings and, in turn, these songs provided too many opportunities to experiment; predictably, the breadth and scope of the studio was simply too vast. The temptation to push the sound to the limits, to become lost in a dizzying maze of gadgetry, to fine tune ad infinitum, was simply too strong for band and producer. Time and time again, a song would finish in a cul de sac with the band straining to find some way forward. James, in particular, argued for long painful hours, clashing with Eringa over possible directions for the music, and attempting to find some way back to the impassioned intensity that had been and would always be the band's trademark. Three weeks in and the new album had already veered wildly away from the very things that the band held so dear. The signs of over-indulgence lay everywhere. The famous story that twenty-five microphones were used to capture the drum sound on 'Life Becoming A Landslide' was an ironic reflection of the situation surrounding the Manics' favourite album, Joy Division's *Unknown Pleasures*. On that occasion, the band's erratic, eccentric producer Martin Hannett spent three days systematically dismantling and piecing back together Stephen Morris's drum kit. Such instances are the stuff of studio mythology, marvellous anecdotes for awestruck engineers and producers. They weren't necessarily productive as far as a new band's musical identity is concerned. And that was the whole problem at Hook End Manor. The band, and, in fairness, the producer too, were constantly wrestling to retain that streak of genuine identity against a studio specifically designed to soften and perfect. Nothing wrong with that, if the band in question are a musically sophisticated and mature unit. But the Manics were still full of youthful fire. It was essential that they kept those raw edges; they were what made the Manics unique.

Against the odds, and with six tracks binned along the way, the recording reached completion and the whole circus was shifted to Olympic Studios in Barnes, where the mixing could begin in earnest. This proved less traumatic and the break between recording and mixing had seen both band and producer suitably refreshed. The new environment certainly provided an added thrust of enthusiasm, especially for James who worked tirelessly in the control booth, suddenly taking delight in the vastness of the sound – a sound now expanded by keyboards (supplied by ex-Q Tips muso Ian Kewly) and future M People percussionist, Shovel. James: "It was the first time I really began to feel confident in the studio . . . which is a strange thing to admit as it's generally not regarded as one of our better albums. I didn't enjoy the recording but, once we had got to the mix, things certainly improved." James was eager to learn, eager to guide the course of the album's sound and delighted to be behind a mixing desk that didn't seem way beyond his still naïve technical knowledge.

Perhaps more than any other studio session, the time at Olympic seemed to outline the fractured dynamics of the band at work. James, studious, responsible, intense, earnest, fired by a ferocious longing to hold onto the band's identity. That latter desire also fired the artistic muse of Nicky Wire who, while the mixes thumped away in the background, deliberated over ideas for the album's sleeve. A task he rightly saw as equal to the musical guidance of James. It was different for Sean who, despite having an enormous input at the recordings themselves, now felt rather estranged, but managed to amuse himself without too much problem. Of course, this entire process served only to push Richey to the extreme edge of the artistic process. He had equipped himself well, back at Hook End Manor, managing to show enough confidence to play under the pressurised isolation of the studio, and not feel unduly oppressed by the critical ears of producer and engineers. But the extent of Richey's input, from strongly influencing the entire affair with the initial batch of lyrics, would naturally weaken as the recording neared its conclusion. As such, at Olympic, he slipped more and more frequently into a detached state, glassy-eyed and aloof, carting his vodka around like a comforting Teddy Bear, collapsing in the corners of the recreation room, head in hands.

This was also a period which saw the band visited by a number of journalists, and it may be presumed that Richey's public image as the 'difficult one' can be traced back to this point. Unlike Sean, he didn't feel he had the musical knowledge to be able to drop into the control booth and add his contribution that way. He could, of course, have opted for the kind of romantic truancy he indulged in during the recording of the first album. This time around, however, things were so much darker. There has been no confirmation that his drinking had quite reached the levels mentioned in the music press at the time – up to two bottles of vodka a day. A more conservative estimate of half a bottle topped up by infrequent forays to the pub seems more realistic. Of more concern was the way he simply slipped from the day-to-day problems of the band. Once his main task – that of writing lyrics – had been completed, he seemed to have time on his hands to wither and worry too much about everything.

The new album was preceded by an eerily portentous single, entitled 'From Despair To Where'. A strange record, and for many strange reasons. For example, there is part of a beer mat bearing some scribbled writing, sitting proudly in a gilt frame, in the bedroom of a modern semi-detached house in Holmfirth, Yorkshire. The owner of the beer mat display, an ex-punk (Manchester Electric Circus Circa 1976), wouldn't allow me to photograph his little piece of rock ephemera (although, should you frequently visit the record fairs of Yorkshire, you will surely have seen it hanging behind the 'Elvis' stall). No matter. The beer mat sports, in spidery handwriting, the words, "From despair to where? Ian Curtis. Warsaw." It is genuine and, in light of the Manics single, genuinely intriguing. Maybe it's just one of those coincidences. God knows, Richey Edwards surely read many of the same books as Ian Curtis. That is, however, where the similarity ends. 'From Despair To Where?' turned out to be a disarmingly soft rock affair, barely lifting above FM mush and possibly the most disappointing single in the Manics' lengthy catalogue. Within that track you can sense the plush, dull atmosphere of the top-notch studio. You can sense a lazy band, stretched beyond their limits, believing they had finally arrived. You can even sense their most inspirational member, absent from the melody, languishing in some distant haze. The track simply lacked hunger, excitement, verve. The title begged more from the song. The re-mix B-sides on the 12″ version bore the suitably complementary titles 'Spectators Of Suicide (Heavenly Version)' and 'Star Lover (Heavenly Version)', both of which had seen service before on the 12″ of 'You Love Us'.

'From Despair To Where?' climbed to a respectable 25 in the British charts. Not high enough to launch the band as mainstream popsters, but high enough to maintain momentum and provide a little promotional push for the oncoming *Gold Against The Soul*. It proved to be a pristine affair which fell between two stools. The angry push of *Generation Terrorists* was still there somewhere, but it was blanketed by a more controlled, buffed, careful sound, typified by the lead-off single.

The first song, 'Sleepflower', recalled the moment when dumb but wealthy Sheffield mega-rockers Def Leppard dropped the hard-edged noise premiered on their own Bludgeon Riffola label and hit upon a new, American-orientated style of muffled rock. Indeed, the song that achieved this twist was prophetically called 'Hello America' . . . and off they jolly well went. I'm not suggesting that the Manics were aiming at the US stadium circuit, but 'Sleepflower' – not, it must be said, a bad song – held that same sense of metallic punch-pulling. It almost rocks. But not quite. That said, it was much livelier than most of the things which followed. Immediately after this track, subtle acoustic strains lured the listener through images of 11 minutes past 11 on November 11: solemn, dignified remembrance. Aged, impassioned faces, hiding proud dark truths. The track was 'La Tristesse Durera (Scream To A Sigh)', named after Van Gogh's last words. For once, we find a rock band blessed with the courage – this was substantially pre-Pulp's 'Help The Aged', of course – to champion the impeccable cause of their elders and draw a comparison with the young of today that seemed almost shameful. It was a Richey lyric. Strange to see such respectfulness in one with such a youthful hedonistic bent. And, as the track exploded into vast anthemic sound it was possible to glimpse, if only fleetingly, the wide-screen epic quality that would come to define the Manics' future sound. Anyone who believes, as many do, that the Manics didn't manage to hone their sound until the post-Richey period should check this track out pronto.

Much of Richey's encroaching angst might be found in the self-deprecating 'Yourself', in which the song's hero coils within himself, torturing himself with his lack of self-esteem, the entire thing crumbling into hopeless depression. Hardly the most inspiring of songs, it seemed designed for self-obsessive bed-sit dwellers; quite the antithesis of the 'La Tristesse Durera' lyric.

On 'Life Becoming A Landslide' we discover a curious streak of the kind of femininity one finds only within the male psyche. (A theme strangely close to that of Tears For Fears' dreary 'Woman In Chains'.) We might be dealing with Nicky Wire's alter ego here. Camped-up and rouged, eye-lined and be-skirted, ungainly and draggy. It is an image we would glimpse again and again, and on all albums, latterly in 'Born A Girl' from the *This Is My Truth* album. There is great darkness, however, to the theme, as the track flickers between the confused borders of lust and love, casting a dark shadow over the mind of a pre-teen, about to enter that terrifying and exhilarating period known as adolescence.

The track leads neatly into the surprisingly upbeat 'Drug, Drug, Druggy', in which that familiar Manics' bête noir – small-town mentality – is ruthlessly worked over. We can imagine the streets of Blackwood, the cycle of gossip, the archaic put down, "Oh, he's on drugs." Even if the 'he' in question, or she for that matter, was nothing more than a bored teenager who occasionally went in for a bit of dope to pass the time. The power of that 'on drugs' line remains and, more often than not, would be uttered by beer boys who rarely ventured away from the tap rooms. The hypocritical criticism has less impact today, as drugs awareness continues to improve but, nevertheless, it still holds a grip in the Blackwoods of this world. Here, the Manics rewind to that moment when their growing awareness and intelligence clashed awkwardly with the prevailing wisdom of those around them. Again, it is a song which seemingly contradicts the passion of 'La Tristesse Durera', both musically and lyrically. Not surprisingly, as it surfaced in a slightly different form in the *Generation Terrorists* sessions.

Richey's dark glam epic 'Roses In The Hospital' would become a key Manics single (reaching number 15 in September 1993). Dark glam indeed. A guttersnipe Ziggy wrapped up in a bleak lyric. Impossible not to play with the imagery of the title – the stark, cold place adorned by an object of simple beauty; the horror of an ageing intellect slowly fading, of a brilliant compassionate mind amongst a riot of football thuggery, an artistic bent in a small-minded environment, an aesthetic core in a political office, compassion in a prison. My images, not Richey's, but the song always takes me to that same place. The lone flower fighting oppression. The playwright battling against philistine critics. It is a sad song because, one feels, the true cause is lost in the face of apathy, stupidity. It's impossible not to think of Richey here, too. A mind with much to say, battling with his own musical ineptitude and yet, somewhat ironically, winning in the end. Getting the message across. That's the true tragedy of Richey Edwards. He actually managed to find his outlet, to get his art across to thousands and inspire so many. It would have been far more tragic, surely, had he never managed to rise above the factory floor or the dole queue, like millions of others whose talents have never been realised. 'Roses In The Hospital' became emblematic of this paradox. In Richey's lyric we are taken into a metaphorical hospital ward where affliction controls intellect. Not for the first, or last, time the Manics serve up a track that is as unappetising as a dome of hospital mash potato, and yet contains a germ of pure beauty.

'Nostalgic Pushead' proved to be one of the album's less endearing moments, casting a nod towards The Smiths' anti-record company tirade on 'Paint A Vulgar Picture'. Like The Smiths, the Manics might stand accused of displaying a certain amount of naïve hypocrisy here, as attacking the very forces that combine to bring this song into published existence is, at best, a confused way of getting your message across.

The album's final cut, 'Gold Against The Soul', rallied forcibly against the fall-out of the Eighties' 'Greed is Good' era. In the song – another Richey lyric – you can sense a defeated working class, an honest worker content to be just that and nothing more. Allowing the spoils to float towards besuited oafs who drift to and from London on commuter trains. The distance between those two worlds – the quaint Surrey train station car park on Monday morning and the silent submissiveness of a quiet Blackwood (metaphorically speaking) on the same day is all too evident. Richey's notion of a two-tier Britain may seem simplistic, but it is also an ironic acknowledgement that Thatcher emerged victorious despite it all. The song is also, in part, a call to arms, a longing for the days of surging idealistic socialism. That brief period of time, in Britain at least, before the unions became famously empowered and, with almost poetic inevitability, emerged as a beast as suppressive as the forces it initially attacked. Perhaps that's the true sadness of 'Gold Against The Soul', the towering inevitability of the failure of the British working class. Or, perhaps more pointedly, the sad final futility of Welsh socialism, at one time the political backbone of Labour-controlled Britain. Again, the experience of growing up in a South Wales valley town is crucial to the tenor of the song. An area in which politics was part of the very air. It is no surprise to find that the local MP throughout the teen years of the Manics was the great Neil Kinnock – perhaps the last of Labour's romantic idealists; almost certainly the last Labour leader to display true heart. How ironic that in these days of soulless New Labour we should look back upon the Kinnock era with misty eyes. 'Gold Against The Soul' is a song etched in defeat. It would have been sadder still, I believe, had Richey been able to sense Labour's move towards the centre ground, and the rise and rise of Tony Blair. Ironically, the dulled melody of 'Gold Against The Soul', with its cushioned FM rock feeling, might itself seem to be an attempt to move into a more commercially successful central ground. A suspicion arose that the band had bowed to Sony's belief that a softer Manics would be considerably more successful, and that the company's idea to place them in all that luxurious studio comfort had been a less than subtle nudge in that particular direction. *Gold Against The Soul* was never going to be a record that the average Manics fanatic would treasure. It just didn't tug the heart strings in the way that previous releases had. The album might make a reasonable background noise for a smoky bedsit Friday night, but it was never going to be anybody's reason to live. And surely that was what the Manics were all about.

I'm sure nobody at Sony batted an eyelid when critical response to the record was universally lukewarm. Indeed, to be condemned by the left-field British music press might have been seen as perversely encouraging. This was no longer a band interested in any kind of cult market. There is no doubt that the Manics had reservations about the record or that these reservations were somewhat tempered by anticipation that it might ultimately make up for its creative shortcomings by delivering financially. That would only be natural for a band who bought into the rock'n'roll dream lock, stock and barrel: nobody wanted to be a *poor* rock'n'roll star – the words just didn't go together. It has to be remembered also that, with the first album hardly setting the world alight, the Manics were now precariously balanced. Should *Gold Against The Soul* have proved significantly less successful than its brash predecessor, then Sony, who held all the contractual options, might be tempted to cut their losses and drop the band. In retrospect, such a suggestion seems positively absurd, but things weren't quite that clear-cut at the time. The truth is that Sony had always intended to steer the band towards becoming the new U2, into making music that would appeal not just to the feverish rock fan, but to the more casual record buyers as well. (It is no secret that U2's real success began when *NME* readers turned away in disgust, while simultaneously the ears of the girl on the till at Sainsbury's, or the car mechanic at the garage, or perhaps even their 'classic' rock-living parents, pricked up.)

Reflecting back in 1996, James commented: "We have never really felt record company pressure but, in a sense, that was because we were just too naïve. I'm sure it was there, especially during that *Gold Against The Soul* period. We found ourselves making music that was, let's say, slightly different. But it just seemed like a natural progression at the time. I'm still really proud of that record. We all are. But it could have been better." There is an obvious hint of mistrust in that statement. Whether the Manics had been cleverly manipulated into softer waters, or not, will have to remain one of pop's intangibles, as nobody, aside, perhaps, from some bright spark from the upper echelons of the Sony hierarchical pyramid, knows the truth. The management fought hard to retain the band's principles, but even they might not be party to the psychological tugs of such a power. All this may seem rather paranoid thinking, but then *Gold Against The Soul* is that kind of album.

Not that the stadium circuit was beckoning too loudly. The Manics seemed tied to mid-sized venues. It was a frustrating period for them; all the more because the album was a distinctly odd success story, climbing to an eminently successful number eight and yet still failing to reach that level where the band could be said to have truly 'arrived'. To put it simply, they still failed the rock star test. They were a large band in every respect and yet could still wander through most British towns without attracting undue attention. If it all fell through after *Gold Against The Soul* – and that seemed quite possible – they would swiftly become one of rock'n'roll's also-rans. Nicky Wire: "We were definitely stuck in the shadows. I don't know if we liked it or not, to be honest. On the one hand we were moving forward without being troubled by the tabloids, or any of that shit. But, then again, I can't deny that we wanted to be pop stars. I mean, I'm still not comfortable with all the PR stuff, although James is brilliant at it, but, well, when it wasn't there we desired it. And that was a really strange period because we were on the fringe. The funny thing is that, later on, I would yearn for those days. In one sense we were in a perfect position. I suppose that's the big lesson in all this. The fact that you always want something else. You are never happy. The human condition. Same for everyone and rock bands are certainly no different."

As Nicky suggests, James was showing every sign of having adapted to the role of a rock'n'roller with enviable ease: "I love the life. Probably more than the others but even I have spent so many evenings drinking to escape it. Back in the days of *Gold Against The Soul* we were still hungry and still pretty mad ... manic, I suppose. We still had that edge even if it wasn't apparent on the album, which is possibly a bad thing. But then I'd get the guilt trip. I'd look at nurses, politicians. Great people and ordinary people and I'd wonder why rock bands think they are special. They are not special at all really, but everyone thinks you are. That's the lie you have to live with. I suppose you shouldn't take it all so seriously."

Which always was, and still remains, the Manics' quandary. They are a serious band. So serious that, at times, they dip into the dangerous waters of pretension and seem to invite ridicule. Sheer force of melody, sincerity and talent generally rescues them. But it's a fine line between emerging as one of the most important bands of their generation, kick-starting pop music again in their own country, and wobbling into self-indulgence. They are not alone in that; indeed they are in good company. Joy Division always teetered on that same line, between self-realisation and self-indulgence.

Quite clearly, the Manics wanted to perform to larger audiences and the simplest way to achieve this was to get onto the festival circuit which, in 1993, was just managing to edge back into respectability in the wake of the rave/rock crossover. Suddenly it didn't seem to be too sad to spend the summers drifting from festival site to festival site, bargaining for soft drugs in local pubs, soaking it all in, and lying in mud . . . All of which didn't necessarily agree with the Manics. True, festivals were a marvellous way of connecting with a large crowd but somehow the whole experience still seemed to grate against their punk mentality. It was a difficult one. They had to think of The Clash at the Victoria Park Anti-Nazi rally rather than the New Age market stall rigmarole of Glastonbury. Still, there was no doubting the skill of the festival promoters, and in particular the organisers of the comparatively recent Phoenix Festival, in bringing the whole concept kicking and screaming out of its hippie infancy. Nevertheless, it was a reluctant and uncharacteristically surly Manic Street Preachers who strolled onto the Phoenix stage in July of that year.

James retained quite definite views of the Phoenix experience: "I fucking hated it. The whole smelly idea of it. The crap PA. The fucking crowd who were moronic, the backstage. The whole thing was horrible." One can surmise that he wasn't completely satisfied with the affair. Perhaps his irritation was exacerbated by his frequent altercations with a gang of rather gormless female mud wallowers. Were they fans? Were they fans of someone else? Why were they there? Nobody seemed to know. Certainly, they didn't seem like the average festival goers. They were too young and were dressed in High Street secretary chic, albeit secretary chic that was splattered with mud and soaked with beer by the time the Manics went on stage. When one screamed "Welsh slaaags" at the band, Richey stood back and failed to suppress uncharacteristic laughter. Whether, as reported, he really did retort with the line, "Look who's fucking talking" remains unclear. James, however, certainly did call the uncouth gaggle a "bunch of fat little cunts", which seems a pretty good indication of his mood that day. Nicky seemed happier than his bandmates, resplendent in headscarf, glasses, the kind of dress that would later be associated with Mrs Merton, and stockings. It was an ungainly and profoundly unconvincing form of drag and an outfit that he subsequently wore as often as possible. An ironic kiss-off, perhaps, to the band's receding glamour look.

Interestingly, at the less prestigious Singleton Park Festival in Swansea, Nicky combined his new look with his time-honoured love of leopard-skin by proudly donning a spotty headscarf. It wasn't an image to which one would have imagined a Swansea crowd would easily relate. And indeed they didn't. The moment the Manics took the stage, taunts and jeers hurtled towards them. Hardly the kind of homecoming the band might have expected. The swell of cheers was challenged, throughout the Manics' set, by an alarming number of people who had, it seemed, turned up with just one thing on their minds: to cause as much disruption as possible. Things had nearly turned nasty during the set by Pele, one of the more promising bands of the period who, during one song, faced a hail of beer glasses. But the intensity of these attacks increased noticeably for the Manics. According to Martin Clarke's *Sweet Venom*, it was an empty Liebfraumilch bottle that crashed into Nicky's head. Other reports state it was Piesporter. Anyway, it was crap German wine and it succeeded in felling our idiosyncratically dressed hero. It might be noted that there are few stranger sights in rock than a horizontal Nicky Wire in a leopard-print headscarf. This surreal sight, although arresting, was little cause for amusement; moreover, rather than calming things down, the incident merely preceded a hail of beer bottles, which splintered dangerously across the stage, forcing the band to make an immediate retreat. "One concussed, three to go you brainless wankers," retorted James as he fled, scowling, backstage.

Why such bile against the Manics? It was suggested that the mindless catalyst for all this was nothing other than a touch of the old Swansea/Newport rivalry. Presumably the argument went that the Manics were a Newport band (even though they weren't), and were therefore fair game for a bit of bother. Perhaps the ludicrous attack was nothing more profound than a case of simple jealousy – something that, increasingly, the Manics have had to live with as they became more and more successful. Courageously, perhaps stupidly, the Manics returned to finish the set. Naturally another beer bottle storm immediately broke upon them but, strangely, it then dissipated just when it appeared that things might become seriously ugly. When the band finally crashed back into the dressing room, they were buzzing with fury; statements like, ". . . never playing in fucking shit South Wales again . . . they can all fuck off" peppered the post-gig discussion. Their anger was only tempered by concern for Nicky's raging headache; mercifully, the local hospital casualty ward was within 100 yards of the stage.

One of the problems with the Singleton Park event, and this problem has been repeated throughout the UK in recent years, was the fact that it was a free concert. Far from eliciting gratitude from the punters, free concerts, especially open air affairs, do tend to attract an element of thuggery. Perhaps it's simple logic. If someone has paid £12 to see their favourite band, they are rather less likely to disrupt the proceedings than if they have just wandered in from some local tap room. "It was a football thing," one fan noted in the local press and, indeed, the football matches of Swansea and Cardiff are often tainted with 'an element'. All of which makes it intriguing to note that rugby, still the most prevalent participation sport in the area, has never suffered from such thuggery. Richey: "It was the most disappointing gig of all, simply because I think we really did expect it to be a kind of welcoming back. And it wasn't like that at all. It felt really alien. Loads of idiots with fat bellies chucking lager at me in a really arrogant and pathetic way. We have nothing whatsoever in common with those people. If they think their machismo is an indication of their being Welsh, then all I can say is that they are so stupid they don't even understand anything about their own culture. Which is so sad and certainly made me feel ashamed."

And there was another problem. The Manics were topping bills now but, in achieving that, they had necessarily transcended the insular borders of Welsh rock. And as a result, that old nugget "Welsh bands should sing in Welsh" emerged to haunt them. It is unrealistic, however, to expect a rock band's music to seep gradually across the world while they restrict themselves to singing in Welsh. Unrealistic and pointless. That attitude is fine, if you wish to remain small-time and small-circuit. But the very point of the Manics was always to emerge as a world force. Whatever, the major criticism one might level at the Manic Street Preachers, from the first time they wandered through Blackwood looking like the illegitimate children of The New York Dolls, to the release *of Gold Against the Soul* is that of their desperate need to grasp attention. And desperate really is the word. The Manic Street Preachers always knew that they simply had to make it. This may cut against the credible edge of their image, but that's how it was. And boy, did it show. On the one hand, they cleverly distilled this desperation into their music, using it for the motivating fire and spirit, a feature that always spilled into their interviews, making them eminently quotable. On the other hand, such desperation for success can come across as a somewhat immature need for love and approval from individuals not confident enough to be satisfied with what they are. The Manics were far from the only band of the time to have to face this quandary. One of their great rivals, Suede, also embraced 'glam' in a curiously respectful manner, rather than using it ironically, and were also treated with a certain amount of distrust. It's not just the glam touches; it's the cocktail of glam and artistic sincerity. It is the difference between Slade, who everybody enjoyed but nobody ever really loved, and Cockney Rebel, who a few people would have died for but many more regarded with deep suspicion.

No one can blame the Manics. Coming from Wales you have to pull every trick in the book, and invent a few more besides, to get what you want. But equally, no one can doubt that the band's intellect, their aesthetic awareness and their heart was often masked by their physical appearance. The early Manics, in particular, delighted in sub-Clash visuals; blouses with spray-painted slogans, drainpipe jeans and spiky-topped heads. And people really did distrust those images. Why wouldn't they? The Clash were, of course, one of the great bands of the past twenty years. But they played dumb music. That's no put-down. There is dumb music and there is smart music and whichever side of that divide a band may lie has absolutely no bearing whatsoever on whether they are any 'good' or not. The Sex Pistols played dumb music. Wishbone Ash played smart music. Who would you rather listen to? Elvis was a dumb act. Peter, Paul and Mary were smart. Then again, Sweet were dumb, T-Rex were smart. Oasis are dumb, Blur are smart. The curious thing about the Manics is that they were smart music wrapped in a dumb package. (The New York Dolls were exactly the same; Morrissey always appreciated that paradox.) To some extent that might be seen as a good thing. But it does lead to a general misconception. And, though *Gold Against The Soul* was clearly an attempt to expand the band's audience, most people were still of the opinion that the Manics were just a bunch of Welsh beer-heads armed with Clash-style Mickey Mouse politics and a line in tired three-chord tricks. And there lay the problem. How would they put across the intelligence that ultimately lay at their very heart, one of the things that made the Manics so special; indeed, potentially so revolutionary? Not an easy task, to say the least.

Martin and Philip Hall had a plan. It was simple and potentially dangerous. Phoenix and Singleton Park were the start, really. Play the festivals. If you can't get that audience for yourselves, grab hold of a general crowd and simply convince them by being one of the most exciting things that crowd will ever see. Challenge them to disbelieve the evidence of their own eyes and ears. Still . . . open air and mud, cans of beer and massive backstage ego clashes; that was the flip-side of standing on a stage in front of a mass of people, most of whom hadn't come to see you. At Glastonbury they became embroiled in a (rather polite) ego battle with Suede. Consider it from Suede's point of view. They were, in truth, the bigger band at that point in 1993, but no way would they wish to follow the Manics. This was a great compliment, of course, and the Manics, almost apologetically, slipped down the order. And why not? Why not let the music speak for itself? After all, at a festival, you tend to play to the same number of people, whatever time you are shoved on. What's more, the best sets often come early in the day. The Manics swallowed their pride . . . and stole the show.

However, the year was to end on a sour note for the band. As the run-in to Christmas 1993 had started the news of Philip Hall's death, following a one-year battle with lung cancer, rippled through the music industry. He was 34. Ex-Stone Roses manager, Gareth Evans: "It wasn't a complete shock, but it was something that I found hard to grasp . . . I think his management of the Manics was simply perfect because he allowed them the space to grow in their own way. Even when they were being ridiculed for being punks . . . and he was under tremendous pressure to try to change them . . . from all areas of the industry. But he just allowed them to develop. But the main thing as far as I was concerned was that I could always talk to Philip. Any time. He was always positive, and that's a rare thing." Gareth's unofficial accolade accurately reflects the band's own statement which portrayed Philip as "a very close member of our family". He deserves special credit because, frankly, it's difficult to imagine another manager with genuine industry contacts, seeing that the true magic of this young band lay within their own idea of themselves. He didn't bulldoze into the Manics' ideologies, however naïve they may have seemed to him. Though this writer never met Philip Hall, I have yet to hear a single bad word spoken about him. In these days when 95 per cent of band managers are, effectively, mere accountants, four per cent are egocentric lunatics intent on building their own name on the back of the artist, one per cent – Philip Hall and, I would suggest, the late, great Rob Gretton of Joy Division and New Order, not to mention a slew of maverick pioneers from the Sixties, many also now dead – actually take time to become an essential part of the band. This takes courage and vision, but in this case one senses that it came quite naturally. Philip Hall was always destined to be a Manic.

5

THE HOLY BIBLE

"Cutting myself up . . . I find it attractive . . . I find it sexual."
– Richey Edwards

It was to be another of those moments of Manic controversy. Again, it was somewhat lacking in subtlety, and somewhat lacking in taste, too. And it occurred on *Top Of The Pops*. To fully appreciate it we could perhaps spin forwards to the autumn 1998 series of *Later With Jools Holland*, and that jokey little interview spot where Jools spikes the chat with a brief and often rather embarrassing clip from the artist's BBC history. This time he was mumbling away with Nicky Wire, before turning to the monitors to see the Manic Street Preachers performing the upbeat anarcho-pop trash anthem 'Revol', in front of a startled *TOTP* crowd. The sight may not have been quite as gruesome and obnoxious as, say, an early Seventies appearance by Little Jimmy Osmond or Paper Lace, but it was, visually speaking, certainly in the same league. The sight consisted of a band garbed in combat gear, fronted by a singer screaming from beneath a black balaclava.

As Holland turned away from the monitor, he fell back into his charming banter, loved by Friday night inebriates across the country. This time, however, his eyes were screaming a different message. "How could you?" he seemed to be asking Wire. "How could you?" Curiously, while Wire started muttering something about the performance attracting more complaints than anything that had ever appeared on *Top Of The Pops* before, his eyes seemed to scream a similar message: "How could we? How could we?" A good question but, of course, Wire and Holland were looking back on a different band, in those long-lost days before they became universally accepted, when life seemed like an eternal scrap against the tide. Sitting before Jools was this erudite and thoughtful young man. Blasting from that monitor was a band achingly desperate to make a statement.

The *Top Of The Pops* performance was awkward, spiky, ill-fitting and uncomfortable. In all the myriad performances of all the disparate acts who have grabbed themselves a moment of glory on that stage through 30 years, I cannot think of a single performance comparable to the Manics that night. They were not better or worse; they were just wildly different. (Mark E. Smith guesting with Inspiral Carpets, perhaps, come the closest. If avant-garde funksters The Pop Group had had a hit with 'She Is Beyond Good And Evil', that would have been pretty close, too.) That, perhaps, was the point. We weren't dealing with Wham! here.

"Mr Lenin-awaken the boy-Mr Stalin-bisexual epoch-Kruschev-Seld love in his mirrors, Breznev-married into group sex . . ." sang Bradfield, punching his point across like a Portobello Road crockery salesman in front of an intrigued but cautious circle of potential punters. "Revol, Revol Revol!!!" Leaders from far left and far right, merging in sexual ambiguity, idealistic hearts slayed by human failings, revolutionaries slowly succumbing to the Establishment. The Manic Street Preachers, in August 1994, presented themselves as mock terrorists battling ferociously to retain their own idealism. A band standing on the brink, staring down into the dark well of compromise. Perhaps this was to be one of their last few genuine acts of rock'n'roll defiance. This single and, lurking behind it like a large black shadow, the album they had just recorded at Cardiff's low-rent Sound Space Studios.

It had been a band decision to go for Sound Space, based on an agreement of the need to return to something approaching their roots. Bizarrely, they had been offered Compass Point Studios; Sony believed in the marketable kudos of recording expensively in exotic places but, at a Manics band meeting, it was pointed out that Joy Division, the band who had been soundtracking the Manics' collective life during the past few months, had always recorded very cheaply indeed. (Actually, not strictly true, Joy Division were always striving for better technology; but the heart of the argument remains valid.) There was no doubt, at all, that in making *Gold Against The Soul* in the luxurious surroundings of a hyper-expensive studio, something had been lost. Here was a band with a new-found desire to record quickly and get out, the aural equivalent of a smash and grab. The key to this change of heart lies in that *Top Of The Pops* performance, in the Manics' all-consuming desire to be different. The band felt they needed some kind of reality injection, and they certainly received it at Cardiff's Sound Space. The choice of studio and city both proved significant.

It was partly a lazy choice: Cardiff is just a commuter ride down the valley from Blackwood. Cardiff is the capital of Wales but not the heart of it. Unless, of course, you visited the city on a day when Welsh songs echo through the streets around Cardiff Arms Park. On such days it can be the most riveting and distinctive Welsh place of all; and then, two hours later, after the voices have faded, the city wears its shy face again. The fact is, it doesn't really feel like a Welsh city at all. It has no particular focus and little soul. Once, when it was the Marquis of Bute's coal port, it had a serious, determined function and it must have felt as though the wealth of Wales flowed in and out of Tiger Bay, as though the city were an artery for the lifeblood of the country. But in the Nineties Cardiff is more indicative of the political impotence of Wales, than of its cultural power. It is a strange mixture now. Part café-bar polite and part rough as-you-like. Pretty parkland surrounds the unimposing castle; the Taff drifts along to the Glamorgan cricket ground, itself tiny in scale. Like a microcosm of the city itself, the Glamorgan ground is unimposing, sullen.

This writer spent some time there in the early Nineties, working on a book about West Indian cricketer Viv Richards, then playing – rather implausibly, given the man's glorious history – for Glamorgan. I swiftly learnt where Cardiff's dark heart lay, where only the dubious and sex-starved businessmen, invariably English, tended to wander. And, right there, slap-bang in the centre of darkest Cardiff, lay Sound Space. It was a distant relative of old Soho, a place which once saw regular battles at night between visiting sailors. To anyone blessed with an imagination, the area is hauntingly evocative. One can only imagine how it affected the mind of Richey Edwards, who would tramp along those streets during lapses in the recording, frequently dragging his garishly garbed frame into some bar not noted for its liberal tolerance. If the Manics desired an environment with 'edge', then here it was, in spades. Personally I would have opted for Nassau, but there is no accounting for taste. And anyway, the Manics had their hearts set on something approaching kitchen sink realism. But the truth of their experiences at Sound Space wasn't quite as romantic as that.

Things were changing within the band, and changing fast. If Richey Edwards had been the artistic focus of the Manics, and if his forays across Soho had helped to give that first album some of its sleazy appeal, things were now becoming a lot darker. In retrospect, even the above description of Cardiff seems to be on the verge of flippancy, for Richey Edwards had already crossed the line. The artistic glamour of blackness, that very rock'n'roll glamour from which the very best emotive music – from Joy Division to The Doors – tends to flow is, by its very nature, a dangerous area. Everyone knew that Richey was treading precariously, drinking down and touching despair, enticed by the strange exhilaration of being in such a state. And yet, unlike most people, who tend to be able to pull back from the brink at the crucial moment, there were always clear signals that Richey might just dip all the way. Whatever his mental and physical state, his writing had reached a welcome peak in terms of both quality and quantity. The lyrics he was passing across to Nicky Wire were intense and convoluted. It was clear that this would be an album where the music would be shaped by those lyrics. Richey, in particular, had much to say, and he wanted to say it quickly.

Strangely, the sessions began calmly. For months, Richey's mood had darkened and he seemed to be perpetually on the verge of tears. He had started to flirt with self-mutilation, albeit in a mild form, openly and often under the gaze of the media. Understandably, this would often be misinterpreted as some kind of Sid-style trip, in which an individual, restrained by lack of technical ability, would damage himself physically in an inarticulate effort to express deep-seated unhappiness or frustration. That was the image of Richey which now started to feature more consistently in the music press. I cannot say how true that was and, after scouring every remark the rest of the band ever made about Richey in the press, one strongly senses that even they were never completely sure about his state of mind. The Manics were a conventional rock beast consistently shaken off their natural musical course by the very existence of Richey Edwards. But there is no doubt at all that Richey's state had altered following Philip Hall's tragic death and, indeed, the parallel tragedy of an old university friend. Always intrigued by death – Richey even subscribed to the metaphorical equation of death and sex, and certainly saw the final curtain as something beckoningly romantic – his interest in the subject was starting to hover on the fringe of obsession.

Nineteen-ninety-four was filled with rumours about Richey. They were everywhere – peppered across the music press, filtered through backstage gossip, seeping into radio DJ patter. The talk was impossible to ignore. Alcohol was now featuring heavily in his day-to-day existence, and from early each day at that. Richey seemed to feel the need to be distanced, to be 'dislodged' from experiencing life too directly. Too many ideas seemed to flood from him, as if he couldn't stop the flow of thoughts in his head, and he appeared, on-stage and in press shots, lost in some adjacent world. A classic portrait graced the cover of *NME* on October 1, 1994, in which a spindly Richey was depicted placing a tattooed, scarred arm around a statue. The headline, "THE SCARRED REVIVAL. RICHEY MANIC BACK FROM THE BRINK" screamed from beneath the paper's famous masthead. Check out Richey's eyes, one peering from the shadow of the statue and the other disturbingly blank. A rabbit trapped in headlights. A further irony, I suggest, came in the form of a smaller headline, "Radiohead cut the 'Creep'" printed on a level with Richey's eyes. Radiohead's classic 'Creep', most people would agree, stands as one of the most affecting statements about alienation since The Doors' 'People Are Strange'. And there on the front cover was a photograph of a man who didn't seem to feel that he belonged anywhere either. Most tellingly, Richey openly admitted that drink helped sidetrack him from ". . . the sheer terror of going on stage". This wasn't rock star posing. This was a man with serious problems.

Richey's skeletal frame was also becoming cause for great concern. For two years this wasting away had seemed gradual but, during the summer of 1994, as his drinking increased, his food intake shrank and he began to appear gaunt. And all this despite being sent regularly to health farms at the band's insistence, where he could relax and detoxify. Trouble was, the core problem didn't seem to be something that could be treated at a health farm.

In July, Richey willingly submitted to a spell in a mental hospital.

This, too, was widely reported, as were rumours about *two* suicide attempts. Whether this was a simple case of Chinese whispers, the idea that his bouts of self-mutilation may have been aborted attempts to kill himself remains a matter of considerable conjecture. Reports were conflicting – *Melody Maker* said Richey had 'slashed his wrists in the bath' while in February 1999, one of Richey's Blackwood friends told this author of an impromptu drinking session in a local pub which, as hours and drinks passed by, became increasingly bizarre. Richey's glazed, serious expression seemed to be hinting strongly that something other than mere drunken hi-jinx was taking place.

"I can say that his mood was disturbing that night," said one regular. "I wasn't a close friend of Richey, or anything like that, but I did know him reasonably well and I had never seen him quite like that. He seemed 'twitchy', strange. I couldn't take my eyes off him because at first I thought he was just acting the rock star. I thought, 'You prat . . . you are in some band and you are just trying it on'. But it soon dawned on me that it was something genuine, something serious. I felt guilty then and felt sorry for him. There were a few people in the pub who were shouting things, y'know, having a bit of a go at him. It wasn't nasty but he seemed scared. I've thought about that night ever since. I don't know whether he is alive or not, but . . . how can I put it? I've never seen anyone look so alone."

So alone, whether in Blackwood or amongst friends. There isn't much evidence to suggest that Richey's estrangement had anything to do with aggression from envious locals. It would seem that his pain lay in coming to terms with his band responsibilities: being a primary driving force between the Manics' aesthete as well as struggling to improve his musicianship. But it was a lonely pain. Both the band and the management searched for ways to help. It has been previously reported that he attended a cold, stark NHS hospital in Whitchurch, where his mental state rapidly deteriorated. Whitchurch, despite its austere atmosphere, is a good hospital. It was not, however, equipped to deal with the exotic problems of a pop musician on a downward spiral. By direct contrast, the Priory Clinic in Roehampton, although cripplingly expensive, had little problem in understanding the complex and unusual nature of the situation, if not the problem. The list of celebrity patients who have checked in at the Priory reads like a guest list at a Rod Stewart concert. Its treatment methods, such as the

12-point recovery programme for alcoholics and drug abusers, are no different from the methods used in dozens of similar institutions. Apart, that is, from one crucial exception. At the Priory they understand celebrity ego, and how it can, and more often than not does, gnaw away at the patient's emotional stability. Ego is rarely the root cause of the problem but it does accentuate and warp the condition.

That aside, the 12-point-plan is conventional and hinges, at step three, on a solid belief, either in God or in some kind of superior being. The patient needs a crutch to help them through the early stages of recovery and if he or she is antipathetic towards God, or religion in general, then he or she is advised to replace the image of a deity with that of a particularly close member of the family. This is the most controversial aspect of the entire programme and there are reports that, as the faith factor is the hinge of the entire process, the programme is less effective when it is not used. When Shaun Ryder went through a similar programme at the Charter Clinic, he used his grandmother as his emotional crutch. Although his particular rehab was deemed to have been successful, he did emerge with his cynicism intact; it was if he had only drifted through partial rehab.

Partial or not, Richey accepted his rehab regime with a genuine desire to re-attune himself and, before the gaze of the band, who, to their credit, devoted large amounts of time to visiting the clinic, his gaunt, frightened expression began to soften, to be encouragingly replaced with glimmers of optimism. Through the murk, the old Richey began to appear. There is a misconception, actually, that the 'artist' is a person who lives an emotional life at a higher pitch than anybody else; that emotional light and shade is more profound for such a gifted individual. This isn't actually true (source: Manchester University Dept Of Psychology). There is no reason why a pop star or playwright should 'feel' things more intensely that a bricklayer going through the traumas of divorce or, for that matter, the overworked health worker who has to endure the daily drama of the hospital ward. It could also be argued that to persistently succumb to emotional pits and falls is simply a weakness. There is nothing wrong with that argument, but, romantic notions aside, it is not the prerogative of the artist to stagger around beneath the weight of emotional wounds. With rock stars, the situation is different simply because their lifestyle gathers pace and mental anaesthetic is not only on offer at every waking hour. A rock star, if he or she is worth their salt, is in many ways expected to be out of control to a certain degree. If the rock star in question suffers from a certain emotional weakness, then the downward spiral beckons. It is a clear-cut and, some might say, unholy path.

Rumours about Richey's precarious state of health came from all corners of the media. Even broadsheets and tabloids carried the story, albeit in short, sharp snatches of reportage or in sensationalist chunks, respectively. Interesting to note that, when this writer phoned then *Sun* showbiz writer Peter Willis about a typical 'Errant punk guitarist in overdose shock' report, Willis freely admitted that, "I've never actually heard of the Manic Street Preachers, but it is a good story." Which is fair enough but it did indicate that a minefield of potentially damaging misinformation was beginning to form around the band. Commendably, the music press distanced themselves from this simmering mass of half-truths and lies, a situation undoubtedly helped by Martin Hall's PR skills. He fully understood the music press and also respected their thirst for a good story; through a series of press releases and candid interviews with the other band members, the truth began to filter through. Richey's penchant for self-mutilation emerged as an unglamorous very dangerous habit. The image that emerged of him was that of an intelligent, obsessive character, who succumbed to strange and, to outsiders, apparently pointless pressures. It was clear that Nicky Wire, in particular, had trouble understanding the nature of these pressures: "I always thought he was incredibly intelligent . . . but with that intelligence came an inability to see solutions to very simple problems. Things would worry him," he recalled to *NME* in 1996. "There are aspects of Richey that I don't quite understand . . . but it isn't the problem that people think it is. The self-mutilation thing, for example, we . . . the band . . . the people around him . . . we understand that. And it is part of what he is and always was. It's easy to come to the wrong conclusion about it. People should be careful."

Despite Wire's comments, it's debatable whether anyone around Richey Edwards truly realised what he was going through in those dark days of 1994. In March 1996 Wire admitted to *Melody Maker*, "Richey just reached a point where something clicked. His self abuse has just escalated so fucking badly – he's drinking, he's mutilating himself, he's on the verge of anorexia." However profoundly the band would strive to accommodate his problems, and however much they would stress that his contribution towards the band, in lyrics, in guidance, in spirit, was absolutely vital, Richey's comparative musical ineptitude could only force him further and further inside himself. Given his propensity for snowballing an apparently small problem into an avalanche of crises, it was no surprise that his self-confidence and self-esteem began to crumble. This fact wasn't missed by the rest of the band who, even while he was in rehab, continued to coax Richey back towards the centre of things, talking over logistical tactics about promoting the forthcoming album as well as seeking his artistic opinion on the sleeve.

Of course, there was still a great deal of media murk about Richey which Martin Hall courageously decided to confront head on. He released a statement declaring: "Richey is still active in the band and he's getting better. He is, however, very ill at the moment and things have developed to the point where the band, but more importantly, Richey, have realised that he needs to seek out professional help to deal with what is basically a sickness." The point about the illness not being an artistic condition was supported by the vast and encouraging surge of letters that began to gather in the music press, and in the corner of the Hall Or Nothing office. Richey's condition had proved effective in drawing a large fan base towards the heart of the band, and from this fan base came a huge swell of support. Whatever was being written elsewhere, it was clear that fans of the Manic Street Preachers related closely to Richey's dilemma. This could have been seen as mere fan infatuation, and indeed to some extent it was, but Richey was swift to condemn the notion that there was anything remotely romantic about his condition. Curiously, his widely reported retort, "Fucking bullshit . . ." served only to draw more and more letters of support. And, for once, the letters were genuinely helpful, stressing, as they clearly did, Richey's true worth within the band. Whichever way you look at this problem, Richey's musical insecurity lay at the root and there was little the band could do to alleviate that. The letters, as Richey later declared, were crucial to whatever degree of recovery he attained.

To add to the irony, the Manics were forced to fulfil their contractual live performance commitments without Richey. Although today this might not seem such a problem, it was an extremely tentative and unhappy band who performed, *sans* the member who, more than any of the rest, symbolised the spirit of the Manics, at the T In The Park and Reading. On the positive side, the latter was fast becoming something of a triumphant regular gig for the band. It was possible to see these shows and not realise the turmoil burning within the musicians on stage. Moore, Bradfield and Wire slammed away with a ferocity that attempted to cover the gaping hole that had been ripped into their essence of the band itself, if not its sound. More than this, all three band members admitted to a growing feeling of guilt, of "spiritual betrayal" at playing without Richey, even if there was no alternative. It was the most uncomfortable and, in all probability, the least enjoyable period in the band's history. Ironically, the band, on-stage, were aching for their missing member while their very appearance must have compounded Richey's sense of estrangement. Reports of the three-piece Reading appearance, and in particular the demands from the crowd for his reappearance, seemed to galvanise Richey, who now seemed driven by a burning desire to get back on stage.

To suggest that perhaps Richey's desperate mental state might have been reflected in the ironically titled *The Holy Bible* album, is rather like saying that Joy Division's *Closer* was a 'bit of a downer'. But what another glorious irony. Here's a musician tortured because of his own insecurities and yet those same insecurities, that same depression, becomes the fuel and the fire and the spirit of the album he is the primary force behind. I realise in suggesting this that I might be doing Nicky Wire something of a disservice, especially as his expertise in shaping and moulding the torrent of words flowing from Richey, in becoming the conduit between Richey and James, cannot be underestimated. But the source of *The Holy Bible* simply has to be attributed to Richey Edwards. More than that, the album, taken as a whole, represents a dramatic mood swing, from deep blue to black, from morose to wholly disconsolate. I cannot think of a single rock album from the past 25 years that occupies the same ground, the place where anger meets despair. Joy Division's *Closer* was a dark, serious trawl, strikingly 'for real'; there was a curious documentary feel to the album, as if it was a non-fiction rock album. Even Leonard Cohen's most dour epics were still etched with lyrical cuteness. Lou Reed kissed the floor with the tragic and gripping *Berlin*, but even that seemed like some kind of fiction, while John Lennon's harrowing yet rigorously self-analytical *Plastic Ono Band* LP was largely inspired by his recent adoption of Dr Arthur Janov's primal scream philosophy which he would subsequently reject. *The Holy Bible*, by contrast, seemed strikingly for real. Anyone who doubts the degree to which Richey influenced the album should sit with the record blasting out in a darkened room, with a bottle of Shiraz, perhaps. *The Holy Bible* lacks any real musical diversity – three or four casual listens would not be enough to allow the record's power to seep through. But it's not enough just to listen; you also have to read.

Words cascade from *The Holy Bible* like a waterfall in Snowdonia. The comparison isn't as lazy as it seems, for the album's bleakness is similarly misty, similarly compellingly stark. Its power, like that of most Manics albums, was underestimated; too many would be discouraged by its apparent inaccessibility. And admittedly, listening to the album can be like staring at a particularly meaty Francis Bacon painting: it has an austerity, a starkness, that can be both depressing and intellectually rewarding at the same time. You simply have to be in the mood but, if you are . . . then it works beautifully. That may sound like a put-down, perhaps it is, but you could say the same thing about John Coltrane's mighty *Giant Steps*. Sometimes you have to do a little work yourself to get the greatest rewards from a piece of music.

The album begins with a rush and a push: 'Yes'. A full-frontal assault that suggests we are in for a punk epic. And how could anyone dislike an album that begins with the words, "Yes. For sale. Some dumb cunt's questions. Virgin? Listen. All virgins are liars, honey"? Just one line in, and you are already in a very different place from anywhere else in contemporary rock'n'roll. Say what? Virgin? What's he talking about? Branson's Virgin? Schoolgirl virgins? I'd guess at the former. After all, 'Yes' is a simple variation on the old hippie poster statement, 'We are all prostitutes.' There are shades here of Bristol's finest, The Pop Group. Uncompromising ragged funksters, highly innovative and fired by a vicious polemic. But 'Yes' isn't an attack, or a claim of moral purity, it's a simple admission of guilt. Here we are, the Manics, on Sony for God's sake. Who are we to preach? In the land of 'Yes', everything is for sale and everything is eagerly snapped up. Religion. Sex. A change of sex. A change of faith. It's all up for grabs. Life's giant car boot sale. The strange thing about 'Yes' is that, although it runs at a furious pace, it has a disarmingly pretty tune. And the words really do rush so torrentially over it, they are difficult, if not impossible, to grasp without clutching the lyric sheet. (Even then, somehow they still don't sound quite right.) The phrasing is extraordinary – a novelistic approach, at times it's like listening to a William Burroughs reading with a band thrashing away. But, eventually, it does gel. The words undoubtedly shape the melody although strangely, the melody manages to keep its strength.

The accusatory tone continues on the next song, which carries the meandering title, 'IfwhiteAmericatoldthetruthforjustonedayitsworld-wouldfallapart'. Again, the lyrics drive the message home, surging through the shattered American dream, returning, again and again, to racism that still permeates that country. There is a comparison, mid-song, with the racism inherent in the British colonial heart (or, rather, from a Welsh perspective, the English colonial heart): "and we say there's not enough black in the Union Jack . . . and we say there's too much white in the stars and stripes . . ." counters Bradfield, his voice reminiscent of the Rock Against Racism marches in 1978, when the streets of London, particularly around Victoria Park, became a flashpoint for left and right, when London witnessed skinhead pseudo-patriots spoiling for a fight with punk-cropped pseudo-lefties. A big lesson was learnt, in those Clash/Tom Robinson Band days (although, alas, the nailbomb outrages of summer 1999 would see the ugly form of racism make news in the capital again), and, curiously, the Manics seem to be reaching for a kind of purity that existed before this flashpoint. Some may call it naïvety. The jury is open. Direct your attention to a four-chord crash about ten seconds before the song's conclusion, which strongly evokes images of The Clash, of the Notting Hill Riot, of shadows beneath the Westway. 'IfwhiteAmerica . . .' is, profoundly, a London song. As to the American angle, it remains astonishing that the US punk revolution of the mid- to late Seventies threw up so little in terms of anti-government rebellion. The fact remains that if one single American punk band, or latter-day metal band, had seriously attacked their own government, they would have become the most potent force in world music. (Actually, that would have been an impossibility. Such a band would be instantly filed under 'cult' in the industry, which is a safe place to keep the wilfully eccentric, the potentially revolutionary. A far cry from the days of Country Joe McDonald's Woodstock 'Fuck' cheer, a far cry also from the relaxed subversion of The Grateful Dead. All serious US punk or metal acts seemed merely hedonistic, or just acting, unlike many Rap artists. But that's another story.) It never happened on a mainstream scale. Worth thinking about and the Manics, with this song, have done just that.

'Of Walking Abortion'. Not a title that lets you in gently to the song itself. There is a real sense of intellectual seriousness here, and one cannot help wonder if pop music was designed to carry such a weight. It is a disturbing dirge of a song to begin with, a rusty grunge, with Bradfield's grainy voice running through a string of images. "Mussolini hangs from a butcher's hook, Hitler reprised in the worm of your soul, Horthy's Corpse screened to a million . . ." Let's just spool back a minute. "Hitler reprised in the worm of your soul?" Who would write such a line? What kind of emotional state would you have to be in to unleash that upon 200,000 committed fans? You couldn't listen to such a line and say that the Manics are no different from Take That although, having waded through this song, the temptation to go all giddy with Kylie had never seemed so utterly compelling.

But the album's heart of darkness was yet to come. 'She Is Suffering' hacks away at the modern-day worship of beauty, at skin-deep gratification. The evil, in this song, is lust; the pull of desire and the empty goddesses of pornographic magazine covers. "Beauty she is scarred into man's soul . . . a flower attracting lust, vice and sin . . ." As a song, it is as sad and empty as a man leaving a strip club, or having a hidden stash of porno mags. It's not an attack on male or female. It's an attack on lust and the way lust can warp and destroy genuine emotional warmth. It is not, by any means, an easy song. But the listener, this listener anyway, does begin to wonder why he hasn't ever heard a song quite like this before. Why is it so affecting? It is not a pleasant aural experience – indeed 'She Is Suffering' is about as welcoming as a NHS casualty ward. Intriguingly, the song appears to be championing celibacy and, through celibacy, a kind of purity. (If celibacy is next to orgasm, you won't find it here.) Odd words from a man who revelled in the plastic delights of Soho and, while writing this song, drifted into the more dubious side of Cardiff. But then again, his experiences of the seamier side of life had obviously left their mark on Richey Edwards. Even if he occasionally dipped into that world, he was still clear-headed enough to know how damaging it could be. Damaging for the women who are sold like slabs of meat on the covers of porn mags, or in shop doorways, and ultimately, of course, damaging for Richey himself. Being intelligent enough to see the way pornography can dull the finer emotions, can actually prevent a sensitive individual from forming meaningful relationships; Richey's dabblings in the sex trade were their own punishment.

You will find little relief in 'Archives Of Pain' either. One searches hard for irony here, as the lyric runs through an ambuscade of famous serial killers and sordid despots. The song is built around the concept that even the most horrific crimes of the century have been glossed and repackaged and sold through Hollywood's glamorising. The narrator appears to be bound up in 'an eye for an eye' rhetoric straight out of the Old Testament. Again, the listener is confronted with horrific imagery. "Tear the torso with horses and chains, killers view themselves like they view the world, they pick at the holes, not punish less, rise the pain, sterilise rapists, all I preach is extinction." Perhaps only that last line offers some idea of salvation. 'Revol' may offer no lyrical lightness, but it is at least a refreshing punky blast which hurries the listener away from the desperate horror of 'Archives Of Pain' to '4st 7lb', arguably the bleakest and most beautiful song on the album. Terrifyingly portentous, too. At 4st 7lb, a young girl, seeking to transform herself into an emaciated ideal of rarefied beauty, finally stares death full in the face after years of anorexia. The song is set at that final, haunting moment, when her caring and bewildered family, still vainly attempt to bring her out of her self-imposed fast, offer her some of the Sunday roast: "diet's not a big enough word" sighs the lyric, as the girl's frame becomes skeletal and her emotional state begins to flake away until there is nothing left at all, just a girl staring at her navel and her impending death. The imagery is painfully vivid and relates not only to an earlier track, 'She Is Suffering', but also very obviously to Richey's own condition. Most worrying of all, perhaps, is the suggestion that the girl, once seemingly past the point of no return, finds a painless and dignified sense of surreal peace as life finally begins to slip away. The song stops intriguingly before the actual death.

'4st 7lb' is one of the songs that gave rise to comparisons between the Manics and Joy Division although, once past the theme of suicide – visited, and much more obviously, three times on Radiohead's *OK Computer* – the comparison doesn't really hold up. Richey Edwards, though arguably still writing from an autobiographical viewpoint, does manage to translate his emotions and experiences into another situation and, in this case, another sex. Ian Curtis never seemed to indicate that the emotive heart of his songs was anything other than his own. Whereas Curtis was self-absorbed, Edwards always attempted to cast a wider net, as his dismissive comments about wounded artists indicated.

However, the two bands clearly operated, to a certain extent, in similar territory. Perhaps unwisely, the Manics had visited the sites of concentration camps Dachau and Belsen during their European trek of 1993. Many bands have felt strangely compelled to do the very same although it was difficult not to think of Joy Division wandering over that same turf back in 1979, with a stunned Bernard Sumner – Albrecht, as he was then – remarking that you could "feel the violence". Richey Edwards certainly 'felt' the violence in Dachau; a place of too many ghosts, of too much history. For an active mind, Dachau remains an unholy catalyst. How could Richey, if not the rest of the band, remain unaffected? How could they not feel driven to present that world with a subsequent song, 'The Intense Humming Of Evil'? It is, fittingly perhaps, the least ambiguous song on the album, as if the sheer horror of what went on in those concentration camps leaves no room for artistic subtleties and tricks. "Six million screaming souls". 'Mausoleum' takes a similar route. Perhaps the sombre atmosphere of *The Holy Bible* began with that particular trip to see reminders of Europe's darkest history, and with the desire not to fall into the forced grandeur of *Gold Against The Soul*. There is, one cannot help feeling, something ironic, if not actually hypocritical, in the use of such subject matter for songwriting material. In its baldest terms, this is a rock band who draws its emotional strength from acts of horrific, unprecedented evil, and in that sense is perhaps not too far removed from a Hollywood film-maker who receives box office rewards for romanticising a serial killer. And perhaps much of that stems from Richey Edwards' inability to grasp the full picture. Certainly, he was deeply affected by a broadsheet report, back in the early

Nineties, that suggested the possibility of a Scorsese/De Niro film based on the Yorkshire Ripper. The idea, and it was only ever an idea, was swiftly quashed following strong complaints from the families of the victims. It might be argued that the Manics were part of the same process; the simple fact that such subject matter is filtered through the medium of rock'n'roll could be regarded as flippant.

'Die In The Summertime' hardly lightened the tone of the album, tracing as it did the journey from childhood to death; or, at least, to a death wish. The song inhabits a hollow place, where the narrator mourns the loss of innocence, at the massive disappointment of maturity, thinking back to whole days spent throwing sticks in the river, and forwards to the final resting place where, "the hole in my life even stains the soil". A grimly poetic image; again, you have to trawl through the blackest edges of rock history to find any comparable vision. (One cannot help thinking during this song of Richey Edwards' happy childhood and wondering where and why things started to close in on him.)

'. . . Sumertime' is a song that conjures up images of desolate hills, craggy coastlines and dark valleys. A poetic vision, perhaps not of the traditional variety, but of a kind that offers some comparison with that most famous of Welsh writers, Dylan Thomas. Certainly there are some parallels between Thomas and Richey Edwards that may be touched upon here. Thomas, a hedonist with an omnipresent sense of melancholy, lived the classic lifestyle of the Welsh poet. Restless, moody, a copious drinker, Dylan Thomas sank away in an increasingly curmudgeonly manner during his brief life. Thomas, from Swansea, was curiously displaced from the heritage of his own country. Although both his parents spoke Welsh, and the family lived in a profoundly Welsh community, Dylan Thomas, inexplicably, was never brought up to speak his native language. All Thomas's work was written in English, only later to be translated into Welsh. And Thomas never really came to terms with this; it was as if he felt that he had a Welsh heart but had not been granted the natural power to express it. An absurd view, of course, given that it is he more than perhaps any other writer who epitomises the country of Wales; but it would have been difficult to convince someone of that whose mind was becoming steadily more blurred by alcoholism. The fact is that Dylan Thomas came to represent the somewhat contradictory state of Anglo-Welshness, battling against his own sense of guilt – he saw himself as a failure as a poet – and dreaming of a final demise, deep within Welsh soil. As it turned out, his grave was to be in Laugharne, on the Dyfed coast, and his gravestone bore an epitaph in English. To this writer, 'Die In The Summertime' strongly evokes a similar image of a personality spliced between two cultures. And here it's worth looking back to an interview in the Glasgow fanzine *Ravaged* from 1993, in which Richey stated, "I spent long periods wondering about being Welsh ... and whether I really was Welsh or just how much Englishness had seeped in." It's that sense of being caught between two cultures, of not belonging, that had informed so much of the Manics' work up to this point. They didn't feel they belonged in Blackwood, but they resented so much about London too. They were rebellious rock'n'rollers, but they defended Welsh farmers in print against incursions onto their lands by New Age Travellers. The music of the Manic Street Preachers is shot through with this cultural schizophrenia. That sense of being an outsider, even within one's own culture, is one of the things that makes the Manics so distinctive.

'PCP' revolves around the repressive taint of political correctness, and how well-meaning intentions can soon become repressive. The subject matter – rather more straightforward than that of other songs on the album – has, perhaps, dulled the impact of the song a little since it first appeared. Over the interim period, lad culture has reared its head – initially a refreshing reaction against the prissier and more stultifying aspects of PC culture, before being attacked in its turn for supposedly encouraging a cultural dumbing down. As such, 'PCP' is now a dated song. At the time of the song's composition, however, it was an isolated and courageous slap at the kind of humourless, immovable and ultimately dangerous political correctness that was sweeping through the County Halls of Britain. Perhaps closer to Richey's heart, political correctness was infiltrating the art world at grass-roots level, in the classrooms, in the universities and art schools, where barriers of political correctness were actively encouraged. A paradox, to say the least. In Richey's eyes, art had to be free from any constraints. It had to have that anarchic edge, to exist without parameters.

All in all, a predominantly lyric-driven album although James Dean

Bradfield must be commended for his exquisite handling of such heavy wordplay, twisting his own personality into the songs and, in places, seamlessly adopting the narrator's character. Sean Moore, too, must take the credit for powerfully driving along the music. There are moments on the album – 'Revol', 'Yes' – where the music actually dominates the lyrics. The choice of artwork for the album is equally intriguing. While one might have envisaged a shadowy tombstone scene, or a picture of a soulless Sixties block of flats to symbolise modern-day bleakness, the Manics opted for a triptych by Jenny Saville showing front and side views of an obese woman. Richey had seen Saville's work on display at the Saatchi Gallery, and she readily gave permission for its use when he approached her. It was featured respectfully on the sleeve, sitting beneath the title, set low against a white background, as if hanging in a gallery. Of course, an obese female is, perhaps unintentionally, the ironic antithesis of an anorexic male.

The Holy Bible was greeted with understandable nervousness by critics who, while not daring to slam the band for producing such a bleak and difficult record, went easy with the superlatives. It was never going to be an all-conquering commercial success, wedged for months between *Now That's What I Call Music* . . . compilations. That said, perhaps surprisingly, it reached number six in Britain – two places higher than *Gold Against The Soul* and seven higher than *Generation Terrorists* which, considering the difficult nature of most of the tracks, was a strong indication of the band's growing stature. People were prepared to listen, and listen hard. The album entered the chart in August 1994, and swiftly established itself as a significantly bleak marker in a curiously mixed year for rock music. The tone of the year seemed set by the springtime death of Kurt Cobain. In the wake of the Seattle grunge explosion, there was something distinctly traditional about mid-Nineties rock music. Oasis were becoming the dominant force in UK rock, their mighty *Definitely Maybe* album shooting straight in at number one during the same month that *The Holy Bible* appeared. There couldn't be two more widely contrasting records, with Oasis producing a noisy barrage of rock, fundamentally beer'n'fags British, that proved irresistible; a dumbed-down Stone Roses, complete with all the requisite Mancunian arrogance. Oasis instantly became the band of the people and, if that suggests that there was something about them as simplistic as, say, Status Quo, well, why not? The mood in the country was still hinged on blind hedonistic enjoyment and Oasis had caught the moment perfectly. Their commercial rivals, Blur, a cleverer band, though less credible to many, had reinvented themselves in April, with the laddish *Park Life*. Such were the twin peaks of the era to come, known as Brit Pop. Again, it's difficult to imagine quite where a record like *The Holy Bible*, with all its intellectual soul-searching, could possibly fit into this scramble to climb back into Doc Martens, swig beer and argue over football and girls. Perhaps a clue lies in the fact that Blur and Oasis, and the steady stream of bands who were beginning to bubble in their respective wakes, were fundamentally English. Philistine English, if you like. The Welsh Manics were striving to create something more subversive and sneak it into the mainstream. And slowly but surely, they were succeeding.

6

INTO THE VALLEY

"On tour I drink all day, just so I don't have to think about going on stage. That's why as a live band we fucked up so many times."
– Richey Edwards

Strangely, the atmosphere of depression that permeated *The Holy Bible* seemed also to work its way into the dynamics of the band. Things had changed. Sean, James, Richey and Nicky were different people now from the four idealistic Blackwood boys who had united against the world in their teens. Now in their mid-twenties, and having hurtled through such an intense period of collective growing awareness, the Manics found that their parochial stance had somewhat receded. Although it had proved a refreshing bonus not to be tied to every nuance of fashion or fad, to not be stiflingly hip, that sense of detachment from their pop peers obviously couldn't last. The Manics had been pulled to the centre and they could no longer lay a genuine claim to be the outsiders' band. There were other changes too. When a group of male friends reach their mid-twenties, their desire and need to be part of a gang generally slackens off. In normal life, people drift apart, spend more time with work-mates, if not with wives and girlfriends. It is the age of diversification. Everyone goes through it, that point when the older names in your Filofax tend to gather dust. You don't genuinely wish to lose contact but, all of a sudden, there just doesn't seem any point in making the phone call to that person. There are new pressures, new friends, new families. People split and evolve. And if a band wants to stay together, it has to somehow find a way to stand against this natural tide.

Every band that evolved from teenage camaraderie faces the same pressure. Even while working so closely together, and often because of living together in such close proximity for so long, personalities drift and alter, the initial dynamic shifts. For the Manics, the pressures and implications of change to that original unit were particularly strong. After all, the young Manic Street Preachers had been born out of a reactionary punkish rebellion. And the whole point of punk was that it was a young person's game.

With *The Holy Bible* the Manics had stretched into another area altogether, where anger now filtered through a studied and, some might say, still naïve intellectualism. As personalities, they were no longer scowling adolescents quoting Sartre; intellectual angst had given way to the very real traumas resulting from Richey's condition. It is interesting to note that Richey was the only member of the band who didn't express a desire to live, if only for a short while, away from the grip of the band. In so many ways, it was his safety net as well as a vital means of self-expression.

By mid-1994, the Manics had started to achieve the levels of critical and commercial success that they had always sought. And were they happy? Check out Nicky Wire's comments to *Melody Maker*; he felt "wretched ... I don't feel the need for anyone to like me any more, Jesus, it's hard enough to like myself ...". Sean, too, noted: "I don't know if we are where we want to be ... it's a big anticlimax ... very disappointing in a way ..." This sense of an unexpected letdown, experienced by everyone who acquires a certain degree of fame, was further exacerbated by a growing sense of embarrassment. It was as if the band now realised that, in making *Generation Terrorists* and *Gold Against The Soul*, they had exposed themselves too early in their career.

Their personal lives had changed, too, by 1993. Most famously, James left Blackwood for a considerably more cosmopolitan lifestyle in Bayswater, west London. Suddenly he was seen flitting around the music business parties of the capital, wandering merrily from Soho coffee bars to trendy restaurants to gritty 'scene' pubs, loving the thrill of being a face in the capital. Nicky, by stark contrast, rarely ventured to London, preferring to enjoy married bliss in a Blackwood terrace. At no point in the Manics history had the gulf between James and Nicky seemed so vast. There had always been, and there always

139

would be, a social difference between the two. Even in 1998, at the *Q* Awards, Nicky Wire was quoted as saying, "James knows more people and he smokes and he has a glass of whisky in his hand, he schmoozes more. I've never found it easy to converse with other people." James the social butterfly? Not quite, but as one who enjoyed a drink and a good conversation, he rightly saw nothing wrong in his new life and rather relished the idea of a valley boy beginning to pop up in the gossip columns. And not just in the music press, either. James even wandered within the tabloids' line of vision. It was marvellous to see him mentioned, if only fleetingly, alongside such powerful socialites as Minogues Kylie and Danni. Quite extraordinary. In a sense this was a perfect reflection of his social position within the framework of the Manics while Nicky, Richey and Sean all retreated into comforting Welsh domesticity.

This amiable split in cultures highlighted the Anglo/Welsh quandary at the heart of the Manics and it was fascinating to see James leaping to the other side, if only temporarily. I'm not suggesting that James's living in London is, in any way, a betrayal of his Welsh roots – the London Welsh are the perfect answer to that accusation. Culture is a state of mind and can be carried everywhere, but there is something about living physically in Wales that the rest of the band clearly found valuable and comforting and it was something that, for many people, is just too special to leave. It is important to mention it at this point, simply because, in terms of pop music in 1994, there was absolutely no credibility to be gained by openly pledging allegiance to Wales. Indeed, despite the swell of rather good rock bands which were beginning to emerge from the country at that time, the music press still tended to regard the entire country as a musical backwater. The success of the Manic Street Preachers aside, it was impossible to guess that, within a few years, Wales would become, musically speaking, one of the hippest parts of Britain. How absurd that prospect seemed back then.

Richey's condition improved towards the close of the year. Somehow, apparently against the odds, he seemed capable of devoting himself to the band again; indeed, the band had become his emotional crutch, his icon. Through the band he seemed to see a way forward; he could try to stop his overactive intellect from taking over by applying himself to the practical task of touring the Manics' last album.

140

There was a famous *NME* interview, conducted while the band were rehearsing for their *Holy Bible* tour, that saw a positively skeletal Richey repeatedly dodging the attentions of journalist Stuart Baillie. Far from being a tetchy, confrontational encounter, *NME* respectfully skirted the problem of Richey's non-cooperation and seemed to respect the bands' quandary – that pushing Richey to the fore would be tantamount to cashing in on his condition. Then again, Richey's problem was etched into his face, into his behaviour too. When the band played live, he knew full well that he was the focus of attention. This terrifying prospect caused him to (twice) make the suggestion that he pull out of the live arena, concentrating on the task of lyric writing. None of the band regarded this as a serious proposition; it was instilled into their collective mindset that, despite their performance as a three-piece at Reading, Richey was an integral member of the band on stage. He loathed touring but, as he noted to *NME*, "All bands hate touring but that's the hard work part of it. If I ducked out it just wouldn't have been fair . . ."

It was, therefore, a weakened and tentative Richey who took the stage in August 1994 for the Manics' British tour. Support band Dub War, were outspoken about playing with the Manics, chastising them as a "complete sham . . . pop star wankers who pretend to go around in an inebriated state." Louise Wener, from Sleeper, who also supported the Manics on the *Holy Bible* tour, was rather more perceptive, and certainly kinder, telling *NME*, "We were supporting a lot of people at the time, but the Manics were different. They were very close-knit, very guarded. They were friendly, no problems like that, but you always felt that there was something else going on, something a bit odd. I didn't ponder on it too much, we had our own work to do, but that's how it was. They were very professional. Very clinical."

This short but encouraging tour was followed by a significantly more demanding trek across Europe, alternating on a bill featuring Therapy? and Suede. An intriguing cocktail, to say the least, as the latter were using the trip to wean in Richard Oakes, the 17-year-old replacement for the recently departed Bernard Butler. Thus, both Oakes and Richey found themselves under close scrutiny during the gigs. If nothing else, the three-band shunt would surely help to take some of the attention away from the Manics and, in particular, from Richey, and it was a terrific managerial decision to share the bill in this way. Unfortunately for all concerned, Richey's improvement had been somewhat overstated. As both Therapy? and Suede seemed to hit their form, the Manics were uncharacteristically static on stage, with only James, ever the passionate performer, seemingly enjoying the experience. Nicky, for his part, occasionally fell into a Hookey-esque bass lunge, but even that seemed somewhat forced. Richey stood stock still, looking uncomfortable, casting scared eyes towards the crowd while contributing little to the overall sound. It would be unfair to suggest, as some have, that the Manics were blown away by an exuberant, ruthlessly ambitious Suede who had a thing or two to prove themselves, but they were clearly a band in trouble. The fact is that, while James carried the Manics visually, Nicky was standing back to cast a nervous eye over Richey who, he knew only too well, would be at his most vulnerable on stage.

Whether this on-stage tension transmitted to the crowd or not is a matter of some debate – critical notices at the time were curiously mixed – but the backstage tension was almost unbearable. Richey would sit in silence, or read from strange medical manuals, apparently given to him at The Priory (the 'library' at The Priory must be one of the most bizarre places on Earth). As well as worrying about his band-mate, Nicky Wire was suffering from homesickness. For his wife, of course, but also for Wales. This tension similarly affected Sean, who refused to talk to journalists or fans (or, apparently, members of the other bands), and seemed to be content to sit in the background, keeping himself to himself. This cautious atmosphere was broken only by James who, fuelled with a growing daily intake of alcohol, practically carried the band through their public and press responsibilities, chatting freely with whoever gathered at the dressing room door, papering over the cracks that were becoming clearer and clearer, keeping it together. It was a nightmare, a band heading for disaster. It's interesting to note just how much restraint was still being shown in the music papers. Perhaps the music journalists, for once, noticed that there was something going on that was beyond the flippancy of pop music reportage? At times said journos were treated with curious disdain, and yet remained generally reverential towards the band.

If anything, the band dynamic worsened as the tour rolled on, with the Manics finding unbecoming relief in the dates where they took the stage first. That way, they could leave as soon as they finished their set and get back to their hotel rooms and the bars. Everyone, of course, was concerned about Richey. His eating habits had not improved since his spell at The Priory and the clinic was beginning to lose credibility in the eyes of the rest of the band. It was becoming blatantly clear that Richey was still obsessing over things, still allowing trivialities to govern his thoughts, to bring him down. His unpredictability was becoming a liability. Anything could set him off – a snippet from the television news, a headline glanced from a newspaper or memories of fellow patients at The Priory. This was something that, to a certain extent, angered the rest of the band. Both Nicky and Sean complained about, "that fucking clinic". Perhaps it was just natural envy; a part of Richey's life that lay beyond the scope of the band. But Richey increasingly seemed to be living in another place anyway. There would be vacant stares, occasional mumbles, incomprehensible sentences. His distance from the rest of the band was becoming unbearable. Dub War had got it very wrong. This band didn't need to fake it.

For Richey, curbing his hedonistic streak was proving impossible. In the past he had taken to drink in an effort to make time flash by, to get himself through live sets, through the after-show comedown and leave him blissfully unconscious in some hotel room in the early hours of the morning. The drinking had made touring half bearable; had made it possible to walk on that stage and not crumble away inside. Now alcohol didn't anaesthetise the pain any more. But without the alcohol, there was a gaping hole of painful nothingness each and every day, all day, and all night. Such a lot of time to be filled. Easy, one might think, for a musician drifting from town to town, from hotel to hotel. That lifestyle can be frantic and glamorous and exactly the reason the Manics wanted to start a band in the first place. Because fame is meant to make a difference. But, as all four were now experiencing a massive disappointment with the realisation that it feels no different when you're finally up there; no different at all. There's just a greater sense of stress, a greater pressure to perform, to keep it up. And no one was more affected by that pressure than Richey Edwards.

Richey embraced extremes. If his drinking really had subsided, he had started smoking to ludicrous extremes. Sixty, seventy cigarettes a day – and he was well aware of Nicky Wire's aversion to smoke. Thing is, when you get that far inside yourself, you can't accommodate other people, however much you might want to. In Hamburg, when approached by two fans in the hotel bar, Richey was sitting in a hanging cloud of smoke, endlessly pouring coffee, glassy-eyed; he offered only brief, surreal blurts of speech in response to typically harmless questions from the two. To say this affected the rest of the band would be a sizeable understatement. James's drinking had now become an everyday routine. His cheery banter with local journalists was becoming increasingly slurred. On one occasion, after Nicky had thrown his hand in the air and declared, "I'm leaving, I just can't take this crap any more," James swerved onto a frightening bender. As Nicky later recounted to *Select*, "In the morning James couldn't remember what I'd said to him. Everyone was totally oblivious to everyone else's needs."

Richey flirted briefly with an exercise regime but, typically, it comprised short manic bursts of activity, rather than any kind of prolonged attempt to attain fitness. Push-ups, sit-ups and star jumps, conducted at a furious rate, leaving him in a disgruntled heap, and still unfit. Relaxation would have been better, accompanied by nutritious eating, but that would never be the Richey way. He was still miserable, perhaps even more so than before his treatment, and complained to the rest of the band about it. One incident, in particular, made the headlines. In Amsterdam, following a particularly miserable set, Richey's mouth was set in a glassy grin, his mood noticeably lighter than it had been. Disturbingly so. It was Nicky Wire who, with an almost fatherly concern, opened Richey's shirt to discover a lengthy slash fringed with blood. This proved something of a turning point; the whole band promptly decided that Richey would have to be 'mollycoddled' until the end of the tour. He was subsequently kept away from fans, journalists and record company executives, put to bed and watched carefully. However, this didn't prevent a second widely reported incident, in Hamburg this time, when Richey was found smashing his head, again and again, against the wall of his hotel room. Nicky later recalled to *Select*, "The situation stopped us from enjoying ourselves. We had no interest in the places we visited which was very sad, to be honest. We all just wanted to get home. I mean, Hamburg! We passed through it in a horrible blur." "It was probably the worst time I have ever experienced in my life," Wire admitted to *Select*'s John Harris. "In some respects it was worse than when Richey actually disappeared because he was on the verge of madness."

They made it through. The Manics finally arrived back in London for three shows at the London Astoria, shows that had initially been booked as the final climax of a triumphant year. There is no doubt that, by December 1994, and once back on British soil, a sigh of relief passed through the entire band. Homesickness faded swiftly as, reunited with family and friends, they attacked London with all the fervour of American tourists on a two-day jaunt. There was work to do but it didn't prevent a curiously cheerful Richey from drifting back through his beloved Soho, or the rest of the band rifling through the Virgin Megastore and Dillons book shop on Oxford Street, occasionally pausing to chat amiably with fans – some of whom had travelled to London from South Wales for the shows. Their mood certainly didn't square with recent press reports concerning the band's traumas on their European tour.

Perhaps it was nothing more than sheer delight to get back but something fired them up for the final night of the Astoria dates. And years later, Manics fans would talk about that night, December 21, 1994, when the Manic Street Preachers rediscovered their lost spark, overcame potentially crippling sound problems, and regained a good deal of their former glory. A fearsome punk unit, launching a barrage of soaring anthemic noise, their infectious band dynamic lifting the spirits of everyone present. There seemed to be an almost palpable sense of relief up there on stage, genuine surprise that they still had it, that they could still blend together, inspire each other, swap in-jokes and simply enjoy themselves. Even Richey, forgetting for once the statuesque grimace that had become a grim trademark on the European dates, turned in a frenetic performance. Nicky swept across the stage like a vulture, his bass dangling around his knees, while James swirled round and round, tying himself up in his guitar lead, and screaming with sheer delight. Naturally, the instruments were trashed in celebratory manner at the end. Well, it *was* Christmas. It would have been a mite churlish for Martin Hall to have castigated the band for reducing a ten thousand-pound stage set-up to a smoking heap of whining electronic rubble. Roadies looked on in horror, the crowd looked on in delight, and journalists crammed superlatives into their notebooks. The whole horrific mess of the past two months seemed to vanish in those five minutes of glorious destruction. Afterwards the band crumpled into a jovial fleshy heap in the dressing room while the crowd filed out, their sweat stinging in the cold December air.

It was over. The band could now look forward to a boozy and work-free Christmas. Blackwood beckoned.

7

FROM DESPAIR TO WHERE?

"Two months ago I was out having a drink in London. And someone says to me, 'How can you be out having a drink?' I say, 'What the fuck are you on about?' He says, 'If I were you I'd be in my room chopping myself up for Richey'."

– James Dean Bradfield

Christmas 1994 passed by calmly. It was a chance to forget everything that had happened on that traumatic European tour, and the London gigs had helped to restore a little optimism. Without them, without that return to form, there would have been little hope of relaxation, of forgetting the band, for a short, sweet break. Even Richey seemed to enjoy the Christmas break, spending long hours at Nicky's house, chatting in an easy manner that had all but deserted him during the previous year. Naturally, friends in Blackwood eyed him with some trepidation. His wasted appearance still gave cause for concern, but he certainly didn't seem to have much in common with the manic depressive they had read so much about. It can be concluded that the old Richey was flickering encouragingly to the surface during the festive break. He wasn't exactly the party animal about town, but had been cheerful enough to exchange presents with family, band and friends, and to give the illusion that he might be able to make a new start in 1995.

That said, a few odd incidents occurred involving Richey around that time. There was the night when the four band members, drying out after their Christmas overindulgence, sat around Nicky's front room, enjoying a slobby 'couch spud' evening in front of the TV. The video they were watching was a shaky recording of the band's Clapham Grand gig which had taken place in March 1994, when the Manics shared a stage with Suede's Bernard Butler, a one-off stand-in for the absent Richey. Did the sight of Butler, an unnervingly talented guitarist, unsettle Richey? The band denied this, but it remains a possibility. Although comparisons between Butler and Richey are about as pointless as comparing Sid Vicious with Stanley Clarke, the sight of Butler's virtuosity could certainly play all sorts of games with the mind of someone battling with his own lack of self-confidence. Maybe that's what happened. Asking for a bowl, Richey crushed two bars of chocolate into crumbs into the bowl before licking the bowl clean and looking up, an unsettling devilish grin crossing his facial features.

For a few long seconds the band fell into silence. A brisk, laddish remark – from Sean, by all accounts – broke the tension. None of the band quite recall the words, but "You fucking daft cunt," is probably pretty near the mark. This was followed by a swirling bout of raucous band laughter and a gentle easing of tension. The rest of the evening seemed light and congenial and, for days afterwards, the band openly mocked Richey's unorthodox method of chocolate intake. Richey accepted such banter in good humour, even instigating some of the jokes himself. For a while the band forgot about the incident. But something had happened that night. In that one brief action, the entire dynamic of the band had shifted again. In his own ambiguous way, he had challenged the rest of the band. As Nicky would later recall to *NME*, "He didn't have to do it in front of me . . . I knew he was fucked up."

Indeed, the band's attempt to make light of the incident didn't really work. From here on in, there was an edge to Richey's actions that would, naturally considering the events of the following months, stick in the minds of Nicky, James and Sean. And here's the rub. Richey knew the impact that the strange violence of his action had made. He knew exactly what he was doing. But at the time, the incident seemed to be an isolated one. Two days later, Richey was merrily wandering the Blackwood pavements, chatting to all and sundry, and apparently overflowing with goodwill. He even ducked into the Red Lion – alone! An entirely out-of-character move, witnessed by a number of regulars. "He stood there," one of them told me, "and he just seemed really friendly. I mean, he wasn't ever a star in here. Only with the youngsters. Most people couldn't give a fuck. But he wasn't trying to be a star, either. I can definitely state that. He wasn't patronising. He didn't seem like someone in a top band either . . . it was as if he wanted something from us. As if we were the pop stars and he was the fan . . . I think he was desperate to belong. I don't know . . . maybe I'm imagining it all. After he vanished and all that . . . it was just natural for your mind to start wondering . . . to look for clues." The interviewee in question doesn't know, or care, whether the Manics are any good or not, but some kind of pride did seem to sneak through when he was talking about them. There was a sense of them being "our band".

When a band finally makes it big, it's tempting to say that they always had something special, that there was always something about the band that marked them out from their peers. It's therefore all the more interesting to hear a local from the Red Lion remember the Manics as young men devoid of that inherent star quality: "The funny thing is that they never really seemed to have any charisma . . . you know. There were, and still are, people who come in this pub who are maybe on the dole who have more presence . . . who have . . . more personality. I think that is the thing that has shocked most people around here. It's a sense of, 'Whaaat? Them?' You know, total disbelief that they could have ever got anywhere. It was only when that one disappeared . . . and so soon after we were talking to him. It was only then that people started to realise just what they had achieved. Of course, later on, we saw them on The Brits. That was a mind-blower too. But they must have something. Are they any good?" This revelation may seem to work against the Manics – after all, what pop star wants to hear that they were regarded as being less charismatic than people who sign on down at the DSS? But that's one of the delicious ironies about the Manics, and also, paradoxically, one of the things about them that is so inspirational. They were like a lot of other people around them, *but they made it*. They proved that anyone can do it, if they have enough self-belief, and that determined DIY attitude marks them out as punks more genuinely than those early raucous singles or all the spray-painted blouses in creation.

In January the refreshed band reconvened at the House In The Woods rehearsal studios in Surrey. Richey, for his part, seemed to take a far greater interest in practising than before. This was a highly significant period in the band's musical development. *The Holy Bible* had closed a chapter. It had been a difficult, dour and musically stifling album to make. An essential album, and certainly one that, lyric-wise, the band simply had to get out of the way, but somewhere along the line some of the colour had drained from their melodies. Now the desire to regain that colour, to make a new start, was felt strongly by all members of the band. This time the music would be melody-led. An opportunity to work on an instrumental for the soundtrack of the upcoming *Judge Dredd* movie served only to encourage the band to experiment more, with Sean adding a depth and resonance to the overall sound. At some rehearsals, a band will simply work over their existing style, become tight and professional, often at the expense of a more experimental approach. But at other times, if the mood is right, a new direction can unfold naturally, just by virtue of the band being relaxed and open enough to let it.

By all accounts (Sean in *NME*, Nicky in *The Times*) this particular rehearsal was loose and enjoyable. There were small distractions – Nicky's relaxation time was disrupted by endless phone calls from Richey, checking on the time the next rehearsal would begin – but even this was seen as *positive* paranoia. It was Richey being Richey, but he did seem to have the band's interests at heart, and he didn't seem so focused on himself any more. Much to Nicky's relief, the smoking had eased up too. It was still there, the smell still hung on his clothes, but he no longer lit up all day, every day. Latterly, this little period would be generally regarded as a brief respite, as that moment, perhaps, of calm after a decision had been made. Several investigative newspaper features would suggest this but, in truth, nobody will ever know for sure. Nicky would later inform *NME* that it seemed as though "Richey was back to being Iggy rather than Ian Curtis . . ." The idea of positive nihilism replacing negative soul-searching must have seemed attractive to the band, given the previous six months. Had Richey finally learned to channel that excess energy to the good of himself and the band? The fat pile of lyrics that he cheerfully handed to Nicky, lyrics which would significantly flavour the next album, surely indicated that this might have been the case. Nobody, however, seemed to pick up on the most ominous portent of all. The Manic Street Preachers were poised to embark on an extensive ground-breaking tour of America. A tour that would, surely, finally break the band in the Stateside market.

Ring any bells?

* * *

Following the rehearsals, Nicky took his wife for a short break in Barcelona. For him, this was a big deal. Hardly addicted to travel, he always preferred to take his leisure breaks in Wales, or in England, preferring not to suffer the rigours of modern-day flying unless absolutely necessary. Barcelona, though, was inspirational and romantic – a famous line, "I've walked La Ramblas but not with real intent . . ." would later surface on 'If You Tolerate This Your Children Will Be Next'. It might also be noted that Nicky's intention, this time around, in Barca, was simply to relax and forget all about the band. It seemed to be good timing. Against the odds, the corner seemed to have been turned.

Back in Blackwood, things were not looking quite so rosy. In tandem with Nicky's break, Richey had vanished from his flat although he would later claim that it was nothing more significant than a "little time out in Swansea". Reports from distant friends of Richey do suggest that he was generally 'out and about' in Swansea and Newport during this period; he even appeared at a post-gig party at TJ's night-club in the town, but nobody seems able to characterise his demeanour at the time other than to report him looking, "Pale . . . a bit moody." The band had been expecting him in London but now he seemed reluctant to join them. His tendency to explode seemingly insignificant events into major traumas might have been the most obvious reason for this brief AWOL. Newspaper features during the next few months, would highlight this mysterious little interlude as being of huge significance. Famously, he learned of an old university friend's suicide that week. It must be noted that Richey's dog, Snoopy, had also died recently. Given Richey's obsessive nature, it is all too tempting to build a huge case for these events causing the darkness to close in once more. But the band have always rigorously denied this. Nicky to *NME*, 1996: "Yes, when he returned he cried over his dog but we didn't see that as anything truly significant. In fact, I think we felt it was healthy in a way. It's a natural thing to do. We all would have been upset. We were all looking forward to America and the mood was generally positive. Richey seemed to fall in line with that. People have made a great deal out of how Richey was during this period. That's fair enough, but I'm not convinced, really, that he knew what was going to happen. I mean I just don't know. Nobody knows."

Many loose comparisons have been made between Richey's tendency towards depression, and his ultimate disappearance, and the character and untimely demise of Ian Curtis. Curtis committed suicide immediately prior to Joy Division's American tour. But Ian Curtis's personal situation at the time immediately prior to his death was extremely complicated. He had a wife and a daughter, and a lover. Prone to epileptic fits, which were increasing in intensity, he had been prescribed a course of drugs that were having alarming side-effects. Curtis was getting out of control, and his domestic strife served only to accelerate the process. Immediately prior to the night he killed himself, Ian Curtis telephoned fellow Factory artist, Vini Reilly, a charming man, and another depressive who survived on an alarming array of drugs. When Reilly learned of the seriousness of Curtis's condition, he was shocked; he subsequently admitted to the author that he believed there was no way out for the Joy Division singer. The added stress of fronting a band and, indeed, a band that was about to take on America, was quite possibly the final push.

Richey, one must swiftly add, at the time of writing (February 1999) and I'm willing to bet, at the time of publication, is still officially a 'missing person'. A thin straw of hope remains intact, despite dozens of investigative features, television documentaries, Martin Clarke's book, Simon Price's book, and interview quotations from the remaining Manics, all of which suggest the worst. Perhaps he really is in Goa, bunking down with the hippies, or in York, busking for breakfast, or in Cyprus, or in Birmingham or even in Newport. It has been generally acknowledged, as time goes by, that these possibilities are becoming increasingly unlikely. But we will probably never know the truth.

It is difficult, I'd suggest impossible, for anyone to make a genuine causal link between Richey's obsession with Ian Curtis and his own disappearance. There is no doubt that that obsession was very real, and shadowed so many of his thoughts. But what we don't know, and can never know, is just how much Richey really knew about Curtis's situation. I speak from a somewhat biased point of view here, because I do know how the strange blend of rising star exhilaration, worsening health and domestic strife combined to lead Curtis to that final drunken night spent with Iggy Pop's album *The Idiot*, a bottle of whisky and a Werner Herzog film. There is, and I know Deborah Curtis will forgive me for suggesting this, a certain glamour that has become attached to that scene. Not in the event of Curtis's suicide itself – that was merely sad and sordid; no, the glamour arose with the Curtis myth which developed after the death of this young, talented, unstable man.

It is a pity, perhaps, that Richey couldn't have read Deborah Curtis's tragic memoir, *Touching From A Distance*, published in the year that he disappeared. The book refreshingly demystifies the entire story, pinning Curtis down as a human who stumbled through life with little sense of control, who made mistakes. But Richey had only ever seen the other Ian Curtis. He thought of the Ian Curtis whose transfixing voice added a Scott Walker depth to those two Joy Division albums, and whose take on the human condition had been controlled by extremely naïve rock'n'roll circumstances. His deep involvement with rock'n'roll was somewhat more advanced than his experience of life. The truth is, Curtis's hero, Iggy Pop, managed to pull back from the brink despite a decade of awesome hedonism. Iggy would survive to eat rocket salad in Manhattan eateries and attend art galleries, while the Iggy that Curtis adored – the mythical Iggy who lived perpetually on the edge – never quite existed in the first place. Similarly, I would suggest, the Ian Curtis that Richey knew, or thought he knew so well, was more a product of his recordings with Joy Division, and worshipful articles in the music press. I'm not suggesting that this image of Curtis was false – perhaps the recorded Curtis was ultimately nearer to the real man than the flawed physical being – but it wasn't true to life. Ian Curtis was not, in everyday life, a particularly intense person. Richey was influenced by an Ian Curtis who was a creation. Not by the truth.

Richey Edwards had (or has) little in common with Ian Curtis. Curtis wouldn't have approved of the Manics' adoration of The Clash, let alone their love of Guns'n'Roses and rock'n'roll clichés in general. His musical heart lay with the innovators, such as German avant-gardists Can

153

and English absurdists Throbbing Gristle. One senses that if Curtis were alive today, he would probably be a particularly sussed club DJ, or dance producer, such was his thirst for breaking new boundaries. It is, ironically, unlikely that Curtis would have given house room to *Generation Terrorists*, or *Gold Against The Soul. The Holy Bible*, for obvious reasons, might have caught his attention, but it's difficult to imagine him ever being a fan of the Manics. Curtis was active at a time when innovation meant everything. Retrospective credibility simply didn't exist in 1979. The whole concept of the Manic Street Preachers would probably have seemed anathema to Ian Curtis, apart, maybe, from the impact of Richey's dark lyrics.

But a few clear parallels do exist. Part of the appeal of Curtis, as a live performer, was the fact that he was at once crippled and fuelled by his own nerves. He was one of the least confident live performers this writer has ever seen, and yet he would summon up, from somewhere within, a tremendous burst of confidence which powered him through. This constant battle within himself was the very foundation of his charisma. He was a non-musician and, therefore, suffered in the presence of more musically gifted individuals. Exactly the same might be said of Richey. A musical novice thrust into the limelight, he battled with himself to keep his own confidence afloat, to be able to conquer his own demons while the band were accelerating forward at an exhilarating pace. Fighting not to be left behind. And, unlike the musicians around him, he couldn't just pick up an instrument and allow his talent to silence his critics. His talent, and it was an immense talent, wasn't so easily definable.

As such, there was added pressure on Richey to remain in control, to retain his rock star good looks, to guard the aesthetic heart of the band, so to speak. This in itself added to the pressure that he was under, and he would worry and drink to alleviate that worry. Then his drinking would worry him – he would worry about putting on weight, developing a beer belly, the totem of those he had fled Blackwood to escape. To counter this, he would stop eating (as is the case with so many rock stars who slide towards alcoholism), and he smoked to alleviate hunger and to give himself a quick buzz of excitement. The buzz would build and build and, in the end, obsessions would take over. Unable to sleep during this period, Richey found himself worrying endlessly over his hairstyle; a problem he solved by shaving the lot off which, naturally, alarmed the rest of the band when he joined up with them again after his temporary disappearing act. It was a nervy little reunion, softened by excited talk about America and, perhaps surprisingly, yet another batch of lyrics from Richey. In an oft-quoted interview with the Japanese magazine writer, Midori Tsukagoshi (famously, it was Richey's last known interview) he stated optimistically, "I want to write. It makes me feel better in myself. I do regard myself as a good poet. I work hard. Songwriting is an art and I really try my best at it." The general mood of that particular interview was upbeat. Then again, maybe Midori caught Richey at the right time of day, after the third coffee, the fourth cigarette. Half an hour later, things may have been different.

The sequence of events that followed have been worked over and over and over by the media until we all seem to think we know something concrete about Richey's disappearance. But we don't. There are gaping holes in the story that may never be filled. When you are talking about a man acting on his own, how can you divine his inner thoughts? One of the problems with such introspection is that, in believing oneself to be a victim, in reality one does actually become a victim. The mind creates and the mind destroys. We can't know everything that Richey Edwards thought or did during the last few days of January and first few of February. This is what we do know.

On January 31, 1995, Richey checked into the Embassy Hotel on the Bayswater Road – a popular rock'n'roll hotel for those bands who hadn't quite made it to the Columbia – the day before the band were due to fly to America. On January 30, Richey had been heavily involved in a band demo recording session, during which the foundations for the next Manics album had been laid. It has been largely reported that Richey was in a relaxed mood, chatting with fans and friends on January 31, presenting one of them with a copy of *Novel With Cocaine*, a courageous tale of teenage drug addiction written by an enigmatic Russian author under the pseudonym 'Ageyev' who had spent time in an asylum in soviet Russia. Part of the very appeal of the book lies in those mysteries which surround the unknown author. Richey was absolutely fascinated by the notion of an anti-celebrity, of a work that could exist, be critically acclaimed and commercially successful, the author of which remained aloof and unreachable.

The Embassy Hotel was quiet that day, as Richey and James

wandered down the corridor, slipping, apparently on excellent terms, into adjoining rooms. It was agreed that they would 'settle in' for half an hour before venturing out into Bayswater to take in the shops and perhaps visit the local cinema. It was a typically loose arrangement and when James knocked on Richey's door for the second time to be told by Richey that he thought he'd stay in, he thought little of it, and wandered out onto Queensway with a friend, visiting shops, the cinema and a pub afterwards. It was a small slice of relaxation before the big day tomorrow and what would surely be an arduous American tour.

Richey didn't surface that night but, tellingly, he put together a small parcel of presents for a girl he knew. She was a girl for whom he may have harboured strong feelings, although, in typical Richey fashion, he had kept these feelings largely suppressed. He knew her as a close friend and confessed that she was the one person capable of breaking through his inner shell. Inside the package he placed a few disparate notes and press quotations, books and videos – Mike Leigh's *Naked*, as well as the deeply disturbing *Equus*. It was a highly personal collection presented with the simple note, 'I Love You'. The box had been left on the bed next to his suitcase, neatly packed for America, his bag of toiletries and a bottle of Prozac.

He stayed in the hotel until 7 am where, safe in the knowledge that James wouldn't have surfaced, he strode briskly out into the already teeming Bayswater Road. Within half an hour, the London roads would have been naturally grid-locked. He must have crawled through Chiswick before joining the M5 and driving to his Cardiff flat, some 150 miles away. It may have been around midday when he arrived there. Nobody saw him enter or leave, he made no phone calls. He must have filtered through his bag, as a second bottle of Prozac and, most significantly of all, his credit cards and passport, lay scattered on his bed.

Back in London, Martin Hall had been alerted by James. Richey would not answer his door. Hall phoned repeatedly and when no reply was forthcoming, passed his concern on to the hotel management. The band's anticipation at the exhilarating prospect of their second US tour turned rapidly into dark concern. They began to worry about Richey. The door to Room 516 was duly opened and, on discovering the parcel, the band's worries escalated. Something was obviously very wrong. It didn't fully hit them at first, as Richey had already disappeared once since the New Year, but the parcel hinted that this might be a different situation altogether. Back at the Hall Or Nothing office, phone-calls were made – to London friends, to friends in Blackwood, Newport and Cardiff. There had been no sign of him in any of these places. Again, the worry stopped short of panic. The trip could be rescheduled. Richey, surely, would be found.

As the next morning, and February, dawned, it became clear that the matter needed more serious attention. Absolutely nobody had heard from Richey. That was unusual. For all his unpredictability, for all his introversion, Richey Edwards needed people. Someone must have seen him. Martin Hall had no choice but to file Richey as a 'Missing Person' with Harrow Road Police Station. Hall then drove to Blackwood to have a meeting with Richey's concerned parents, Sherry and Graham. Even at this point it was felt that he would turn up, somewhere, full of remorse, possibly full of renewed optimism again. A drive down to Richey's Cardiff flat provided a few clues. He had obviously been back. Newspapers from January 31 proved he had been there, his unmade bed suggested that he had spent the night, though they couldn't be sure. The encouraging thing was that his trail was now warm.

The situation was incredibly difficult for Hall. US promoters are not noted for their tolerance of 'artistic temperament' and were bombarding the Hall Or Nothing office with concerned calls. They were informed that the guitarist was suffering from an 'infection', although, deep down, Hall knew that the excuse wouldn't hold water for long. Sheepishly, he informed promoters in Prague and Vienna, where the Manics were heading immediately after America, that there may be some kind of problem. Everything was put on hold. But Hall knew he could only stall things for a day or so.

Richey's family covered the local angle, placing an advert in the local paper, asking for Richey to get in touch. If he was in the vicinity, someone would surely see him and tell him about the advert. For everyone concerned, the following elastic thirteen days seemed an eternity. It actually wasn't in Richey's character to put his family, let alone his friends, through such torment. That thought, more than any other, weighed heavily on the minds of the people who cared about him, and still does. He might vanish, he might turn up unexpectedly in some distant town, but he wouldn't put his family through such trauma. It wasn't in his nature. Finally, out of sheer desperation, Richey's disappearance was made public. A web of concern spread across the whole music industry. Richey's dad made an appeal via Radio One's *Newsbeat*. In the background, in the shadows of Newport and Blackwood, private detectives hired by Hall Or Nothing took up the case, alongside local and then national journalists, who realised by now that there was a big story brewing.

On reflection, Richey's general improvement immediately prior to his disappearance seemed to provide both hope and despair. Had he genuinely improved? Was it real optimism or simply a front for the benefit of other people, to stop them worrying? Was he intending to give America his best shot or had he always known he would opt out at the last minute? The fact was that his lighter mood during Christmas and, allowing for that one blip, during January could now be seen to be pointing in either direction. And suddenly, little things began to take on a greater significance. Why had he been so keen to hand over so many lyrics lately? Why had he thrown himself into those demo sessions with uncharacteristic zeal? Why had he purchased a pair of sneakers identical to the ones so famously worn by Kurt Cobain during his final days? Why had he recently started listening so intently to Joy Division's *Closer*? The questions invite tantalising answers, they seem to suggest links, motivation, a process; but ultimately Richey's actions in the weeks previous to his disappearance could mean everything, or nothing.

A breakthrough, of sorts, came on February 16. Over two weeks after his disappearance, Richey's silver L Registration Vauxhall Cavalier was found parked at the Severn View Service Station, next to the Severn Bridge. According to the local press, more abandoned cars have been found in that particular area, originally known as Aust Service Station, than any other car park in the country, presumably due to its close proximity to the bridge, one of two notorious suicide spots in the area. Given that fact, many people have noted how odd it was that a car could stand for several days there before attracting attention. Despite a barrage of interviews with local people, service station workers and customers, despite the widespread media coverage that the disappearance now attracted, there were no sightings of Richey whatsoever, at least not in the area immediately surrounding the discovery of the car. Further afield, and much to the confusion of both police and press, reports started to flood in of sightings before and after the car had been found. The problem then, as now, was that the entire issue would be confused by bogus calls. There was even a fanzine, from York, dedicated solely to reports of Richey sightings. Even though it later emerged that the reports in the publication, rather tastelessly entitled *Spectators Of Suicide* after the song on *Generation Terrorists*, had been the invention of the editor, it still managed to catch the attention of local press. It added to the intrigue of the case, which snowballed further following an alleged sighting of Richey busking in York, in 1998. (If it was him, it's amazing he didn't end up as a member of The Seahorses.) That, perhaps, was the most extreme case of false reports, although it soon became rather wearing to see Richey's name suddenly featuring in every teenage runaway story in every freesheet in Britain.

With no body, and no way of closing the story, the stage was set for widespread speculation. When reports filtered into the music press that Richey had, for weeks prior to his disappearance, been contemplating orchestrating the 'perfect disappearance', it served to bring speculation to fever pitch. The facts of the case – the credit cards, the passport, the 'eve of the American tour' parallel with Ian Curtis – were twisted to support the theory. The evidence would certainly support a staged disappearance. The possibility of Richey's engineering the perfect disappearance couldn't be dismissed.

Little comfort could be found in the official line. The police stated that the most likely answer was, indeed, suicide, given the sketchy nature of most of the alleged sightings to date. Then again, the sheer volume of sightings created a smoke screen in itself. As for the remaining Manics, they forced themselves to assume a bravely practical front: "I've given up thinking about it," James commented to *NME* in 1996. "Maybe he is alive, maybe he isn't. But he's not in the Manics and we have to get on with it." Nicky Wire was optimistic about the chances of Richey turning up, but confessed that in order to get through life day by day, he had to consciously lock off from thinking about his friend so often: "I still think he's alive but I've pushed that thought away. You can only spend so much time speculating over this, life goes on. To some extent I'm annoyed. I'm annoyed that he's done this, but I'm not subjecting myself to endless speculation. There are no real clues one way or another." The band's pragmatism was wholly understandable and, although since Richey's disappearance a disturbing number of fans had contacted the music papers to disclose their own suicidal tendencies, a general air of resignation seemed to descend. Nobody believed anything any more. A page had been turned.

Whether Richey perfected a brilliant though uncharacteristically cruel disappearance, or a suicide with no trace, it must be conceded that he had been successful. Either way, he achieved some kind of freedom. Freedom from whatever demons were so clearly haunting him, freedom from that crippling pain that fame and success had only made worse for him. Deep down, to survive and thrive at pop's peak, it seems that an individual has to grow a few protective layers of skin, and in the process potentially lose something of their character. Try, if you will, to square the humble lovelorn Morrissey of 'Hand In Glove' with the distant, self-absorbed despot that he became. Look at Jarvis Cocker furiously fighting to retain that humble edge, that touch of Sheffield humility, while simultaneously maintaining his position as one of London's pop elite.

People change and Richey may have changed accordingly, but it is increasingly difficult to see just how he would have fitted in with the world the Manics have survived and thrived in after his disappearance. Aesthetically speaking, Richey was a throwback – to the naïvety of punk, if you like, but certainly to a time when a band's music was considered rather more important than their PR. To an age when people read *NME* and believed it. Glance back to any section of the music press in the late Seventies or early Eighties. The level of solemn pretension in comparison with the jokey cynicism of today is astonishing. The post-Richey Edwards pop world is the Robbie Williams era. A smile, an arrogant career step, a failed relationship made public, a battalion of Brit Awards on the mantelpiece. A world in which *Q* magazine, once the home of the thinking music fan, has been whittled down to little more than pointless lists, schoolboy jokes about trousers or *Hello!*-style pics of partying popsters at the magazine's own awards ceremony. A Warholian nightmare in which celebrity is everything and Patti Smith is usurped by Natalie Imbruglia, where a smile and a pout is worth more than a stack of Velvet Underground albums. In the late Nineties, pop is more than ever measured in terms of record sales and public profile. It's difficult to imagine Richey Edwards lasting five minutes in such an environment.

There's one final difference between Richey Edwards and his hero, Ian Curtis, that we haven't looked at yet. Without any shadow of a doubt, Ian Curtis was a ferociously ambitious individual and would have played the pop game with all the shameless panache of a Damon Albarn or a Brett Anderson. But Richey Edwards' motivation for being in a band was never simply to make money. He did it because he was driven to. It's perhaps wrong to label Richey a 'genius', though his lyrics were certainly some of the decade's most distinctive and arresting, but he was, undeniably, completely genuine. The key moment in the Richey Edwards story was when he carved '4 Real' into his arm in front of Steve Lamacq, back in May 1991. Whether this was a courageous heartfelt statement or a pathetic display of rock star insecurity isn't really the issue. Because Richey believed it. Rock music will never, one senses, provide a reasonable canvas for the determined, uncompromising artist. As, arguably, Kurt Cobain realised, the precarious balance between artistic integrity and the mechanical commercialism of large corporations seems impossible to maintain. Perhaps the battle has been long lost and it is that realisation that is all too often the catalyst for self-destruction.

8

EVERYTHING MUST GO

"I do love cleaning. It gives me such a sense of fulfilment."
– Nicky Wire

Picture Nicky Wire. Back in the valley, in his terrace house, his long legs curled beneath him on the sofa, television blaring away, S4C flickering into the room, alarming static adverts for furniture shops in Cardiff, stilted soap operas and, arguably the ultimate Welsh cliché, the Friday night televisual treat of poems and pubs, bad R'n'B bands and folk singers.

Wire retreated into Wales. He even shunned the cosmopolitan culinary delights he had become accustomed to in favour of local fish'n'chips. But it didn't stop there. Rock'n'roll had dominated Wire's life for too many years. Richey's disappearance was now the catalyst for him to withdraw from the life that he had once craved. Indeed, there is nothing particularly odd about adopting a more conservative approach to life as the late twenties approach. For most people, a day dawns when *NME* doesn't quite pack the punch that it used to; when Radio Four suddenly seems more appealing than Radio One or the local dance station. With Richey's disappearance and the traumas of the Manics' European tour immediately prior to that, it's understandable that Nicky Wire's withdrawal from the youth culture that had made his band one of the UK's top acts should be all the more violent. If he could have secured a job in a local Building Society at this point, one senses he might have taken it. Wire needed a spell of obscurity and, for a while, he even constructed an alternative world for himself that had nothing to do with his musical past. He started to play for the local cricket team and spent long hours on the golf course. In an unlikely throwback to his student days, he decked himself out once more in slacks and Pringle sweaters, golf shoes and waterproofs. It was about as far from the white-jeaned slogan-daubed punky apparel of the early Manics as it was humanly possible to get. And that, surely, was the point. Curiously, in an interview with *Hot Press*, in 1996, Nicky Wire admitted, "There was always part of me that longed for that middle-class way of life. That may sound like a betrayal but, you know, the detached house, nice car, good job in sales, chatting to the neighbour over the fence. Who knows, I may end up like that anyway . . . I would just have taken a more unusual route." A job as a sales manager via rock'n'roll – certainly not a conventional career path.

As a further antidote to his pop star life, Wire began to take an interest in anything and everything about sport. Sport provided him with a further fantasy world. Although this isn't a distinctively Welsh trait, it is true that the Welsh are one of the few nations who elevate their sport to the levels of a religion. Wire wasn't exactly a regular at Cardiff Arms Park, bellowing 'Men Of Harlech', but he started to take a more active interest in sport, which would probably have alarmed Richey Edwards, had be been around to observe it.

During the spring of 1995, the band maintained a regular though distant contact with each other. Sean stayed mainly in Bristol, where he enjoyed a pint at his local and developed a greater interest in domestic affairs: tripping down to the local B&Q, fixing the flat he shared with his girlfriend and maintaining a deliberately low profile. James, in London, fought shy of even the most tempting parties, although he later complained that rumours of his time spent at various bars was somewhat overplayed. He was also susceptible to beer blubber, so he had more than one reason for a spot of abstinence. As he told *Mojo*, "My double chin was getting out of hand, it was slapping round my ankles." But James couldn't contemplate a return to Wales. As he would later tell *Q*'s veteran reporter Phil Sutcliffe, "I've got to live in London – for the band. It's the only way I can stay detached. If I went home I'd become obsessed with my own history. 'Too many fookin' ghosts, maan.' I remember so many things, good things, that don't exist any more. I get maudlin and lose all my energy. Whereas there is a transience in London that keeps me ticking over."

It was a classic example of the spirit of London Welsh. It's more than just the buzz of the big city. It's different from, say, the young girl down from Todmorden for a PR job in the West End, taken aback by the change in pace. A sense of being cut adrift, culturally and spiritually, permeates Wales to this day, despite modern communications. As for the Richey situation, James's physical and emotional distance was the most obvious way to cope. For him. But not for Wire.

Continuing in this way was, obviously, just treading water; all the Manics were still hopeful that Richey's deafening silence would somehow be broken. The period was a blank, hopeful space, interrupted only by infrequent band get-togethers, during which, apparently, musical issues were never even mentioned. Finally, naturally, something simply had to crack. James, in particular, felt it impossible to cope with the lack of routine. The tight, at times crushingly intense, rigours of band life were suddenly there no more, leaving elastic days and nights that merged together in an unpunctuated existence. Unlike the other two, James had no domestic commitments, had no desire to develop his DIY skills, and would frankly have looked ridiculous in a Pringle. As the months passed it became all too clear that, if Richey was still out there and if he was to be tempted back into place, it would take more than mere silence from the rest of them. Perhaps band activities should be resumed. A meeting involving the band, Martin Hall and Richey's parents was arranged. Initial media speculation that the Manics would immediately splinter seemed pretty much on the ball. There had been speculation about James offering his services to other bands. Had this been a genuine option, then one wonders if Nicky, if not Sean, would ever have been tempted back into music. Probably not. One strongly senses that Nicky would have chosen his new freedom to develop his writing skills, perhaps start that screenplay, perhaps work with his brother, Patrick Jones, a burgeoning playwright whose work remains eerily spiked by the same verbal attack found in Manics' lyrics. The truth is that the band, in shock from the moment that Richey's car was found and the possibility that its driver had actually committed suicide began to dawn on them, found it simply impossible to focus their attentions on band matters at all. Neither splitting up nor continuing as a trio seemed the right answer. They needed the time, just to see how things turned out. But by the time they had that meeting in May of 1995, a way forward seemed clear. If Richey was still alive, and was to be tempted back, then surely an active band would be one way of achieving that. Especially if it became known that the Manics were working their way through that stack of lyrics, setting them to music. If Richey could see this happening, well ... Whatever the outcome, nobody in the meeting could come up with any reason why the band should not continue.

There was simply nothing else for it. James had started to take an active interest in the booze again. Wandering through Soho's neon-lit streets, losing himself amid the daytime drinkers and coffee bar dwellers might seem romantic, in a Tom Waits kind of way. But it soon becomes a fairly empty experience. The main pull of Bradfield's life, for so long, had been the Manics. Without them, what else could he do? A life spent guesting on other people's albums, the Johnny Marr butterfly technique, never managing to settle with anything to match your former glories, wasn't really on the cards. Perhaps it became clear, at this point, that being a member of the Manic Street Preachers was a one-off. The magic they had created belonged to them all and, even without Richey, it was the most valuable thing they had. There was nothing else for it. It was time to start again.

Nevertheless, it was a nervous three-piece Manics who booked rehearsal time at Sound Space that May. Wire brought Richey's stack of lyrics, now heavily modified by his own scribblings, and ready to be worked, knocked into songs. Immediately the experience proved rewarding. Somewhat to their surprise, the time spent in the studio became something of a relief, as their initially loose jamming acted as a focus for the three musicians. Tentative melodies and chord sequences started to germinate, and Richey's lyrics simply begged to be used. The gap in band activities, albeit due to dreadful circumstances, proved an artistic bonus. The Manics felt refreshed, empowered even and pleased to be back on familiar ground in Cardiff. One week into the rehearsals it became clear that the Manic Street Preachers would not only continue to exist, but would have some exciting product in the pipeline before long. Naturally, this came as an almighty relief to the record company, who, Martin Hall would acknowledge, had unexpectedly maintained a dignified distance, unwilling to push or pull the band in any manner. That said, the decision to continue as a recording unit was made entirely without record company intervention, the band spending considerable time with Richey's family before mutually deciding to proceed.

The idea was to take things very, very slowly. They had two dozen songs, of varying quality and in different stages of development. It soon transpired that the band could work without Richey's on-the-spot input. Richey's lyrics had clearly guided the band in a certain direction. It was a fleetingly beautiful direction, and it had provided the Manics with a unique appeal but, to be frank, the dangers of that direction had become apparent with *The Holy Bible*. It is difficult to imagine the band continuing up this path. As the Manics pointed out in the wake of Richey's disappearance, many fans, who had identified with Richey for what he was, also tended to underrate Nicky Wire's immense lyrical input. True enough, he was a less commanding character, less enigmatic, perhaps and certainly less of a romantic figure than Richey, but it was Wire who had perfected a method of using words in a fractured, commanding manner, moving away from bare skeletal sloganeering.

The band had already realised that the lack of Richey's guiding influence, although essential to their early development, wasn't going to damage their future songwriting. Indeed, as they later told *Select*, Richey's absence actually "freed us a bit. We don't feel the need to justify ourselves because we've done enough of that." There is no doubt that the previously intense nature of the Manics' lyrics could now ease up a little. As any artist must, the band would have to evolve – the situation had been forced on them, but they could now use it to their advantage. Nicky felt curiously empowered by this, numbed perhaps by the knowledge that he could now write about anything he wanted. The barriers had been taken away. One wonders, speculatively, if part of Richey had sensed this also; that his intellectual 'demons', such as they were, were restricting the band's direction, perhaps in direct contrast to their increasing prowess as musicians. All kinds of different musical areas had started to beckon during, and even before, *The Holy Bible*. Glimpses of a softer, more composed Manics sound had started to surface. While it would have been fascinating to see how Richey's lyrics developed over time, there was also the worry that he might not have been able to adapt his intensely emotional style, to broaden his lyrical palette, to suit the developing Manic Street Preachers.

*   *   *

The troubled and now tragically demolished Hacienda Club in Manchester may have achieved its global fame due to the innovative dance policy of its DJs, and the vivacity of the Manchester clubbers, but it is often forgotten that it also housed innumerable classic gigs. Indeed it was primarily designed as a rock venue back in 1982, during a period when Manchester nightclubbing meant little more than posing from beneath cheekfuls of rouge in some chromed and mirrored disco in Oldham.

But there was always something about the Hac. The faint aroma of rubber, the airiness, the modern angles – dated towards the end of the club's life, but still impressive in the café bar age – and, purely by accident this, its curious atmospheric capabilities. Perhaps it was the size and shape of the dance floor. Perhaps it was just the mood of the clubbers but, at two-thirds full, the whole place carried an intoxicating, positive vibe. This was always extraordinary to witness. When The Hacienda was rocking, it always felt like the centre of the world. Strangely enough, that feeling went way back to the days when it would lurch from night to night on a shoestring, surviving only by virtue of the occasional huge gig.

The Manic Street Preachers, to their credit really, never harboured a grudge against Manchester, or The Hacienda, which initially treated the band with profound indifference. As to the club, they took every opportunity to voice their admiration of a place that was, in every sense, the ultimate three-dimensional piece of Factory artwork, even if the label itself had faded in the wake of the club's success. The Manics were still refreshingly naïve enough to believe in the romance of the place – after all, Joy Division and New Order were high on their list of musical heroes.

When the band were initially asked to support Oasis for their monumental shows at Manchester City's Maine Road stadium, their excitement was understandably tempered by a genuine fear. Could they cut it without Richey? Their fourth member would be especially missed, one might presume, on such a vast stage, where more than ever the band had to feel like an invincible gang. Nevertheless, they hadn't hesitated in accepting the offer. It was Martin Hall's clever idea to initiate a warm-up gig at Manchester's Hacienda a couple of nights before. It could be low-key. As low as you could get in The Hacienda. In fact, it was in the downstairs bar, the original chill out area named, by Tony Wilson, 'The Kim Philby Bar' and one where the band would be crammed into a corner, staring the crowd directly in the face. It would be an intense experience. More importantly, it would see the band performing in an environment that was totally appropriate for a three-piece. Down there, in that little sweat box, they might not miss Richey. So went the theory.

It is regarded as one of the strangest gigs in the Manics' history – a ferociously powerful performance which proved that their new upbeat, anthemic material could be produced very effectively by this stripped-down version of the original band. In that respect the gig was a great relief, and the band slammed through the set with ear-splitting vigour. There was only a small space, too, where Richey would have stood. But, rather like a cat asleep on a bed at night, the area seems to grow and grow as the gig progressed. And despite being, literally, face to face with the audience, Nicky Wire felt the hollowness of that space acutely. Nobody else could really sense it. And at one moment, per-haps only that moment, he allowed the music to carry him away from reality, he turned to allow Richey to jump into the instrumental break as usual. It was only for a split-second. And though not many present saw it, it was enough to reduce Nicky to near tears. At the end of the set he rushed to the dressing room, noticeably distressed.

Much has been made – too much, in fact – of the apparent similarities between the Manic Street Preachers pre- and post-Richey and the transition from Joy Division into New Order. I have already discussed why I see little substance to the mythical links between Edwards and Curtis, two vastly different characters living in different bands in different circumstances in different times. Nevertheless, as both bands saw their most romantic, passionate member vanish with a violent immediacy, one perhaps should acknowledge that New Order and the Manics can, at least, both claim to have gone through a similar life-changing experience. It is difficult to believe that any band could survive such tragedies without moving on to encompass a very different musical direction. It would be the healthiest and most artistically valuable way to proceed. As far as New Order were concerned, their first thoughts were, given the vocal limitations of guitarist Bernard Sumner, to replace Curtis with a new singer. Bizarre auditions featuring Factory singers Alan Hempstall (from Crispy Ambulance) and Kevin Hewick came to nothing. Subsequently, via a series of clumsy accidents and the addition of drummer Steve Morris's girl-friend, Gillian Gilbert, on tentative keyboards, the transition from a dark howl to lighter and more punchy sound was achieved. And, curiously, the legacy of Joy Division seemed to add soul to the New Order's tendency towards flippancy. There was also the fact that, in attaining a lighter mood, New Order had been lucky enough to reflect a general change in the early Eighties, from introverted indie rock to the second age of glam, from dour rock to bright dance.

It wasn't quite the same for the Manic Street Preachers. Things were not so simple in the mid-Nineties. No Clash, Pistols or Iggy in 1996. But the Manics, despite their often rather sweet intellectual pretensions, were still as dumb as the best of the dumbest. And that, I can promise you, is the highest compliment I could possibly pay them. They were a rarity indeed. A band with true heart, with real passion – even though Bradfield openly despised being labelled 'passionate', believing it would make the Manics seem like some second-rate punk band. It's difficult to think of too many other successful bands at the present time who could make the same claim. Passion, it seems, is for loser bands. Whatever they might have said to *NME*, it always seemed obvious that, should everything fall apart, the Manic Street Preachers would not be able to sink smoothly into quality vocations. There was too much tap room stink for that. Too much grass roots braggadocio. New Order's glory was always the fact that they were deft enough, clever enough, smart enough and lucky enough to rise away from the masses. Rather as a precursor to Oasis (though not The Stone Roses), New Order were a flash car/top hotel kind of a band. The Manic Street Preachers, by stark comparison, have always shouted for the glory of the people from whom they emerged. Indeed, it's difficult to imagine two more different bands. Nicky Wire and Hookey? Barney and James Dean Bradfield? Leave it out. Working class as they all are, these pairs have never really had anything in common.

Did the Manics lighten up to attain commercial success? I don't think so. 'A Design For Life' – the first song written after Richey's disappearance and, fittingly, the first post-Richey single release – was neither dourly introspective or trivial and poppy. Although rumours of a surging new Manics sound were rife among the music press, and, indeed, among the Roses fans who could be bothered to listen to the Manics' support spot at Wembley Arena, it wasn't until this single surfaced, like a galleon surfing the Radio One play list, that it was possible to believe the rumours to be anything other than hype. The real surprise was that the song was a full-blooded working-class riposte against the café bar society that had started to adopt working-class pretensions – in short, the rise of *Loaded* culture. Interestingly the song fell firmly on the side of the Burnage boys in the rather pointless Oasis/Blur media battle. Not for the Manics, the patronising world of pseudo guttersnipes, the Hornby set, tripping down to The Groucho following an afternoon at Highbury. 'A Design For Life' was solid, downbeat, levelling, unglamorous and as rousing as a Cardiff Arms Park chant. The song's famous opening line, "Libraries give us power", was swiped cleanly from a graffito Wire had discovered at the library in Pwll. Transposed to 'A Design For Life', the sentence attained a new significance. It might initially seem rather po-faced but there is simple honesty in the line. Libraries presented the Manics with the power to move away from the restrictions of their home town, onwards and upwards.

For Bradfield, the lyrics, uncomplicated as they were, demanded a vast musical noise, a place where Tamla Motown and infectious modern rock might meet, against a background of Phil Spector's wall of sound. It was the sound that the band had strived for on 'Motorcycle Emptiness', although their inability to flesh out that particular song had actually provided a certain intriguing eeriness. This time around, the improved musicianship of the band had all but closed the gap that lay between the sound in Bradfield's mind and the end result in the recording studio. There was nothing sad or mournful here. It was an instant triumph.

In a sense, and with an irony that, surely, even Richey would appreciate, the lack of his intellectual input had freed the band. 'A Design For Life' was in many ways a dumbing-down from *The Holy Bible* and the fact that it is a better song than anything on that particular album was always a little difficult to admit. A song for the masses? Well not quite, but as the song was a rally against middle-class pretensions, the dumb-down worked perfectly. Its finest hour came during the band's celebratory performance at the 1997 Brit Awards ceremony. As the television camera panned across the crowd, it rested on Richard Branson, caught in a state of deep adoration. Noel Gallagher, too, paid his respects, acknowledging that he knew a working-class anthem when he heard one. A Welsh anthem, too. How fitting perhaps, that the soaring strings of 'A Design For Life' would be used by the Welsh Tourist Board's television adverts of 1998–99. In what seemed a direct response to the way the music of The Cranberries had hauntingly soundtracked images of rolling Irish fields, crashing waves, white cottages and towering mountains (during an advertising campaign by the Irish Tourist Board), so 'A Design For Life' provided the background music as a camera swept through the awesome valleys of Gwynedd. It was all somewhat removed from the rather less obvious beauties of Blackwood, but still. The fact that, on mainstream TV, Wales would be instantly associated with the music of the Manic Street Preachers, was indeed something special. Rather like the association between London streets and The Clash, or Manhattan and Lou Reed. It was where they came from.

It seems incredible to note, considering the song's universal appeal, that 'Design . . .' was not an immediate choice for a single. Its release was surrounded by trepidation, from both record company and band. The problem was that it was such an odd record and, as such, its commercial appeal was impossible to confidently predict. It would be a hit, of course, but how big? This was not a question that would have worried the Manics with previous releases, but this time around things were different. They were at a pivotal moment forced upon them by Richey's disappearance. Could they continue to flourish, maybe even attaining greater status than before, or would they begin to fade from the music scene, another case of a band that might have been great? There was no doubt that the fate of this strange and compelling record would set the trajectory, one way or another.

That it shot into the charts at number two amazed everyone concerned. The band were relaxing in their respective homes when the news came through. Bradfield, temporarily back from London, rolled out of bed, telephoned his mates and that night shared a pint in the local after watching sport on S4C. Nicky Wire, after a bout of dusting and mowing, took Sunday tea with his parents. A deep sense of satisfaction settled upon the band. A bridge had been quietly crossed. It augured well for the album.

With *Everything Must Go*, the Manics had finally arrived. It was a defining album, a special moment. And it was such an inspiringly old-fashioned record. Old-fashioned in the sense that it immediately energised the listener, body and mind, firing fractured lyrical imagery into the mind with effortless zeal. It made old punks feel young again. It caught the sound that the band had been ferociously striving for on *Gold Against The Soul*. This time around, that brassy attack had been captured by a powerful and elegant production, showcased by 'A Design For Life' but spread richly across the broader canvas of the album.

Many did not like the opener, 'Elvis Impersonator; Blackpool Pier', with its lilting acoustic intro slammed into submission by full-on rock bombast. Through the lyric we visit the crumbling, paint-peeled, Fifties Americana that settled and strangled the life out of Britain's larger holiday resorts. Blackpool, latterly a hotchpotch of uninspired B&Bs, Formica-filled hotel lounges, bottom drawer attractions, peopled by surging stag and hen party revellers. But on Blackpool Pier, Americana is shrivelled into the grotesque sequinned pottery figure of Elvis. The ultimate in tack, looking down mockingly. One might have preferred the image to be given a wordier description than Wire's savagely pared down lyrics, but his starkness is chillingly effective. It does, however, wrong-foot the first-time listener into thinking that, perhaps, this is *The Holy Bible* revisited. Such thoughts are swept brusquely aside by the sweeping glory of 'A Design For Life'. The first completely non-Richey song – music by Bradfield and Sean Moore, lyrics by Wire – it establishes an altogether different mood, triumphant and celebratory, and seems to look towards the future. However, it is at this point that shades of the Manics' past territory first re-emerge. The photographer Kevin Carter took prize-winning photographs of the Rwanda war, but profiting out of such misery played so heavily on his conscience that he eventually took a shotgun to himself. Richey Edwards, struck by the poignancy of Carter's story, wrote a set of lyrics based around it. Indeed, the story, which parallels the theme of *The Killing Fields*, affected Richey to such an extent that he incorporated a combat 'n' camera look into his stage act. Not an entirely healthy obsession, it might be observed. The track was lifted from its pedantic base by strikingly funky trumpets – played by Sean – which created a brassy pull so strong that, when it eventually surfaced as the third single, many people took to the song before they realised that it was the Manics at all.

And so to 'Enola/Alone', penned by Wire after seeing a photo of his younger self surrounded by Philip Hall and Richey. A statement of the abrupt shock of loneliness that Wire felt at the loss of two such close friends, 'Enola/Alone' is undoubtedly the most courageously personal song on the album, in that it addresses that transitionary stage between being in mourning and moving forward, regaining some kind of optimism, some consolation from even the most basic things. Hence the lines: "I walk on the grass and feel peace at last, I walk on the beach and for once I feel some ease."

This transitionary period is also reflected in the title track, although it was written much further down the line, when genuine optimism had started to return to the Manics. 'Everything Must Go' hurtles like a roller-coaster ride that is impossible to resist. One likes to think of it as a song of freedom, of breaking through to the other side, leaving the negative shadow of Richey's disappearance far behind.

'Small Black Flowers That Grow In The Sky' is an immediate throwback to the moment that Richey watched a BBC television documentary depicting caged animals slowly losing their sanity. The film had a lasting and powerful effect on him and he quickly scribbled down a set of lyrics that, perhaps unintentionally, used the animal metaphor to reach deep into his own heart. For this writer, it's the most intense, personal and arguably distressing song Richey ever wrote. It could be seen as a retreat from the glare of fame, but I tend to think it displays a damaged, fragile psyche that would have struggled with or without the pressures of a public profile. In fact, things might have been worse for Richey had he remained in obscurity. At least the band provided a release for him, if only to push out disturbing and highly evocative lyrics such as this. Lame, caged and wild, untamed and defeated, 'Small Black Flowers . . .' provided the album's most uneasy moment. With *Everything Must Go*, the Manic Street Preachers would enter the households of new fans, of those drawn by

'A Design For Life' and 'Everything Must Go'. But 'Small Black Flowers That Grow In The Sky' is not the kind of song that would lie submissively in the background. It was stark, gaunt and spiky. It didn't fit but one can only be grateful that the Manics chose to include it.

Richey also dominated the lyrical input for 'The Girl Who Wanted To Be God', which drew on the tragic relationship between the American poet Sylvia Plath, who committed suicide in 1963, and her then husband Ted Hughes (although to this day Nicky Wire refuses to acknowledge any awareness of the song's meaning). Unsurprising, perhaps, that Plath's brilliant, peripatetic mind would appeal to Richey Edwards.

'Removables' hardly lightens the atmosphere of the album. A song that pre-dates *The Holy Bible*, its origin lies in a set of Richey's lyrics that hover around the theme of suicide. It's difficult to ignore the significance of the fact that, during the recording of the track, the band learned the news of Kurt Cobain's death. As such we were treated to a one-take acoustic affair, an affecting half-completed demo set in an album of considerable polish. But the 'rushed' feel, no doubt intended to capture Nirvana-style looseness, only serves to unsettle the listener. To my mind, this is a song that remains unfinished business. Whereas it does work in the sense that it is intended to convey an unpremeditated reaction to a sudden loss, artistically it seems to demand more care and attention.

'Australia', the album's fourth single, contained shades of both 'A Design For Life' and 'Everything Must Go'. Light and infectious, surging and irrepressible, it was nothing less than a plea for freedom, for wide open space and some time away. Australia is a metaphor for somewhere to escape to, somewhere far away from the problems that the protagonist of the song has undergone. New listeners might have been forgiven for regarding the song as some kind of desperate plea for the preservation of native Australian culture, for Aboriginal land rights, perhaps. Nothing of the sort. The breeziness of the track is in stark contrast to the next song, 'Interiors'. Through Nicky Wire's fractured lyric, we find a tribute to Willem de Kooning, the Dutch abstract painter who used his work to convey the disorientating state of Alzheimer's disease. The line, 'Your beautiful triangle of distortion' in particular hints that the artist's life, work and illness were all strongly linked. Any triumph to be found in the context of the artist's life is aesthetic, his vision remains untainted by the disease he is suffering from; indeed, his vision, and the art that it will produce, will ultimately make the artist impervious to death. You are what you create and nothing can destroy that. Given the subject of the song, it's probable that Richey Edwards was in Nicky Wire's mind too when he wrote the lyrics. In the background, you may hear the sound of a Peter Hook-style bass line. But that's where the comparison ends. It is impossible to imagine New Order ever attempting a track with such a theme. Not for them this brave journey into deeply uncomfortable lyrical waters. With this track in particular, the Manic Street Preachers were laying claim to a greater depth within the pop format. 'Interiors' was a strong hint that, even with Richey's disappearance, the band were not willing to become lightweight pop stars. Indeed, the gulf between the Manics, fighting to retain their darker moments, and early New Order, fighting to shed themselves of theirs, couldn't be more striking.

The next track, 'Further Away', offers another change of direction. Is this not a love song? Is this the sound of Nicky Wire pining for a distant love, or an old man weeping for a lost youth? Both perhaps. Whatever, it is not the kind of theme usually associated with this particular band. Once again, it's a sign of the Manics tentatively trying out new forms. It was a brave new world in the wake of Richey's disappearance, and the band were eager not to limit themselves to making the same musical statements as they had in the past. A Manics lovesong? Why not?

With the album nudging past the 300,000 sales mark – two months in and it had already become their biggest seller to date – the band had crashed through a psychological barrier it was vital to put behind them. It would be too simplistic to merely call this new three-piece the post-Richey Manics. That said, they had definitely become 'something else' in the wake of his disappearance. 'A Design For Life' instigated this transformation, and the growth of a new Manic Street Preachers continued through a blindingly successful run of singles. Here was a band who accepted their new identity, and had started to go about the responsibilities that go hand in hand with such exposure with good grace, with eloquence even. Perhaps the success was all the sweeter, all the easier to handle coming, as it did, so late in the day.

Back in Blackwood, there was a marked change in the way the band were perceived after *Everything Must Go* took off. No longer were the Manics a cultural secret for those who turned up at the newsagent every Wednesday for their *NME*s and *Melody Maker*s. With the soaring majesty of 'A Design For Life' and 'Everything Must Go' dominating the airwaves, the Manics were becoming a household name. Ordinary people had fallen for the melodies of those tunes, and now recognised the Manics, 'their' Manics, as genuine stars. Talking with *Q* magazine's Phil Sutcliffe, James Bradfield perceptively summarised the secret of meaningful mainstream success thus: "To be universal you have got to stain the consciousness of the people. You've got to dig out a truth that everybody knows, but they don't want to hear, then tell it in a manner so aesthetically indignant, so beautiful, that they've got to accept it back into their lives again. That's what I want to do. Touch something universal with your own language."

Blackwood, Britain and much of the world beyond, had succumbed. But not, it seemed, America. Even as this book was being written, in January 1999, the music business would talk about the 'Manics and the America problem' as the very antithesis of the Garth Brooks and England affair. (The country star is currently one of the largest-selling artists in the world – 100 million albums sold by 1999 – but remains off the spotlight in England, though he has a sizeable following in Ireland and Wales.) There are times when huge acts that have gained huge acceptance on one side of the pond simply fall into a vacuum on the other, for no discernible reason. In his excellent Manics biography *Sweet Venom*, Martin Clarke argues that the Manics fall too easily between the rock and pop markets for the US market to understand them. One tends to think that there's more to it than that, but it's very difficult to understand the States' resistance to a band who, with their wide-screen sound, powerful vocals and hummable tunes, would seem perfect for that market. Tony Michaelides, Manchester-based record plugger, argues: "There are some things in the music industry that simply cannot be explained. You can explain why Garth Brooks never quite made it to the same degree over here despite having quite a lot of fans. It's a radio thing. British radio just isn't geared to promote that kind of music. It's changing, with Radio Two getting so much better, but there is still some way to go. That is an example of a problem that is purely mechanical. But the Manic Street Preachers' comparative failure in America is just impossible to pin down. I don't accept that they fall between rock and pop. You could say that about Bryan Adams . . . about any of a hundred acts that are massive in the States. It could be a record company politics thing. It's impossible to know. Personally, and after 25 years' experience in the music industry, I'd say that the Manic Street Preachers are, like U2, absolutely the perfect act for American ears. More so than for English ears. Someone, somewhere has cocked up . . . but it isn't Hall Or Nothing."

In the autumn of 1996, the Manics continued their association with Oasis by trooping across the Atlantic to support the Mancunians who by now were firmly established as the biggest thing in UK pop since The Beatles. How bittersweet must it have been for the Manics to have achieved such album success only to find themselves scrambling around like hopeful upstarts crashing the gig of their favourite band. "It is humbling," Bradfield admitted to the *Guardian*, "but it doesn't do any harm to realise your place in the scheme of things."

Well, maybe not. But touring with Oasis, in autumn of 1996, must have been like confronting their commercial status and admitting it openly to the world. As the American media circus gathered around the Gallaghers, feverishly scribbling down every monosyllabic grunt with relish, the Manic Street Preachers could literally wander away and sit unobserved in local cafés, wondering why the magic they were working at home just didn't seem to have any potency in America.

9

THE EVERLASTING

"I wish I could be more arrogant about it, but I still don't know what went right with 'Tolerate'. I walked out of here (Top Of The Pops *studio) and it was full of 14 year olds and not one of them fucking knew me."*

– James Dean Bradfield

Never before had British pop music seemed so fluffy, so futile, so juvenile. A soundtrack for primary-coloured children's television, where cute presenters with Zeppelin-sized egos would flash teeth and belly buttons, command raucous games shows for eight year olds and usher the walking grin known as 'Billie' into the spotlight. It was as if we were all living in a hell created by Pete Waterman. Bouncing, perfect bodies everywhere.

It could be argued, of course, that *Top Of The Pops* is certainly no worse today than in the early Seventies when the studio audiences were filled with curiously innocent faces, casting moronic stares towards pouting popsters in glitter. Sometimes it seemed as if the audience had donated all their make-up, all their colourful gear, to the band. By autumn 1998, despite bursts of energy from the likes of Mansun, Placebo and Garbage, it all seemed like one big frantic game of karaoke. Get on, look pretty, make a buck, get off. Any band with a bit of substance would, surely, look preposterous in such an environment?

And the Manics did, indeed, look and seem preposterous, uncomfortable and strangely old. Their appearance on the show should have been celebratory, given that 'If You Tolerate This Your Children Will Be Next' had crashed straight in at number one in the singles chart. It had been a particularly shallow *Top Of The Pops* that week, featuring Steps, All Saints – whose early fresh pop brilliance had already started to take a back seat to the celeb fest they joined during the year – and Courtney Love's Hole, bashing through a pouty 'Celebrity Skin'. The latter came across like a rock band with all the sincerity of a blockbuster novel. The Manic Street Preachers, somewhat out of place in this environment, took the stage looking more like electricians than number one pop stars, which was itself intriguing. The glam element that had been the Manics' early hallmark was now fully erased, replaced by dull cotton and earnest expressions. But as the song began to unfold in all its laid-back glory, and as James Bradfield sang, "so if I can shoot rabbits I can shoot fascists" it was clear that this was one of those *TOTP* moments, rather like The Osmonds' performance of 'Crazy Horses', that seemed captivatingly surreal.

'If You Tolerate This Your Children Will Be Next' was born onto British radio in an almost apologetic fashion. DJs would back announce the track with the words, "Well, actually, I quite like that . . ." or, in the case of Radio One's Jo Whiley, ". . . am I the only person who actually likes the new stuff the Manics are doing?" The expectation was that the carefully measured maturity of the Manics' new music, the sheen of self-confidence, would make the songs rather less effective than the towering anthems from *Everything Must Go*. There wouldn't, after all, even be a chance for James to do his little guitar-wielding twirl with stuff this reserved. This would be static Manics, with Wire, studious before the Welsh flag that covered his amplifier. In the *Top Of The Pops* environment, where an aerobic chant is all that currently seems necessary to command attention, here was a band singing dourly about the Spanish Civil War. (Wire's interest in Spanish history had been sparked by the holiday he spent with his wife in Barcelona.)

It wasn't subversive. It wasn't like the Velvet Underground performing 'Heroin' in front of a café filled with tourists in 1968. It wasn't like The Sex Pistols playing 'Anarchy In The UK' on *So It Goes*, either. For something genuinely subversive to have taken place, a few of those plastic pop kiddies in the audience, or the ones at home itching to plug in their Nintendos and replace James Dean Bradfield's face with Super Marios, would have to have taken in something of what was being sung. Nobody would be at all surprised when, a week later, the Manics would be replaced with a jumble of gaudy bopping popsters like Steps. But for those who were willing to listen, the song contained an awesome power. A power that seemed particularly relevant given the Omagh bomb atrocity of August 15. By singing about a fight against violence, about a future for all, the Manics had, quite unconsciously, captured the zeitgeist. The haunting melody and subtle music inveigled its way into the mind; the song seemed both a requiem and a call to arms at the same time. The refrain, it had been noted by sundry critics, bore more than a passing resemblance to The Stranglers' 'Duchess'.

To John Harris, in a surprisingly perceptive interview in *Select* magazine, James Bradfield later admitted a certain amount of relief when the record hit top spot. "I was just relieved not to be the brides-maid any more," he confessed, "but even now, I'm not quite sure. It could all go fucking wrong." Difficult to see how, to be honest. If you can write a song about the dark heart of Spain, about the clash of extreme politics that tore families apart, and float it to the top of a chart bubbling with teen froth and still not appear to be doing any-thing too subversive; if you can write hit singles about the lonesome death of a war photographer, or the crumbling psyche of the British working class, and still be allowed to spin around and pump away on that stage, then you must be doing something very right.

As Bradfield explained, "I wish I could be more arrogant about it, but I still don't know what went right with '. . . Tolerate . . .' I expected the song to lose out, I really did. I thought it was going to be monumentally embarrassing, to come up against Steps, and to lose out. I've said this a few times, but it would have felt like a really intelligent politician losing to a stumbling Ronnie Reagan. That is what I expected and I was ready for it. I was worried, especially when the DJs first started making strange comments about the song . . . but I was ready . . . and then we went straight in at number one. Pretty strange, to be honest." Therein lay part of the charm of the Manic Street Preachers. They talked a great fight, they built their reputation on confrontational comments and buzzing guitars, but when you looked a little further you saw four – now three – very insecure individuals. For pop stars, they are very human.

If there was a compromise, then it must lie in the aching melodic subtlety of that single and, indeed, much of the new album, which bears an ethereal quality, partly as a result of Bradfield's softened voice and partly because this is music that now seems mapped from the landscape. The Manics' Welsh heritage emerged time and time again on this album that took its title from an Aneurin Bevan speech. The Bevan connection was astute, and seemed perfect for the new, relaxed intelligence of this band. Bevan was as close to being a genuine Welsh hero as it was possible for any politician to be. The historian Jan Morris had described Bevan as both "compelling" and "majestic", two words which might be perfectly suited to the new album which, again not unlike Bevan's style of politics, would have many detractors. Aneurin Bevan was a miner's son, from Tredegar and worked as a miner himself before following his political heart and becoming the Labour MP for Ebbw Vale. The love the Welsh would retain for him could, perhaps, be linked with Bevan's knack of thoroughly 'winding up' the English Establishment, who never took kindly to this pugnacious red-faced Welshman. Churchill loathed him and, during the Second World War, openly referred to him as "that squalid nuisance". Positive proof, if proof were needed, that Bevan was doing his job right. He held the Ebbw Vale seat for thirty years and such was his local charisma that he made it arguably the safest Labour seat in British political history. His passionate fight for the declining Welsh coal fields was a prominent feature of his speeches. If there was a paradox to Bevan, it was his choice to ignore the Welsh language, and much of Welsh culture come to that. His belief was that Wales, to survive in the big world, would have to emerge from its insular circle, much as, admittedly on a more trivial level, the Manic Street Preachers had had to leave Blackwood to achieve pop success.

The cover for *This Is My Truth Tell Me Yours* could have back-fired. A beige-clad band windswept on, of all things, a Harlech beach, with Snowdonia rising in the background! It did seem oddly fitting though, as the album, in sound if not in lyricism, is vast and spacious, cold and open, and as strangely relaxing as a drive through the mountains. Some critics boldly announced the album to be little more than an exercise in treading water, in maintaining the momentum that *Everything Must Go* had created without adding anything of genuine significance. This was a complete misreading of the album, which sees the band attain a staggering maturity without softening to pomp rock. It was a mighty achievement indeed to strike a balance between melodic accessibility and intellectual bite, a perfect reflection of James's point about telling a truth in such an aesthetically striking way that the viewer or listener instantly understands it and accepts it.

To be fair, the album is certainly a 'grower', and it could take seven or eight plays to make its mark. Before that point, melodic similarities between tracks do tend to limit their impact as individual songs. And James's voice, surprisingly beautiful on any isolated track, doesn't have the depth and scope to return, song after song, theme after theme. Until the songs are familiar, there is a certain feeling of the album weakening about halfway through. Most first-time listeners would be startled by the unlikely 'prettiness' of the first three songs. That's no put-down. Quite the reverse. From the outset – 'The Everlasting' – it is clear that the Manics had managed to create a kind of haunting beauty that lay way beyond *The Holy Bible*, a feeling that they had first approached with 'Motorcycle Emptiness' all those years ago. 'The Everlasting' – the follow-up single to '...Tolerate...' – is probably the finest rock song ever written about the greater understanding that comes with growing older. The song battles against the perception of age as a degeneration, making a strong case for the value of the wisdom that comes with time. This is not the bleatings of some beery thirty-five year old crying into his pint down the Welfare Club, pining for lost passions. Here the passion remains, albeit tempered by the more worldly view of someone who has lived a little and learned a lot. The Manics can no longer make noise from the front line, that is the task of younger bands. But as Nicky Wire wrote, "it doesn't mean that I don't care." The song's beauty – the finest, most evocative piece of music made in 1998 in the opinion of this writer, and the best lyrics Nicky Wire had ever written – shone on the airwaves, and its overall power even made us forgive Bradfield's 'unusual' pronunciation of the word 'genuine' – most memorably heard during the band's appearance on *Later With Jools Holland*, when the word came across as the rather affected "Gennnerrrrwinnnn".

'...Tolerate...' followed, continuing the run of slow burners, with lyrics inspired by the fight against fascism in 1930s Spain. Strangely, the song would be reflected in a television programme made by, of all people, Michael Portillo, whose own Spanish family had been spliced in two by this same war. (Portillo's father was a communist, unlikely as it may seem.) But the theme of Portillo's programme, that blood is thicker than politics and, most poignantly, that our modern-day set-backs can seem remarkably trivial when compared to events of the past, was almost directly reflected in these lyrics. The Manics and Portillo. Strange bedfellows, to say the least.

'You Stole The Sun From My Heart' was a pure and simple beauty. A trickle of a guitar riff, like a mountain stream, holding the song's pretty heart in place while, four times, the track explodes into an angry condemnation of a departed lover.

'Ready For Drowning' used the swamping of the Welsh village Capel Celyn, to make way for a reservoir to supply water for Liverpool, as a metaphor for the suppression of Welsh talent. The Manics, it seems, do not feel they are 'ready for drowning', not just yet anyway, whether by a storm of new talent or by the encroaching influence of neighbour-ing England on Welsh culture.

'Tsunami' is, perhaps, the album's strangest song. The track is a heartbreakingly sad tale of twins June and Jennifer Gibbons, lat-terly tagged 'The Silent Twins' in a beguiling biography penned by Marjorie Wallace which, presumably, Nicky read shortly before writ-ing the song. Growing up in the quiet Pembrokeshire town of Haver-fordwest, the twins soon started attracting concern locally for their strange behaviour. Painfully withdrawn, they started to communicate with painstakingly slow movements which would mirror each other exactly. Sometimes, the pair would remain utterly expressionless for long periods of time while, all around them, caring adults tried to tempt them from within their shells. Their refusal to communicate was born directly from their love of each other and their joint dis-trust of the world outside their duel existence. As the years passed, they even developed weird and frantic speech patterns, completely indecipherable to anyone else. Their only means of communication was through writing – they kept meticulous diaries and June even managed to have a novel, *Pepsi Cola Addict*, published. This unlikely literary bent subsided as the twins started to hang around the local RAF base, where they discovered some kind of juvenile excitement by attracting the attentions of the airmen. They subsequently fell into petty crime and vandalism; this, sadly, escalated into arson, which in turn led to their joint arrest. They were imprisoned in Broadmoor where, briefly, their joint demeanour seemed to improve, and the staff allowed them to attend prison social functions. (Hence the line, "disco dancing with rapists".) The tragedy, however, is that two creative, intelligent individuals became stifled by the intensity of their love for each other.

'My Little Empire' takes you into the personal world of Nicky Wire. Nicky in his home, endlessly cleaning, mowing lawns, cutting hedges, blissfully immersed in the domestic life. His world vision, his talent even, shut down in favour of reassuring little chores. It could be that Nicky finds some kind of comfort, of safety, within those walls. "I'm happy being sad" pines the lyric, somewhat self-pityingly. And yet, as the song draws to a conclusion, there is an eerie creeping neurosis, as if Wire's submission to normal life carries its own dangers. A retreat into his own house might seem to represent a much-needed retreat from the insanity of the outside world; but what if the madness is not out in the big bad world, but within Wire himself? It is no accident that 'My Little Empire' features the lead vocals of Wire, rather than Bradfield. And, in a sense, the entire album unfolds from the constraints of that one song, and those four walls. Towards the end of the track, a niggling edginess creeps in. Personally, I find Wire's small explosion – "I'm fucked with being fucked" – uncomfortable, to say the least. Wire would later comment that 'My Little Empire' questions the true value of his style of writing. What right, just because he plays bass in a pop group, does he have to unload his perception of the world on an audience? Of course, he has as much right as the rest of us. But to an individual as sensitive and analytical as Nicky Wire, that's not necessarily of any real comfort. At its most basic, this is nothing more than the standard musings of the artist/poet – an indication of a lack of confidence, perhaps. In truth, Nicky's feelings were certainly rather more complex than that, hence the songs, hence the desire to confront them.

There was a danger with this song, and indeed with this album, that the Manics were producing a shrink-wrapped version of Wire's personality; that it was his obsessions, his dark moods, his joy that dominated the records varied themes. There is no answer to this, other than to say firstly that most groups are dominated by one or two personalities, that democracy is not necessarily compatible with creativity in the songwriting process; and that Bradfield's impassioned and beautiful voice, and Moore's powerful commanding musicianship make *This Is My Truth Tell Me Yours* an ensemble piece.

The second half of the album, from the self loathing of 'I'm Not Working' to the final crushing solemnity of 'S.Y.M.M' (South Yorkshire Mass Murder), reveals the Manics taking a parallel path to Jimmy McGovern's take on the appalling Hillsborough miscarriage of justice. In a sense, this track is the most clear-cut statement on the entire album, with the music succeeding in grinding the whole opus into the dust. Three songs earlier, in 'Be Natural', the band had attained the very opposite effect: a haunting ethereal melody that dominated the album's ragged closing sequence. And it is a ragged run of tracks, too, with brilliance ('Be Natural') and mundanity ('Black Dog On My Shoulder') existing side by side, despite sounding as if they hailed from different eras, if not different bands. Nevertheless, I'd disagree with the many critics who saw *This Is My Truth Tell Me Yours* as merely treading water. Only the truly hard of heart would deny that, given repeated plays, the sheer quality of the album shines through. All in all, the best Manics album to date. In this I would suggest it is a marked contrast to *Everything Must Go*, on which the grandeur of the production on so many songs tends to merge them into one. *This Is My Truth* wins hands-down in terms of diversity.

Strangely enough, the most fascinating song from the Manics intriguing autumn '98 batch never even made it onto the album. Lurking as one of the B-sides to '...Tolerate...', if indeed, extra tracks can still be referred to as B-sides, was an odd little beast with the grand title, 'A Prologue To History'. It might sound like the name of a particularly weighty A J P Taylor tome but the track is, in fact, a much lighter affair, rippling with curious little references, pseudo product placement and name-drops. In a strange way the song sits closer to the heart of the album than even 'My Little Empire'. Sounding like The Charlatans after downing a variety of unidentified pills, 'A Prologue To History' keeps its lyrical base very much within the increasingly curious confines of Wire's abode: "So I water my plants with Evian/A brand new Dyson, that is decadent/Read my papers and the business section/Check out the TESSAs and the pensions". What kind of a deranged rock'n'roll lifestyle could lead to such lyrical subversion? But as well as images drawn from his own domestic setting, Wire mixes in references from the very different worlds of politics and pop. Thus: "Were we the Kinnock factor/Am I talking Private sector/Do I think I'm Shaun William Ryder" and "Remember ethnic cleansing in the highlands/No one says a thing in Middle En-ger-land".

The ferociously marketed bagless vacuum cleaner, 'Dyson' is a reference to Wire's well-documented obsession with cleanliness. Fact is, Wire owns three separate models and has openly marvelled at their incredible suction. The Kinnock Factor is slightly more serious. It is a reference to the horrific mistreatment that Labour leader Neil Kinnock suffered at the hands of the Thatcher-loving English tabloids. This caused much consternation in Wales, as it was seen as a deliberate slant, not just against Kinnock, who was always of far greater intellect than his hapless PR image ever suggested, but against the country as a whole. It had been easy for the media to forget the immense contribution that South Wales had made to British socialism and the Labour party in particular. One often wondered just how Bevan might have faired in the modern era, against Tim Bell's ruthless pro-Thatcher spin-doctoring.

The Shaun Ryder reference is equally interesting. At first glance there might seem to be little common ground between the semi-literate Ryder, whose street-wise vernacular helped to make his idiosyncratic lyrics so striking – and Wire's more consciously intel-lectual approach to songwriting. But there are connections between the two. Moore, Bradfield and Wire had all, separately, expressed their admiration for Happy Mondays, and the Manics had covered the Mondays' dance trance classic 'Wrote For Luck' as one of the extra tracks on the CD version of 1993's 'Roses In The Hospital'. At the time Richey Edwards explained this seemingly odd choice by saying, "We've got the scum factor of the Mondays. We'd have a bag of chips and a fuck in the bus stop on the way home. We wouldn't go to a hotel. It would be, 'Stop here, I want me dick sucked'."

Perhaps more explicable is the reference to "Cleansing in the High-lands" and "Middle En-ger-land". One might look no further than the subject matter which inspired Mel Gibson's *Braveheart* for this, and the English attempts to breed the Scots out of Scotland by passing a sneaky bill allowing Scottish brides to be "taken" by any marauding Englishman. The lyric could also refer to the Highland clearances of

1746 when a law was passed in England which made clan chiefs sole owners of their estates – the point being that they would then be able to wipe non-land-owning Highlanders clean away, thus serving the cause of English wool traders. En-ger-land, meanwhile, is a clear reference to middle-brow football culture, the Hornby set who had permeated the media during the Nineties. The En-ger-land phrase was first captured on a cardboard sign held aloft by Factory boss Tony Wilson in the video for New Order's 1990 football song, 'World In Motion'. You couldn't ask for a finer anti-imperialist pop song for the late Nineties. The Manics could still pack a political punch when they wanted to.

10

THE MATTER OF WALES

"I just wonder about my own mentality, sometimes. Do I have the right to express all these opinions?"

– Nicky Wire

December 1998.

In a concrete tomb, in Manchester, in a giant shell, as ugly as sin and as cold as the worst architectural tragedies of the Sixties, Catatonia are on-stage, triumphant and gloriously loose.

There is warmth, for once, within the concrete, down on the ice rink, beneath the plastic seating which rises steeply to meet the glassy strip of corporate hospitality boxes. This is a major rock venue, in England in the late Nineties, but in many respects it feels like an American ice hockey venue, with a cubic video box hovering overhead, with a dusty grey surround, the obligatory McDonalds glaring yellow and red from the corner. A place of worship, for the inelegantly trendy teens, resplendent in Helly Hanson and Nike, Berghaus and Ellesse. A perfect venue for guzzling Coke, munching burgers and casting envious eyes towards whatever gorgeous popsters happen to be gracing the stage. It is the *Manchester Evening News* Arena, a place still more commonly referred to by the name of its previous sponsor, Nynex.

Most rock gigs, in the *MEN* Arena finish triumphantly. But that's generally because the audiences pay good money to see their heroes, and even if said heroes are whacked-out ageing rock'n'rollers, or brain-crushingly monotonous rappers, the final applause will still bellow appreciatively, before the crowd quickly disperses to attempt the wearisome task of getting a car out of the six-storey car park.

But, on this night, things seemed genuinely different. There is a swell of warmth spreading around the arena. There are Welsh flags billowing everywhere. Not rebel flags, but flags that create a curious feeling of homecoming. It was impossible to tell if these people were Welsh, or were pretending to be Welsh or were just having a bit of fun and, strangely enough, it didn't matter. It was an acknowledgement of Welsh talent – that it had, at last, really arrived in the pop world. What a difference a decade made! Hard to imagine that this was the same town that, as the Nineties began, was recognising the mythical dance state of 'Madchester', and believed itself to be twinned with New York and Chicago, would now be heartily applauding two Welsh rock bands! It was impossible not to sit in the Nynex that night, and not think back to poor Rhys Mwn, from Yr Anrefn, explaining how, in 1988, the tone in promoter's voices would noticeably drop whenever he mentioned he was from a 'Welsh' band. It wasn't racism; it was simple fact. Welsh bands just didn't sell. They couldn't sell. They just weren't sexy.

But something special was in the air that December night as, following Catatonia's gleeful, inspiring appearance, the Manics bounced on-stage to be confronted by a roar that wouldn't have disgraced the Stretford End after Ryan Giggs put Arsenal out of the FA Cup in injury time. And the raging collection of simmering bodies in front of the band, seemed reminiscent of an earlier football age, a golden age of pre-all-seater stadiums and Nick Hornby. The football references are deliberate. This really was like a football crowd. A riot without aggression. The Manic Street Preachers had taken a Manchester audience back in time, to a period before the cool arrogance of New Order, the sullen throb of Joy Division, the coy rock of The Smiths or the acid daze of The Stone Roses or Happy Mondays. This was a rock gig in the old sense, full of simple fire and passion. Even though it was the second time in 18 months that they had stormed this particular arena, the band seemed genuinely surprised by the reaction. Could this be the same Manchester that so studiously ignored them, back in their un-hip days of glammy Clash thrashing?

Most surprising of all, the greatest cheers seemed reserved for the songs from the new album. All of them. So much for the critical flak which had flown around the time of release. The fans made their feelings unmistakable. 'Tsunami', 'You Stole The Sun From My Heart', 'My Little Empire', all treated like standards that had long since been etched into the hearts of the fans. Great to hear them all sing, "I'm bored with being boooored!" A beautiful inversion of the classic punk rock statement.

Yes, of course, there was a thick deep groan of delight as the awesome lyric, "Libraries give us power" was launched over the audience. The Manic Street Preachers, as they exited and strode briskly through the concrete and back to their dressing room, had discovered something valuable on that night. It had been suggested that they had become too clever for their own good. That they had written themselves out of the mainstream. That, like Pulp, like Blur to some extent, they had produced a fine record that had slipped out of step with the times. They hadn't. An unlikely, nay, bizarre procession of flags bearing Welsh dragons, trooped out of the *MEN* Arena, that night, drifting up to Deansgate, surging across the city like some conquering army, dispersing into the multitudinous café bars. For once, that strange little country, clearly visible from the rooftops of Manchester on a fine day, had been allowed to land one inspiring aspect of its fine culture on foreign soil.

* * *

February 16, 1999.

A gleaming little trailer preceded the 1999 Brit Awards on our TV sets. The smug but deserving Robbie Williams was spotted clutching an award, as if he'd just cat burgled the damn thing. Before the Robster, we saw Cerys, belting out 'Road Rage', Andrea Corr's man-crushing pout and a brief snippet of the Manics, spinning slowly upside down in the 'Tolerate' video. That, perhaps, would have been enough for most people. A microcosm of a rather dull year for home-grown music, where the dominant forces came from Ireland and Wales and a new trail blazed by the beautiful Aussie songstress Natalie Imbruglia. That was all we really needed to know. And few people were surprised to discover that the actual screening, on the 17th – clashing messily with a Man Utd/Arsenal game – was an altogether painful affair, full of all the usual nauseating backslapping but somewhat lacking the spark of the highlights of the previous two years – the Manics' classic appearance in 1997 and All Saints' performance of the mighty 'Never Ever' in 1998. This year just wasn't so infectiously triumphant. Undoubtedly this was a reflection of an uneasy year. Even the normally unflappable Johnny Vaughan stumbled in the role of MC as, all around him, pop star smiles hid torrential undertones of ego-clashing stupidity. All Saints toothily handing an award to Natalie. Norman Cook, in the guise of Fatboy Slim, being heartily applauded by his fiancée, Radio One mega-mouth Zoe Ball. And woeful performances by the irksome Steps. Whitney, Cher, Eurythmics . . . even the Placebo/David Bowie pairing seemed strangely unsuccessful.

As to the Manics, winners of two awards – Best British Group, Best Album – they at least attempted to invigorate the proceedings with a spirited performance of 'You Stole The Sun From My Heart', with Nicky Wire, resplendent in leopard-skin and eye-liner, looking like a post-apocalyptic punk in some Ken Russell flick, bouncing all over the stage. They even put on an absurd acceptance speech, featuring the bellowing of the band's name from Bradfield while Nicky Wire put a skipping rope through its paces. Well, it was a daft little stunt, but at least it provided something of a talking point. There was precious little else to talk about. How ironic, then, that *This Is My Truth Tell Me Yours*, universally – and incorrectly – regarded by the critics as little more than a stepping stone record, should finish up grabbing the Best Album Award. Deservedly so, although Pulp's *This Is Hardcore* was an artistic, if not a commercial, landmark, soundtracking the grinding down of pop music in 1998 to absolute perfection.

Backstage, of course, was the proof that British pop, at its worst, could be merely a swarming promo opportunity, a wine-guzzling gathering patronised by tabloid journos with little interest or knowledge of pop music *per se*, but keenly primed for the eye-grabbing headline. Zoe and Norm! What about Robbie and Nicole? How strange, though, to find the Manic Street Preachers not only fitting smugly into this unholy hierarchy but sitting sweetly at the top of the pile. This is not necessarily a criticism, just an observation. Who would have thought it? Of course, ever since the speedy absorption of punk into the mainstream, everyone knows that the natural course for young anarchic acts, from The Clash to Chumbawamba, from The Thompson Twins (check out their early profile as anarcho-punk favourites) to Public Enemy, is always to assume as commercially friendly a state as possible. Either that, or remain right out there in left-field, artistically independent and commercially dead. Even so – the Manic Street Preachers, once bright little valley boys pumped with arrogance, were now heartily prized by the establishment! It still seems difficult to accept. From despair to where? To a suite in The Grosvener, apparently, even though any fair-minded person would be pleased for the band. There was still one remaining question. Was their commercial success a triumph or a failure?

There would, one presumed, have to be a spark of rebellion left. Were the Manics capable of biting the hand? Of delivering a nice Welsh slap to those who had helped them on their way. Well . . . maybe. Something had been fermenting in the band's collective mind, for several months. Perhaps it was a simple fear. A fear of all this dreaded acceptance. A fear of becoming the band that the young kids loathe, that the new punks – I use the term loosely – ferociously rebel against. Of even floating away from those Welsh roots that helped to make them special in the first place. Clearly they knew it. Even backstage at the Brits, it was possible to sense their itchiness to withdraw from it all. A girl from, of all papers, the *Daily Star*, grabbed a quick chat with Sean Moore – he probably didn't have a clue who she was – and by the next day it was an 'exclusive' interview. Three more albums, Sean said. Three more albums and we finish, split, completely. No returns. No reunions. No way would they ever turn into The Rolling Stones.

Behind the "Manics To Split" headline – hardly the hottest story of the year – lay a darker reality. While they had been touring the East, all but swamped by blanket blind adoration, the Manics had been holding band meetings in hotel rooms. The plan, such as it was, had been formed between the three band members and Martin Hall. Three albums, five years, tops. No way could the Manics be allowed to slide into ageing dinosaur territory. They would try to maintain their success, even build on it and, perhaps at last, finally crack the States, but to become a sad parody by overplaying their hand would undermine everything they had stood for. Of course, in the undertone to this decision lay the fear, the knowledge, that in the eyes of their older fans, they had already softened beyond belief. Unlike Oasis, the point wasn't simply to 'have it large' and live a whacked-out existence as professional rock stars. The Manics had always had a deeply moral side; they cared too much, they were too intelligent to just do it for the money. They might have touted themselves as corporate sluts originally, but there are few bands around today with such integrity.

And then, of course, there was the prospect of seeping back into life in Wales, a dream shared by all three, even James. Fast approaching his 30th birthday, in Japan he had expressed the paradoxical desire to return, at some point, to some kind of normal life in his home country. The Manics had, it seemed, learned fame's hardest lesson of all. When they had got to the top of the heap, where every struggling musician longs to be, there was nothing there. It was a place of cosseted emptiness, terrifyingly dislodged from the valuable reality of life back home. And the biggest fear was that they might never be able to get back; the ultimate gruesome example being, of course, The Rolling Stones, whose achievements for so long have been measured out solely in terms of hard cash, their lips and tongue logo identifying a corporate entity with as much cultural significance as the McDonalds arch. There was a touching sign of the Manics' early arrogance in Sean's statement, "I think most of our fans are with us on this one. I think they accept that we shouldn't be a band who are around forever. That thought is horrible. We would hate that. We are not here to fulfil contractual obligation. Contracts exist to help us achieve our natural number of albums." Of course, they had said this before. One thinks back to all those boasts about self-destructing after *Generation Terrorists* had gone global. Thankfully, it didn't; and they didn't.

'You Stole The Sun From My Heart' seemed to hang around the charts for eons. Not a bad thing, of course, and it certainly shone like a jewel in the company of the dreaded Steps, the now very dull Beautiful South and the very beautiful but equally dull Billie (although it did make a beguiling partner to R.E.M.'s 'At My Most Beautiful' on one unusually watchable *Top Of The Pops*). How refreshing to hear that revolving guitar lick ushering in Bradfield's impassioned vocals! In a neat contrast to the resigned jilted lover tantrum of '. . . Heart', the song's B-side was a slab of pure old-fashioned Manic Street Preacher polemic. Entitled 'Socialist Serenade', the track could have fitted quite smugly into *Generation Terrorists*. Within the lyrics one hears Nicky Wire's heartfelt plea for an Old Labour tradition, a plea for small things; like commitment to education. As Wire explained to *The Times*, "If the policy they have got now was the policy they had when I was around, I might not even have gone to university. The song is really about abolishing grants. Everything else they have done hasn't surprised me, but the Tories would never have done that. It would have caused too much of an outcry."

Wire's long-suppressed desire to actually enter into the political arena "rather than writing dumb lyrics about it all for a fucking band" was finally out in the open. 'Socialist Serenade' was a throwback, a cry for old values which, presumably, were on Nicky Wire's personal agenda. His current political heroes, he admitted, were a worryingly ageing breed: Tony Benn and Dennis Skinner were two names, though he had some time for John Prescott. His political ambition seemed serious: Wire appeared intent on a plan of action to encourage talent to flourish regardless of its social situation, a level playing field for working class and middle class alike. A National Health Service unburdened by top-heavy management, stupefying bureaucracy and inadequate funding. A new, healthy, realistic agenda for Wales. How unfashionable can you get? But wouldn't it be fitting, if the Manic Street Preachers were eventually to become the vehicle for this new breed of old-style politics? Of course, Wire would immediately stand accused of gross naïvety. Doesn't everyone enter politics for those very same laudable reasons, only to slowly succumb to the temptations that power brings? Actually, that's how it used to be. Today, tragically, many young politicians don't even seem to bother with that old idealistic launch pad. They opt straight for the fast career track.

And, of course, there are the other problems. Images from one's past, for example. Wire: "Looking at the front cover of the *Sun* . . . there's a picture of me in a dress talking absolute bollocks. You think. 'How could I get out of that?' " Well it would make a change. The Wire lifestyle – outlandishly clad rock star attempts to conceal lifestyle of tedious domesticity – should present a whole new challenge for those doctors of spin. Flippancy aside, Wire seemed serious about this possible change of field, mentioning to *The Times* that Peter Hain, the Welsh Office Industry Minister was "a very nice bloke" and that he would like to think that with the Welsh Assembly he might, one day, try being Minister for Sport and Culture.

"I wouldn't mind doing my bit," Wire stated, earnestly.

* * *

WANT. IGNORANCE. SQUALOR. DISEASE. IDLENESS. The words, white on black, scream from the promotional postcards. They evoke a play. A bleak block of polemic, bitterness and hurt. A block of words so emotionally hungry they touch upon a curious beauty of their own. Not surprisingly, the play is Welsh. It is so 'in yer face' that it positively sticks nut on you. Once you have bought your ticket, and taken your seat, there is simply no backing out. You are in for a cultural slapping.

The play in question is *Everything Must Go*, written by Patrick Jones, soundtracked by the Manics, Catatonia, Super Furry Animals and Stereophonics. Not surprisingly, it proves to be a work which revolves furiously around the generation of the lost Welsh, of the unhinged valley clusters, of the vibrant young talent of Wales drifting sadly away into bitterness and despair. Of course, this concept is rather ironic, given the context. As the play itself, as its esteemed author and as the gaggle of bands who gather in the soundtrack serve to testify, young Welsh culture had risen to unprecedented heights, by the start of 1999.

But it was a curious night, with Manics quotes hurtling from the stage, to be greeted warmly by the hoards of expectant Manics fans in attendance and deftly down-played by the faintly embarrassed Nicky Wire and James Dean Bradfield. The two seemed rather embarrassed that night – not by the play itself, but perhaps by the forceful way that Jones had grasped the basic imagery of the Manics and had, if you can possibly imagine this, actually intensified it.

The play centres on five characters, each one flailing horribly while succumbing to all the intense horrors of the modern world. Irving Welsh haunts the script faintly in places, although it would be most unfair to dwell too strongly on this. A better comparison, which was actually picked up by no less than three separate reviews, would be Derek Jarman's truly manic post-apocalyptic punk flick, *Jubilee*, a film which failed due to the over-ambition of the director. *Everything Must Go* almost suffers a similar fate – the nihilism on display is almost suffocating. It is not a happy tale, and it's almost surprising to realise that only one of the five characters actually dies – a merciful release, perhaps – while the others scrape through, albeit alienated and bitter. The beauty of the play, such as it is, comes from the intensity of the pain and the awesome scale of the sadness. There is little doubt that for "post-apocalyptic" one should read "post-Thatcher", as these characters are clearly stumbling around in the debris left behind by that particularly English dictatorship.

On the plus side, the play is powered along by some great Welsh music and there is a sense that much of this music has finally settled in its true resting home. Whether the play actually manages to scrape something remotely constructive from this sorry scene of dilapidated landscapes and personalities, proved to be a matter of considerable debate. Even the author himself admitted, in *Melody Maker*, that he was finding the nihilism somewhat difficult to handle in an artistic sense, and strongly hinted at a change of direction in the near future. Of equal interest was the prevailing sense of something coming full circle. It was as if Patrick Jones and the Manics had started from the same point, had spun in opposite directions and had finally merged.

* * *

> *Taffy was a Welshman,*
> *Taffy was a thief,*
> *Taffy came to my house and stole a leg of beef,*
> *I went to Taffy's house and found him in bed,*
> *I took a big cudgel and hit him on the head.*

Hard to imagine, in the PC Nineties, that such violence could filter into a playground rhyme. But it did once, long ago. The rhyme surfaced in the border counties of England – in Cheshire, Shropshire and Herefordshire – and was duly filtered down to the children. Simplistic indoctrination. And similar rhymes, of course, fuelled the poems of the Welsh borders, spreading hatred amongst the hard-working adults and, in their turn, becoming part of the playful rituals of the children. To be honest, it must be acknowledged that stupidity and prejudice darkened the minds on both sides of the border, beyond big and small, good and evil, right and wrong. Beyond politics.

Of course, most English people who have spent time in Wales adore the country. Jan Morris, staunch Welsh Nationalist, agrees. That said, resentment lingers in the more nationalist areas of Wales. Maybe it will be eased by the Welsh Assembly. As I write, in April 1999, the Welsh Nationalists are already rejoicing the opinion polls which precede the May 7 Welsh Assembly election. The great Dafydd Wigley, Caernarvon-based leader of Plaid Cymru, was predicting that his party would win at least 15 of the 60 Assembly seats, nudging themselves second only to the Labour Party. Travel anywhere in Wales and the feeling these days is generally upbeat. The Welsh Assembly: surely a change for the better? The rugby team, buoyed by clinching a recent victory against France in Paris, would, within days, achieve an even more important victory over the fiercest rivals of all: the English. Catatonia have just released yet another album chock-a-block with glorious pop songs and inspired lyrics, and Cerys is flavour of the month with the pop inkies.

Meanwhile, in a little office in Manchester, promoter Phil Jones is attempting to piece together a strong musical bill for the Welsh Assembly celebrations, taking place, alas, on the very day that Manchester United stride proudly into their first European Cup Final for thirty-one years. Phil has been struggling. His initial idea was to string together the full spectrum of Welsh music, highlighting the whole occasion with a line-up of Stereophonics, Super Furry Animals, Catatonia and, surely, the crowning glory, the Manic Street Preachers. Tom Jones and Shirley Bassey immediately accepted the offer. But all is not peaceful in the garden. Catatonia, on learning that the Queen and Prince Philip will be in attendance, refuse point blank to perform. The Manic Street Preachers initially agree, and James Dean Bradfield even shunts his richly deserved holiday back by two days, apparently proud to be performing on this most auspicious of occasions. Then comes the first proviso. The Manics, like Catatonia, will not perform in the presence of the Queen. They will, however, be willing to perform if the Queen is *nearby*. Then the story changes again: it appears that Nicky Wire will not perform if the Queen is in the vicinity. James may well have to go on alone, a solo spot with acoustic guitar. The split in opinion explains a great deal about the band's dynamic, about their desire not to lose their own individuality under the umbrella of the Manics. It also indicates that the Manic Street Preachers have grown older in different ways; now, if one of them starts up with "Repeat after me . . .", who can say how many of the others will join in?

Phil Jones, meanwhile, remains bemused. As it stands, the encouraging swell of Welsh pop talent that has grown over that last few years of the decade will be barely represented on the night, with Bradfield's performance, if it happens, complemented only by a coincidental Super Furry Animals gig in Cardiff on the same day. The resentment seems to flow strongest from the younger element. It's a conundrum.

*   *   *

Postscript.

When the Welsh Assembly results came in (after a disappointingly apathetic turnout), Plaid Cymru exceeded Dafydd Wigley's prediction by two seats; Labour took the laurels, though with a mere 28 seats. And as it turned out, the evening itself would be memorable for rather unexpected reasons. The Welsh Assembly may or may not be a step towards a genuine autonomy, if indeed that's what the Welsh want. But history will remember it for another event, taking place in Nicky Wire's beloved Barcelona. Walking down the Ramblas that night, *full* of intent, were 50,000 ecstatic Manchester United supporters, fresh from seeing their team spin a European Cup Final on its head in injury time. The Reds sent mighty Bayern Munich dizzy with total incomprehension and, on what would have been Matt Busby's 90th birthday, regained the mantle of European Champions. The luck of the Welsh. To pick that day, of all days, to try to echo the ghostly battle cry of Owain Glyndwr. He could have rallied a mighty army at Offa's Dyke for all most people cared; they were glued to their TV sets. It was the Welsh showbiz old guard who turned out, all smiles and gush, to meet and greet royalty and Tony Blair (who, famously, had one ear cocked to catch the football score). But not the young bucks.

The Manic Street Preachers have real power now; genuine international commercial clout. Few people can touch them and although they have crossed over to the mainstream with their last two albums, they are still screaming loudly from their Welsh heart. It's good to hear. In the introduction to this book, I lamented the influx of English tourists, the slow erosion of a great and ancient culture on the Llyn Peninsula. The possibility of no future for young Wales seemed, for a while, all too serious. But with the rise of the Manic Street Preachers – intelligent creators of powerful, thought-provoking music – and the stream of bands following in their wake, anything now seems possible.

Croeso I Gymru.

DISCOGRAPHY

SINGLES

Suicide Alley/Tennessee (I Feel So Low)
(SBS 002, 7″) August 1989

New Art Riot (EP)
New Art Riot/Strip It Down/Last Exile On Yesterday/
Teenage 20-20
(Damaged Goods Yubb 004, 12″) June 1990

Motown Junk/Sorrow 16/We Her Majesty's Prisoners
(Heavenly HVN8 12, 12″) January 1991

Motown Junk CD Single
(Heavenly HVN8 CD) January 1991

You Love Us/Spectators Of Suicide
(Heavenly HVN 10, 7″) May 1991

You Love Us/Spectators Of Suicide/Strip It Down (live)
(Heavenly HVN 10 12, 12″) May 1991

New Art Riot EP (Pink vinyl, 3,000 copies)
(Yubb 004P, 12″)
November 1991

Stay Beautiful/R. P. McMurphy
(Columbia 657337 6, 7")
August 1991

Stay Beautiful/R. P. McMurphy/Soul Contamination
(Columbia 657337 6, 12") July 1991

Stay Beautiful
CD Single (Columbia 657337 2) July 1991

Love's Sweet Exile/Repeat
(Columbia 657582 7, 7") November 1991

Love's Sweet Exile/Repeat/Democracy Coma
(Columbia 657626, 12") November 1991

Love's Sweet Exile/Repeat/Democracy Coma
CD Single (Columbia 65758 2) November 1991

You Love Us/A Vision Of Dead Desire
(Columbia 657724 7, 7") January 1992

You Love Us/A Vision Of Dead Desire/It's So Easy (live)
(Columbia 657724 2, 12") January 1992

You Love Us/A Vision Of Dead Desire/We Her Majesty's Prisoners/
It's So Easy (live)
CD Single (Columbia 657724 6) January 1992

Slash'n'Burn/Motown Junk
(Columbia 657873 7, 7") March 1992

Slash'n'Burn/Motown Junk cassette
(Columbia 657873 4) March 1992

Slash'n'Burn/Motown Junk/Ain't Going Down
(Columbia 657873 6, 12") March 1992

Slash'n'Burn/Motown Junk/Sorrow 16/Ain't Going Down
CD Single (Columbia 657873 0) March 1992

Motorcycle Emptiness/Bored Out Of My Mind
(Columbia 658083 7, 7″) June 1992

Motorcycle Emptiness/Bored Out Of My Mind cassette
(Columbia 658083 4) June 1992

Motorcycle Emptiness/Bored Out Of My Mind/Under My Wheels
(Columbia 658083 8, 12″) June 1992

Motorcycle Emptiness/Bored Out Of My Mind/
Crucifix Kiss (live)/Under My Wheels (live)
CD Single (Columbia 658083 9) June 1992

Theme From M.A.S.H. (Suicide Is Painless)/
Everything I Do (By Fatima Mansions)
(Columbia 658382 9, 7″) September 1992

Theme From M.A.S.H. (Suicide Is Painless)/
Everything I Do (by Fatima Mansions)
Cassette (Columbia 658382 4) September 1992

Theme From M.A.S.H. (Mash Mix)/
Everything I Do (By Fatima Mansions)
CD Single (Columbia 658382 2) September 1992

Little Baby Nothing/Never Want Again/Suicide Alley
(Columbia 658796 7, 7″) January 1993

Little Baby Nothing/Never Want Again/Suicide Alley cassette
(Columbia 658796) January 1993

Little Baby Nothing/Never Want Again/
Dead Yankee Drawl/Suicide Alley
CD Single part 1 (Columbia 658796 2) January 1993

Little Baby Nothing/R. P. McMurphy (live)/Tennessee (live)/
You Love Us (live) CD Single part 2
(Columbia 658796 5) January 1993

From Despair To Where?/Hibernation/Spectators Of Suicide
(Columbia 659337 6, 12″) June 1993

From Despair To Where?/Hibernation/Spectators Of Suicide/
Starlover
CD Single (Columbia 659337 2) June 1993

From Despair To Where?/Hibernation
Cassette (Columbia 659337 4) June 1993

La Tristesse Durera (Scream To A Sigh)/Patrick Bateman/
Repeat (live)/Tennessee (live)
(Columbia 659477 6, 12″) July 1993

La Tristesse Durera/Patrick Bateman/
What's My Name (live)/Slash'n'Burn (live)
CD Single (Columbia 659477 2) July 1993

La Tristesse Durera/Patrick Bateman cassette
(Columbia 659477 4) July 1993

Roses In The Hospital/Us Against You/Donkeys
(Columbia 659727 7, 7″) October 1993

Roses In The Hospital
(6 different mixes) (Columbia 659727 6, 12″) October 1993

Roses In The Hospital/Us Against You/
Donkeys/Wrote For Luck
CD Single (Columbia 659727 2) October 1993

Life Becoming A Landslide/Comfort Comes/
Are Mothers Saints (Columbia 660070 6, 12″) January 1994

Life Becoming A Landslide/Comfort Comes/Are Mothers Saints/
Charles Windsor
CD Single (Columbia 660070 2) January 1994

Life Becoming A Landslide/Comfort Comes cassette
(Columbia 660070 4) January 1994

Faster/PCP/Sculptor Of Man/New Art Riot (In E Minor)
CD Single (Epic 660447 2) May 1994

Faster/Sculpture Of Man/PCP
(Epic 660447 0, 10″) May 1994

Faster/PCP
Cassette (Epic 660447 4) May 1994

Revol/Too Cold Here/You Love Us (live)/
Life Becoming A Landslide (live)
(Columbia 660686 0, 10″) August 1994

Revol/Too Cold Here/You Love Us/Love's Sweet Exile
CD Single part 1 (Epic 660686 2) August 1994

Revol/Drug Drug Druggy (live)/
Roses In The Hospital (live)/You Love Us (live)
CD Single part 2 (Epic 660686 5) August 1994

She Is Suffering/The Drowners/Stay With Me (live)
(Epic 660859 0, 10″) October 1994

She Is Suffering/Love Torn Us Down/
The Drowners (live)/Stay With Me (live)
CD Single (Epic 660895 2) October 1994

She Is Suffering/La Tristesse Durera (dub mix)/
La Tristesse Durera (Voval mix)/Faster (dub mix)
(Epic 660895 5) October 1994

A Design For Life/Mr Carbohydrate/Dead Passive/
Dead Trees And Traffic Islands CD Single part 1
(Epic 663070 2) April 1996

A Design For Life (3 mixes)/Faster (vocal mix)
CD Single part 2 (Epic 663070 5) April 1996

A Design For Life/Bright Eyes (live)
Cassette (Epic 663070 4) April 1996

Everything Must Go/Black Garden/Hanging On/
No One Knows What It's Like To Be Me
CD Single part 1 (Epic 663468 2) July 1996

Everything Must Go (3 mixes)
CD Single part 2 (Epic 663468 5) July 1996

Everything Must Go/Raindrops Keep Falling On My Head (live)
Cassette (Epic 663468 2) July 1996

Kevin Carter/Horses Under Starlight/Sepia/First Republic
CD Single part 1 (Epic 663775 2) September 1996

Kevin Carter (3 mixes)
CD Single part 2 (Epic 663775 5) September 1996

Kevin Carter/Everything Must Go (acoustic) cassette
(Epic 663775 4) September 1996

Australia/Velocity Girl/Take The Skinheads Bowling/
Can't Take My Eyes Off You
CD Single part 1 (Epic 664044 2) December 1996

Australia/Australia (lion rock mix)/Motorcycle Emptiness
(2 new mixes)
CD part 2 (Epic 664044 5) December 1996

Australia/A Design For Life
Cassette (Epic 664044 4) December 1996

If You Tolerate This Then Your Children Will Be Next/
Prologue To History/Montana 98
(Epic 666345 2) September 1998

If You Tolerate This Then Your Children Will Be Next/
Massive Attack Remix/David Holmes Remix
(Epic 666345 5) September 1998

The Everlasting/Black Holes For The Young/
Valley Boy
(Epic 66832 2) December 1998

The Everlasting/Small Black Flowers That Grow In The Sky
(Live at Nynex)
(Epic 66832 4) December 1998

You Stole The Sun From My Heart/Socialist Serenade/
Train In Vain (live) CD Single
(Epic 66935 2) February 1999

You Stole The Sun From My Heart/
David Holmes Remix/Mogwai Remix
(Epic 66935 5) February 1999

ALBUMS

Generation Terrorists
Slash'n'Burn/Nat West-Barclays-Midlands-Lloyds/
Born To End/Motorcycle Emptiness/You Love Us/
Love's Sweet Exile/Little Baby Nothing/
Repeat (Stars And Stripes)/Tennessee/
Another Invented Disease/Stay Beautiful/So Dead/
Repeat/Spectators Of Suicide/Damn Dog/Crucifix Kiss/
Methadone Pretty/Condemned To Rock'n'Roll
(Epic 471060 2, CD) February 1992
(Epic 471060 1, Double LP)

Gold Against The Soul
Sleepflower/From Despair To Where/La Tristesse Durera/Yourself/
Life Becoming A Landslide/Drug Drug Druggy/
Roses In The Hospital/Nostalgic Pushead/Symphony Of Tourette/
Gold Against The Soul
(EPIC 477421 2, CD) June 1993
(EPIC 4774212, LP)

The Holy Bible
Yes/IfwhiteAmericatoldthetruthforonedayitsworldwouldfallapart/
Of Walking Abortion/She Is Suffering/Archives Of Pain/Revol/
4st 7lb/Mausoleum/Faster/This Is Yesterday/
Die In The Summertime/The Intense Humming Of Evil/PCP
(Epic 477421 2, CD) August 1994
(Epic 4774212 1, LP)

Everything Must Go
Elvis Impersonator; Blackpool Pier/A Design For Life/
Kevin Carter/Enola/Alone/Everything Must Go/
Small Black Flowers That Grow In The Sky/
The Girl Who Wanted To Be Good/Removables/
Australia/Interiors/Farther Away/No Surface All Feeling
(EPIC 483930 2, CD) May 1996
(EPIC 483930 1, LP)

This Is My Truth Tell Me Yours
The Everlasting/If You Tolerate This Then Your Children Will Be Next/
You Stole The Sun From My Heart/Ready For Drowning/Tsunami/
My Little Empire/I'm Not Working/You're Tender And You're Tired/
Born A Girl/Be Natural/Black Dog On My Shoulder/
Nobody Loved You/S.Y.M.M.
(EPIC 491703 9, CD) October 1998